LOUISE FIROUZ

RIDING THROUGH REVOLUTION

The Memoirs of an American Woman who married a Persian Prince and re-established the original Oriental horse through Revolution, War and Intrigue

WRITTEN by LOUISE FIROUZ
COMPLETED AND EDITED by BRENDA DALTON

1

ACKNOWLEDGEMENTS

On behalf of Louise Firouz, I would like to thank all the people without whose support and assistance this book would not have been produced.

These are just a few:

H.R.H. Prince Philip
Joyce Covington
Ateshe Firouz
Caren Firouz,
Roshan Firouz
David Laylin
Ruth Staines
Gill Suttle

© 2013 Brenda Dalton

ADVANCED GLOBAL PUBLISHING, INC.
P.O. Box 310, Shippensburg, PA 17257-0310

ISBN 13 TP: 978-0-7684-8429-8
ISBN 13 Ebook: 978-0-7684-8428-1

For Worldwide Distribution, Printed in the U.S.A.
1 2 3 4 5 6 7 8 9 10 11 12 13 14

MAP OF APPROXIMATE LOCATIONS

Louise (Laylin) Firouz
24th December 1933 to 25th May 2008

"And as I was riding along, my heart resounded in the lawn-dampened steps, resounded in the snorting and champing on the bit by my grey, and a blissful happiness lit up my heart and I knew: If I now dropped out of the world, I would fall into heaven."

Baron von Munchhausen

At first sight it might seem a bit unusual for a retired Naval Officer to be involved in equestrian matters, but it so happens that when I finished my naval career, I took to playing polo. I was then invited to stand for election as President of the International Equestrian Federation. It was with these connections that I heard the story about the discovery of the ancient Caspian Horse by Louise Firouz. A few years later I was invited to attend the spectacular celebrations of 2,500 years of the Royal Dynasty of Iran. It was on this occasion that I had the pleasure of meeting Mrs Firouz and seeing some of her Caspian Horses.

In the course of our conversation, it occurred to me that, if the whole of the genetic pool of the Caspian breed was isolated in Iran, there was a serious risk that disease, or some other event, might wipe out the whole breed. I discussed this with Mrs Firouz, and offered to look after a breeding unit in England if she thought that this was a good idea. The consequence of this conversation is described in this book. As things turned out, this move made a contribution to the survival of the breed in later years.

That is only one incident in a most remarkable life story of a most remarkable woman. Brenda Dalton is to be commended for putting this enthralling account together.

INTRODUCTION

There was war, revolution, domestic disaster and court intrigue, and there were doubting archaeologists. There were glorious times and there were despairing times, but the pull of the past was an underlying compulsion that drove me to continue the search for the origins of the Oriental horse when all else was failing. There was security and energy in the continuity. The mystery and its solution would be companions whether the Shah was in power or the Clergy were giving the orders. The voices of Herodotus and Strabo were clear reminders that, over two thousand years before, people had tackled the same questions that I was groping to answer.

The unique equine that I named the Caspian, by virtue of the area where it existed, showed me one of the places where man first became friends and partners with the horse and where selective breeding was first practiced to develop what we know now as the Oriental horse.

The Caspian horse is no normal phenomenon. It inspires people to great efforts as in a Russian fairy tale and it leads people into temptation. For me it was a 'unicorn' that drew me deeper and deeper into the mysteries of the Oriental horse. Whether it provided pleasure for my family and friends or a thread by which to find my way through the labyrinth of Oriental politics and intrigue, it provided a purpose to my life that has sustained me through some vividly trying times.

Discovering the Caspian horse gave my life new dimensions which have swept me through Royal Courts to prison cells; from Embassy drawing rooms to Kurdish mud huts. I have had praise heaped on my head and slander slashed across my face. I have been referred to as a lunatic and a seer but, for my family and me, the Caspian became the catalyst to discover Persia; the ancient glories and the excitement of pursuing a dream.

Whenever I was convinced that we had hit rock bottom, there was the beckoning beam of this little horse and what it represented, on the horizon. I have followed this 'unicorn' and it has led me through the valley of death and destruction to untold heights of love of life.

Louise Firouz

CONTENTS

Acknowledgements
Map of approximate locations
Foreword – H.R.H. Prince Philip
Introduction – Louise Firouz

Chapters

Epilogue - Brenda Dalton
Translations
Biography

Note: A pony is defined as an equine measuring under 14.2 hands high (58 inches or 147cm) and the Caspian could therefore be classed as a pony. However, the bone structure, gaits and temperament are that of a horse and it is therefore officially classed as a horse. In this book both descriptions are used.

Chapter 1

Growing up in Virginia and Expulsion from University in Beirut

When I was six years old we moved from Washington D.C. to a farm near Forestville, Virginia, a small rural market town of six houses, a village store, grange and a two-roomed schoolhouse. My parents bought a run-down old pre-Civil-War house, with traditional red barn, in 1939 just as World War II was starting in Europe. Forestville is now called Great Falls and has a shopping mall, office buildings, and is zoned for large plots and million dollar houses for lawyers, Senators, and others who hover around government in Washington, D.C, a half hour's drive beyond the Beltway, depending on rush hour traffic.

In those days we rode to school on horseback along forest trails. In fine weather, when the leaves were golden and dropping in the autumn sun, and the chinquapin nuts were ripe, we found it hard to abandon the horses so instead we abandoned school, along with similarly inclined friends also mounted, and sped towards the Potomac River and its heavily forested banks. We spent the days swimming and speculating what we would do with the rest of our indolent lives.

I learned a little about how to read and write, and a lot about milking cows, harvesting hay, picking potatoes and schooling young horses. I also knew that I always wanted to live out in places where I could smell the seasons turning.

As the second world war was in full swing no one paid attention to our lack of reading or writing skills. As long as we were up in time to milk the cows, make sandwiches for lunch and were off on the horses in the direction of school our Mother was too pre-occupied with her war work to notice our pristine exercise books. To this day, even with a college degree, I cannot write long hand but continue to print.

In spite of the initial lack of formal education I eventually managed to complete a University education at Cornell, returning each summer to Hidden Springs Farm. My brothers, John and David, and I absorbed the smells of milk warm from the cows as we sat drowsily milking them on misty Virginia mornings, fresh hay stacked in the lofts of the barn, honeysuckle on the wood-panel fences and horses flicking flies with their tails under giant black oaks in the forest. These scenes made an indelible impression and left me allergic to the idea of life in a big city. Eventually our parents divorced and after a short, unhappy for me, stint in New York City, my Mother bought a small farm in New Hampshire.

The village was typical New England with a main street lined with old square houses shaded by huge maples and elms, several churches and an impressive inn. Our farm was ten miles away on a dirt road with nothing else in sight except pastures, forest and deer. My brothers were sent off to boarding school while I was enrolled in the local grammar school. At first, when the weather was fine, my Mother drove me to school but when the snows started we were stuck. As we were not on a dairy route the snow ploughs did not come in our direction. We bought a small Morgan mare, a sleigh and a buggy and this was our transportation. Getting up in the dark each morning to hitch up the mare and drive the ten miles to school has given me a life-long aversion to rising in the dark. Whenever I have to catch a plane at an ungodly hour I shudder and remember the valiant little mare, Rhoda.

I was moved on to a private school in nearby Peterborough but still had to drive Rhoda to Hancock, put her in the church stable and take a taxi for the next twelve miles, repeating the process each evening.

When Mother became ill in my final year at Kendall Hall I quit school and stayed home to take care of her. I continued to study, however, and eventually passed the College Board exams in Latin, Maths and English and was accepted by my college of choice, Cornell University. There I joined a childhood friend, Margot Pringle, who had been my co-conspirator in many childhood pranks in Virginia. She and I were both enrolled in the Agriculture College where I was taking pre-veterinary courses with a veterinary career in mind. The courses were difficult and the hours were long. There were classes in chemistry, physics, botany and, of course, English and history but it was the science classes that were the challenge. The first classes started at eight in the morning and went on until sometimes nine at night. I managed to struggle through most but physics defeated me. My sisyphus was incline planes and no matter how much I puzzled over rates of acceleration and deceleration I could not understand it. So, I was rejected as a candidate for Veterinary College.

My father was an international lawyer, a partner in the law firm of Covington Burling in Washington D.C. One of his more celebrated cases was Iran vs. the Soviet Union, argued in the United Nations after the Second World War when Russia was reluctant to leave Azerbaijan. The case dragged on for some time and the Iranian Ambassador to the United States, Hussein Ala, became a good friend and frequent visitor to our farm. We virtually grew up with his son Fereydoun. We rode, swam and skied together, keeping up the friendship even after we had all gone to different colleges in 1951. Fereydoun went to Harvard, my brother John went to Yale and I went to Cornell.

When my problems with incline planes in physics put a stop to my plans for becoming a veterinarian, I decided to branch out into new frontiers and study Arabic instead. John and I both decided to take off for a year and go to the American University of Beirut.

We had both been fascinated by Fereydoun's tales of Persia (although I suspect most were apocryphal since he was brought up in the various capitals of Europe). Everything that I had heard about the Orient intrigued me: the horses, the bazaars, the palaces and the bleak landscape. Life in the United States seemed tame and unchallenging by comparison.

Cornell granted us a year's leave of absence. The American University of Beirut approved our applications so John and I boarded a ship in New York destined for Naples. There we switched to a small ship sailing for Alexandria and Beirut. King Faroukh's palace in Alexandria (he was no longer there) proved the stories of Oriental grandeur but we soon found this was a gilt-edged sophistry and hardly typical of the Orient. The half-clad beggar children with running sores and trachoma who swarmed around us were real. So were the women hurrying along in the dust, their eyes cast down, and parcels of some kind of greens clutched in a hand under their robes. We saw no flashy white Arab stallions charging down the lanes. There were only thin donkeys with sores from badly fitting pack saddles, staggering under heavy loads.

Beirut sat on a promontory which jutted out into the Mediterranean at the foot of an impressive range of mountains. We were met at the port by an Armenian student named Gharo Ovanessian. He helped us with our bags and found a taxi to take us to the University, a frantic fifteen-minute drive away, the driver's hand glued to the horn.

We rented rooms from a Chemistry professor who had a flat off campus and enrolled in classes. Compared to Cornell the student body appeared much more mature. This observation was supported by the black beards and sweeping moustaches of 'students' from Aleppo, Damascus, Amman and various towns of the Lebanon. There were Armenians, Kurds, Palestinians and flashy Arabs from Saudi Arabia and the Emirates, at that time called the Trucial States. The first day in the Political Science class our professor, Cecil Hourani, asked the students to park their side arms on his desk or leave the class. A rattle of guns hit the desk from half the students and the other half left class firmly wedded to their weapons and their right to bear arms.

There were five American students that year including John and me.

We all found our fellow students stimulating: more interested in toppling governments than resorting to 'panty raids' to burn off high spirits. Their long history in an area famous for internecine battles and invasions left them with a kind of quiet dignity and quick temper.

In addition to the native Druse, Christians and Moslems, Beirut was full of Palestinian and Armenian refugees. The latter were still recovering from a more distant relocation but they refreshed their memories with a chapel in their graveyard, the walls of which were lined with bones of relatives massacred while fleeing Turkey. Many of these Armenians had recently left Palestine having made the mistake of thinking they had found a safe haven and they loved nothing more than to wave photographs of Stern Gang atrocities depicting Arabs as the victims for a change. The Palestinians were more subdued, the proximity of rats' den refugee camps on the outskirts of Beirut dampening enthusiasm. This salad of racial genes was spiced with wealthy Arabs from Saudi Arabia and other Moslem countries, who came to Beirut to wallow in the bars and discotheques. Beirut in the 1950's was the playground of the Middle East. No one foresaw the carnage that would be visited on this sybaritic world.

But the seeds had been planted and it did not take many weeks before we discovered that the American University of Beirut was a political proving ground in itself. Pitched battles between students and the army resulted in the University being closed as often as it was open. I had been expelled for an infringement of the rules and we had moved from Dr. Constantine's modern flat to a converted storage area over some donkey stables in Ras, Beirut where we had an undisturbed view of the Mediterranean, a rich aroma of donkey manure and access was along the top of a wall.

My father had not found my being expelled amusing and forthwith cut off any further funds. I found a job, training racehorses early in the morning at the track under Beirut's unique umbrella pines. During the day I worked cataloguing books at Khayat's Book Store opposite the main gate of the University. At weekends I took assignments for the Alumni Magazine and interviewed graduates in Aleppo, Damascus and wherever else the editors decided there were interesting stories. John and I managed to live off my meagre earnings but I was relieved when our mother showed up towards the end of the academic year taking over the shopping.

We rode along the beaches and swam horses in the sea. We skied at the Cedars of Lebanon, explored Crusaders' castles and watched marijuana grow in the Bekaa valley. There were souks (markets) in Damascus to be explored and the walls of the old town in Aleppo to be climbed. And I discovered the Oriental horse. Although I did not realise it at the time, this was a turning point in my life.

Fereydoun had written that he would be in Teheran for the summer and would we come visit him when the academic year was over. My mother and I decided to go to Iran. John decided he had better mend fences at Yale and returned to the United States.

We arrived in Teheran by plane in the beginning of June and were met at the airport by Fereydoun. He drove us to his family's garden in the village of Dezashib in an area known as Shemran north of Teheran, a summer retreat for wealthy Teheranis. That first night, in a garden scented with jasmine and moonlight sliding in the shadows of giant plane trees, with the Alborz Mountains looming black against them and jackals howling faintly in the distance, I met Narcy. Fereydoun's sister, Iran, had married Narcy's brother, Eskandar, two years previously and Narcy was visiting from Shiraz for the evening.

We had stumbled over a small white stray dog in the garden; discovered we both liked dogs and stoutly defended this one against Madame Ala's outraged protests. We lost the argument and the dog was ushered out of the garden by the head gardener but it was the start of a friendship and when Narcy returned to Shiraz, where he was Chief Engineer for the Nemazee Hospital, he invited my mother, Fereydoun and me to visit.

Paved roads existed only in some parts of Teheran, not even between Teheran and Shemran. There were certainly none between Teheran and Shiraz, which is a drive of about a thousand kilometres, south. The landscape was brown and flat except where sharp mountains rose perpendicular to the plain. Every so often an oasis of trees emerged from the heat shimmer. We stopped for melons and tea and a chance to breathe air, not dust.

We reached Shiraz on the evening of the second day. We had passed Persepolis, sixty kilometres before Shiraz and stopped to pay homage to the giant columns and figured reliefs and tried to imagine what Alexander the Great was thinking of when he put the great palace of the Achamaenians to the torch over two thousand years earlier. It stood alone on a vast flat plain, the only solid structure in a civilization of mud hovels. A few goats and sheep were browsing for wisps of dry grass in the cracks of the stone steps watched by a shepherd boy with a felt hat on his head, accompanied by a giant hairy dog.

Narcy met us in his house and announced that he had laid on a special wild boar hunt for us the next day. This was a three hour drive further south to a swamp and village called Dasht-e-Arjan, the valley of lions. We hunted pigs, thigh deep in ooze that gave off gaseous bubbles of foul smelling decayed matter and we swatted mosquitoes. When it became dark we made camp in some near mountains above the valley of Dasht-e-Arjan.

Fereydoun and my mother lay down in their sleeping bags near the embers of the fire soon after we had finished dinner. Narcy suggested he and I go for a leopard hunt. I thought I heard Fereydoun giggle but I wasn't sure. Narcy led the way, his rifle cradled professionally in his arm, while I stumbled in pursuit, tripping over rocks and scratching myself on thorn bushes. We settled on a large rock as a suitable site for spotting leopards and were looking out over Dasht-e-Arjan clear and bright in the moonlight when Narcy suggested I marry him and stay. Tempting as this was I remembered that my mother had always regretted that she had not completed her college course when sent from Argentina to the U.S. many years before. I agreed to a postponement. I would return to Cornell, earn my degree and then join Narcy in Shiraz.

Horses at Hidden Springs were used for farm work as well as pleasure riding
Louise, aged 11, driving Nellie

Louise competing on Firefly

 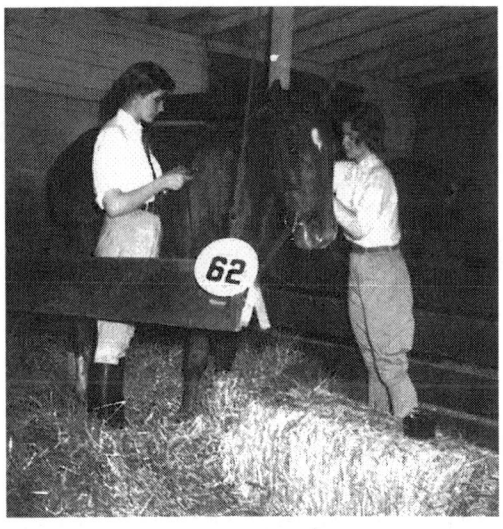

Left: Louise at Hidden Springs Farm   Right: Louise, and Margo Pringle, competing with Wilson at Cornell - Photo courtesy of Margo Liberty

Left: Louise driving Rhoda in New Hampshire
Right: An affinity with horses

Chapter 2

<u>Marriage, Shiraz and Norouzabad</u>

I returned to the U.S. and Cornell to finish my studies, majoring in Classics and English Literature. Narcy and I kept up a sporadic correspondence. I broke my back schooling a young horse over fences for friends and spent my senior year with a maternity jacket covering the body cast. Towards the end of the academic year representatives from companies began interviewing the top third of the senior class for possible jobs. Out of curiosity I attended a few of these interviews. Appalled by the dangling bait of the retirement plan I wrote Narcy a letter asking if his Dasht-e-Arjan proposition was still on.

"Narcy," I wrote," you will not believe what these people are doing to the entire senior class at Cornell. They are telling us at age twenty-one that the height of ambition is a place on a fishing wharf in Florida. Tell me there is more to life!"

"Come live with me and be my love," he quoted, adding, "and meet me at the Marble Arch in London at eleven a.m. on October 3rd."

I went to England, found Fereydoun looking very British studying medicine at Edinburgh and together we were standing under Marble Arch on October 3rd. Narcy was not there. He had forgotten and was hunting in the northern forests with some Pahlavi Prince but he did show up later in Paris where I had gone to see my Mother.

Despite some family doubts that I could adapt to a completely different lifestyle, we were married on 1st February, 1957 at my father's farm, Hidden Springs, in Great Falls, Virginia. The minister who married us was a local Baptist who agreed to perform the service more out of a sense of humour than any serious religious convictions. In name I was Episcopalian and Narcy was a Moslem but religion was not a serious priority in either of our lives. My father was not too pleased by my choice of husband or future. He had hoped that I would marry one of the young lawyers in his firm. In retribution and unknown to me he had sent a notice to the New York Times stating that I had married this Persian Prince and was going to live in Iran because I liked horses! I was glad to be enlightened on one subject. I hadn't known Narcy was a Kadjar Prince.

Narcy had a degree in Engineering from Yale and an M.S. from the University of Michigan. On his return to Iran he had been given the position of Chief Engineer at the Nemazee Hospital in Shiraz. We lived in a staff house on the Nemazee Hospital compound and started a family. First to be born was Roshan, a beautiful curly headed daughter who was riding swaddled at my waist before she was six months old. Eighteen months later we were joined by Ateshe who had survived a fall I took off a horse when she was seven months on. A son, Caren, was born three years later.

Narcy had bought fifteen thousand hectares of land over the mountains in a valley to the south. The area, called 'Siyakh', meaning thirty frosts, was full of migrating Qashghai tribesmen in the spring and autumn and later when the Army (at the suggestion of U.S. military advisors) confiscated the land for a fraction of its value, to create a firing range, was full of soldiers.

There was a river that ran along the southern edge and mountains to the north. There were herds of gazelle, wild sheep, jackals, foxes and wolves. We were told there were leopards and hyenas but we did not see them. We planted fruit trees and wheat. We built a small house and a stable. We raced with the Qashghais on our horses as they passed through.

We had also started a small farm near Shiraz where we built a house, started a chicken business and introduced our children to the rural life. Narcy had already bought himself a horse; a beautiful bay Qashghai stallion he had named Albert. As a wedding present a cousin of Narcy's gave me a black Basseri stallion that I named Kyrie Eleyson to commemorate my four years of choir at Cornell. These two lively stallions were soon joined by two mares that we bought and started our venture into breeding the Oriental horse.

Narcy had been happy to start his career in Iran 'learning the ropes' in Shiraz and dabbling in agriculture. When his first contracting job led to the takeover of his beloved valley, Narcy was persuaded to change his status and, in order to comply with government regulations for First Class contractors, which stated that they be based in the capital, Teheran, instead of the provinces, we rented the remaining small farm to some Point Four advisors and moved the horses, dogs, canary and children to Teheran.

To compensate us for the loss of Siyakh and to encourage us to continue raising horses, Narcy's father, General (Prince) Mohamad Hussein Firouz gave him a property that had been in the family for some time. Norouzabad was one hundred and forty hectares of barren land a half hour's drive west of Teheran. There was little to recommend the situation. It was flat and drab and barely supported some scrub grass poking through the gravel and rocks.

The Firouz/Farmanfarmaian family had once owned much of the land between Teheran and Karaj. This was not surprising considering that Narcy was descended from a long line of Kadjar princes. His grandfather, Farmanfarma, was the son of Firouz Mirza who was the brother of Mohmad Shah and was married to Mamdali Shah's full sister. Farmanfarma (his title) produced over forty children. He was advanced for his time and ensured that all of them were educated abroad, and provided for. Narcy's father, Madsein Mirza, as he was familiarly known, was educated at the Corps de Pages in St. Petersburg and later in Paris. This one hundred and forty hectares was one of the few pieces left of the vast lands they had owned. No one had ever bothered to cultivate it and it did not look like much. It looked like a lot less when we had to sell off two thirds of it to pay for developing the remaining third. Fortunately for the success of the experiment we were too young and inexperienced to realise the amount of work and money that would have to be poured in to make the farm a success. Triumph of optimism over expedience. And we did not have much capital to spare after the confiscation of the farm in Shiraz and the expense of setting up a new company.

On all sides of us empty rocky desert stretched to the trees of distant villages on the lower slopes of the Tochal mountains in the Alborz range. The mountains were the only majestic feature in the unrelieved flatness: dry folds of brown earth and rock rearing in a long uneven line from east to west. In winter they rose white against azure blue. Sand grouse and jack rabbits were the only animals that seemed comfortable in this environment. During the first winter we discovered that wolves followed the flocks of sheep out of the mountains and into the plains, howling around the stable we had built at night. There was a 'nar' or canal, on the north side of the property, which brought water from the Karaj River, forty five kilometres to the west. Although this water was primarily destined for the village of Yaftabad near Teheran, the 'mir ab', or water master, added us to his list of customers. When he wasn't around we resorted to furtive nightly theft.

Sometime in the past an optimist had named the place Norouzabad. Norouz means, literally, new day, and is the name of the Zoroastrian New Year which falls on March 21st, the Vernal Equinox. 'Abad' in Persian means to develop; 'ab' for water and 'bad' for air. Taken together it was either a bad joke or a good omen. It was obvious that it had never been cultivated in spite of its name. Several years later, after we had been labouring on our patch of land, the owner of the adjacent land to the west, observing our efforts, turned his into a gravel pit. We would have been well advised to do the same but we wanted to farm.

We shivered in sub zero temperatures in the winter, planting trees. Sometimes we had to build fires on the ground where the tree holes were to be dug to thaw out the soil. Spring was a semicolon between winter and summer. Suddenly the temperatures would hit forty degrees centigrade and climbing. There was no shade. We planted trees, we sifted rocks from the soil and we piled manure on the land to make humus so the water would at least pause on its way back to the underground water table. Narcy's training had been as a civil engineer so he knew all about what happens to water. His farming skills were more in the way of hereditary landlord managing the feudal lands but those days were gone. He worked during the week at the office of his construction company (Firouz Construction) and spent weekends and lunch hours with a shovel in his hands. I had been raised on a farm in Virginia and had spent two years at the Cornell Agricultural College and knew how to raise crops in a temperate climate where it rains on time. Neither of us knew what we were doing in a place that was never intended to be farmed.

I had found an old house near central Teheran for us to rent. It was three stories tall and narrow and reminded me of the houses in Georgetown, Washington D.C. There was a fireplace in the living room and tall plane trees and a small pool in the garden. It was close to the building where Narcy had established the Firouz Construction Company and close to the Iran Swiss School where we enrolled the children.

Teheran had replaced Isfahan as Iran's capital city when the Kadjar Dynasty took power and, in 1962, when Narcy and I moved there it had a population of around three million. For me it was still bearable as there were vestiges of old world rural smells and sounds. There were horse drawn 'doroshkehs' and donkeys carrying goods for sale piled high on their 'palouns', hawkers crying the price of potatoes and onions, mattresses to be fluffed or snow removed from roofs in winter. But there were cars and taxis and buses which made it bedlam compared to the quiet clip-clop of horse drawn vehicles in Shiraz where tribeswomen flitted quietly along the tree lined streets offering their loomed horse blankets for sale. There was Teheran and there was Shemran. For those who could afford it there were houses in both. Shemran was a collection of old villages nestled at the base of the Tochal range twenty kilometres north of Teheran. There were springs of cold, rushing water from melting snows on the mountains and centuries old plane trees. The villagers tended their crops with hoes watched by their grazing cattle and donkeys while in the summer children of the wealthy, who could afford gardens and country houses, splashed in swimming pools and their parents rode the elegant Turkoman horses brought down from the northern steppes. Between Teheran and Shemran was barren land slowly being filled with houses as the two crept towards each other.

Narcy and I juggled our lives between the town house on Avenue Damghan in Teheran and Norouzabad. We built a small cottage on the farm spending weekends planting trees and riding horses.

We had brought our extended herd of ten horses with us from Shiraz. Roshan and Ateshe also began to ride and that was when we ran into trouble. The Oriental horse is a far cry from the mixed breed Thoroughbred hunters that I had ridden in Virginia as a child; as different as learning to drive in a Jeep and then being given a Jaguar sports car or being told you should marry a Washington, D.C. lawyer and instead attaching yourself to a Persian Prince with a passion for the great outdoors. There is a great deal to the Oriental horse and just about all of it I had to learn myself. There were no books that accurately described this phenomenon.

Louise and Narcy on their wedding day at Hidden Springs Farm, Virginia

Louise and Narcy during a hunting trip

Gashghai migrating near Shiraz

Louise and Narcy raced with the riders that headed the migration

Left: A donkey foal is carried across a saddle during a migration
- (Courtesy of Joan and Kay Taplin)
Right: Firouz first home near Shiraz nicknamed "Little Lou (Louisiana)"

Louise and Narcy – early days in Shiraz

Louise and Narcy Firouz shared a love of horses, dogs and farming
Right: Louise with Ateshe

Chapter 3

Finding my Unicorn

We had abandoned the profitable business of raising chickens when we left Shiraz for a reckless plunge into breeding horses. By this time I was beginning to discover that there was more to the Oriental horse than the Arabian but the horse books at my disposal were dismally lacking in information about horses in the Middle East and, even worse, about the horses of Central Asia. I had figured out that there were Ghashghai, Basseri and Darashuri tribal horses in Iran. There were also several types of Kurdish horses from the Iran-Iraq border as well as horses that were called Arabs and looked like the others. But I was unaware of the wealth of equine diversity that was waiting to be discovered.

Our children shared our enthusiasm for riding but were unable to control the spirited stallions that Narcy and I rode so, in April, 1965, three friends and I left Teheran for the north of Iran to find some ponies. We were not sure whether the Caspian Sea area had any ponies but I remembered seeing small horses grazing on harvested rice paddies when we had visited friends in that area the year before.

The Teheran Zoo did have a pony they were willing to sell at an exorbitant price. It was a short, fat Shetland that reminded me of a similar beast from my childhood in Virginia. Peppermint's bad temper had come close to terminating any further contact with horses, a circumstance that might have altered my future considerably, and my father notwithstanding.

We left Teheran early in the morning while there was still little traffic on roads that were usually a snarl of cars, trucks, horse-drawn doroshkehs (carriages) and donkeys. The road to the Caspian led up the hills to the ski slopes of Ab Ali. Then it climbed steeply over the three thousand metre pass of the shrine, Imam-Zadeh-Hashem, where the late Shah, Mohamad Reza Pahlavi, was once said to have been cured of a near fatal fever while travelling to Teheran by horseback. Mount Demavand loomed high above the road, its six thousand metre snow-covered volcanic cone outlined against a brilliant blue sky.

We were four women travelling alone which, in those days in Iran was unusual as it is once again in these post revolutionary days. Women are supposed to stay at home, cook meals and raise children, not stray alone conversing with strangers. There had been token objection from the more concerned of the husbands but close proximity with the fruits of a western education probably convinced them that the local population would come off second best and that we were competent to deal with any difficulties we might meet. Besides myself there were two Americans; Penny Williams and Jean Engel, both of whose husbands were working in Iran. There was Azizeh Azodi, a distant relative of Narcy's. They were both descendants of the Kadjars, the dynasty preceding the Pahlavis. Azizeh was a brilliant woman who spoke at least seven languages and was somewhat over qualified for this trip but she was determined to find a pony for her nephew, Mahmad Reza. She also managed several large farms in the area of Shahrud in the east of Iran and was a good rider herself.

We followed the road as it wound steeply down towards the Caspian that is twenty four metres below sea level and meant that we were dropping over three thousand metres in the space of two hours, much less by train, causing severe earache for those unfortunate enough to fall asleep during the descent. From the snow covered slopes of Mount Demavand through cold, rocky gorges with the river leaping through fresh spring foliage on the upper reaches of the forest, the landscape metamorphosised into full-blown leaves and lush gardens in Amol at the base of the mountains. For those who knew where to look, the window of an assassins cave could be seen in one of the vast rock faces. We met trucks on the attack at every corner, mules and horses carrying heavy packs of cut green wood plodding by the side of the road and loose cows that took no notice of the traffic.

We stopped at a gas station outside Amol at the beginning of the Caspian plain, still sixty kilometres from the sea. There, stocky horses were waiting to have tins of kerosene for cooking fuel loaded on their packs before climbing back to their landlocked villages in the mountains. As we waited our turn to have gas hand pumped into our car we asked the owners of the pack-horses if they knew of any horses smaller than theirs.

"Sure, we've got plenty of foals," they replied.

"No, we mean an animal that does not grow any bigger when it is the size of a large dog or sheep. You know, a pony."

This word 'pony' has now passed into the Persian language but at the time it had no meaning. We used it for lack of any Persian equivalent. We were rescued from the doubtful stares of the drovers by a young student. He had been listening to the exchange with scarcely disguised amusement. He knew of a tiny horse in Amol. In fact, he said he even knew what a pony was because he had seen a picture of one in a magazine. It had been described as a "Poonie". His only doubt was that the fat, shaggy pony we had described and he had seen in the magazine did not quite fit the description of his small horse.

We drove into the town of Amol and parked the Jeep. Women were squatting beside piles of red radishes. Carts of produce pulled by horses were splashing through pot-holes in the dirt road. Donkeys were staggering under burdens of cucumbers, bricks or cement urged on by impatient small, black-clad, and bow-legged men. We dodged the traffic and leapt potholes and followed the student into a narrow alley. High mud walls with branches of orange blossoms hanging over them gave off the pungent scent of their blossoms that just about won the battle with the equally strong scent of urine and horse dung. After about a hundred metres the alley opened into a small courtyard where women in chadors (an elongated scarf that envelopes the female form from head to toe) were washing clothes in the water of a jube (an open ditch) running down the middle. The water seemed to serve a combined purpose of irrigation and sewage disposal with bits of orange skin and potato peel and other residue floating past in the brown water. The clothes did not seem improved by the bath.

On one side of the courtyard there was a small horse covered with cement dust attached to a crude wooden cart. He was about eleven hands tall, slim, with tiny ears and large bold eyes. He had fine legs and small hooves. He wasn't a fat, shaggy pony. He was a beautiful horse. The boy was apologetic.

"I said he was small," he said, "but I also said he does not look like the pony in the picture."

"Never mind," we said, "we'll take it."

The student stayed to bargain with the owner and we agreed to meet him later at Amol's only hotel. We had had dinner of kebab and dugh (watered down and herbed yoghurt drink) and were squatting on our cots when he returned. He said the pony was ours and he had stabled him in a caravanserai near the hotel. We thanked him and paid him for the pony with a handsome commission to reward him for his initiative.

The small horse we now owned was puzzling. It was the size of a pony but it definitely did not fit the description of a pony. It was a perfectly formed miniature horse. Where could such a perfect creature have been produced? Was it native to Iran; was there more than one? Although we had all visited Persepolis, none of us remembered that a similar horse had been carved into the East stairway of the Apadana two thousand five hundred years earlier and we fell asleep speculating about our brilliant find.

Still puzzling over our purchase of the previous day, we were having breakfast of tea and white goat's cheese in the hotel's dining room when a man with blue eyes and a gold ring in one ear came to our table and introduced himself. He said that he had heard that we were buying horses.

"I am a horse dealer", he said "I can help you."

The commission we had paid had obviously been above the market rate and our reputation was preceding us. We collected our things, paid the bill and joined the horse dealer, Mahmad Ali, by the Jeep. He suggested that we leave Amol and go forty kilometres east to Babol by way of the old road. A new asphalt road had recently been built to connect Amol directly with Babol, part of an overall plan for the ambitious Asian Highway which has never proceeded much beyond the dream, but which did not include any villages where we might find horses. The old road was gravel and wound through rice paddies and thatched-roof hamlets. Geese and ducks blocked the road. Herds of horses and cows grazed the brown rice stubble in the fields, knee deep in mud. Drainage ditches on both sides of the roads were one to two metres deep. In the slow moving brown water, snakes writhed and turtles moved amongst them undisturbed. I don't know if these snakes were poisonous. Probably some were and some weren't. What amazed me were the quantities. There seemed to be more snakes than water. The movement of the water was caused more by great swarms of snakes nudging around each other, rather than by any current.

We took the Jeep as far as possible but the condition of some of the side- tracks left us no alternative but to abandon the Jeep and continue on foot. This made us vulnerable to the scores of small, half-naked children who collected around us. Their mouths were half-open, their noses running, their bare feet sank in the mud and their thin bodies were clad in rags.

Their parents were lethargic with overwork and poor rewards. When their tasks were interrupted by our arrival, they glanced listlessly in our direction. A woman, her hand clutching a partially washed shirt in the snake-infested water, smiled tentatively. A man pulled his yoked oxen to a halt to watch us. The villages consisted of poorly built mud and wattle buildings with thatched roofs. These were perched on stilts to keep them above the mud and water.

We met many people that day in many small villages. The insides of their huts were in sharp contrast to their surroundings. The walls were lined with gay hand-embroidered material. A samovar simmered gently in a corner of the one room. We were always offered tea. We also took off our shoes at the door which, given the ankle deep mud at the door-steps was a sensible practice. The one-room houses were immaculate and the felts on the floor swept clean. Mahmad Ali was not sure what we were looking for but at each village which yielded no horses of interest to us he grew more optimistic.

"In the next village", he said," there are many small horses. "

He was not deterred by the fact that in the next village there were no small horses at all. We were having tea on the porch of a hut when Mahmad Ali came into the yard leading a small chestnut stallion.

"Yes", we said, "this one is good."

Here was another perfect specimen of a miniature horse.

There was an aura about these special horses that set them apart from the hundreds of others that were grazing the rice paddies, or carrying packs. It was difficult to say why one appealed and another did not even though they might have been about the same size.

By now it was late afternoon and we were tired. We left Mahmad Ali to sort out the problem of getting Hawk, as his new owner, Azizeh, had named him, to the same caravanserai in Amol as the bay stallion, which Penny Williams now owned and had decided to call Akai. We found the same hotel again and ordered the ubiquitous menu. The hotel offered no other.

We had made some progress because we owned two beautiful tiny horses. It was clear, however, that although there were pony-sized horses, there were not very many of them. They were not recognized locally as a distinct breed In fact, Mahmad Ali was puzzled why we said 'yes' to one horse and 'no' to another which was the same height. 'What's the difference?' he asked. We admitted that we didn't know either but the ones we had bought was slim and fine and the others resembled shaggy Mongol ponies of no particular distinction. Except for brief visits to swim in the Caspian Sea, none of us had ever been to this part of Iran before and had no idea what to expect, ignorant as we were of the geography, the people and the animals.

We had heard that three hundred kilometres further east there was an area known as the Turkoman Steppes. Horse people in Teheran spoke of the Turkoman and their horses with awe. We decided to abandon Mahmad Ali for the time being and go east to see what other surprises we might find while Mahmad Ali promised to take care of the two ponies in the caravanserai until our return.

Whilst we had been asking Mahmad Ali about horses we had also probed a bit about his people.

"We are Gilakis," he said proudly.

"We are not Fars" (meaning those people on the other side of the Alborz Mountains who were unfortunate enough to live in hovels like Teheran).

They certainly were different. They were short and swarthy and all seemed to have bow-legs. They spoke a different language which did not seem to be related to either Persian or Turkish although Carleton Coon, in his book 'The Seven Caves', identified similarities to the Basque language. They lived by planting rice, netting wild ducks in winter and planting garden crops for the Teheran market. We did discover that they were not particularly friendly to strangers but could tolerate them when a commercial transaction was in process. Once the deal was done there was little interest in furthering the acquaintance. According to Mahmad Ali, unlike other ethnic groups in Iran (Kurd, Azari Turk, Baluch and Arab) the Gilaki tended to stay in their own area and not migrate to other parts of Iran looking for work. They hardly needed to. Their own area was so fertile and intensively worked that they provided Teheran with much of its fresh produce: lettuce, fava beans, radishes, squash and cucumbers. There were plums in the spring, and then peaches, figs, apples and oranges. There were Circassian walnut trees and almonds.

The countryside south of the Alborz range is characterised by savannah and desert. Oases of cultivation have sprung up wherever there is water. To the north of the Alborz the strip of land bordering the Caspian is a geographical cornucopia. The Caspian Sea is rich in sturgeon, herring and other fish and, in the winter, snipe, woodcock, ducks, geese and swans settle on the swamps and are caught by men in boats beating gongs and netting the startled birds. The high, plaintive cry of the Siberian swan sounds mournful against the raucous call of mallards, teal and pintails. It is part of the migratory route between the summer Siberian nesting grounds and winter quarters which stretch from northern Iran to Africa. Tea is grown on the steep mountain slopes near the town of Ramsar and tobacco is grown further east near Turkoman country. The forests are the province of wild sheep, goats, barking deer, red deer, leopard, boar, bear, lynx and wolves. At night jackals trot along the beach looking for fish washed up or a Caspian seal caught in a fish net and left to rot.

The houses of the Gilaki vary according to the amount of rainfall. In the west of the Caspian, where the mountains come close to the sea, the annual rainfall can reach a thousand millimetres per year and the houses are raised on stilts and have steep, thatched roofs. Some are cone shaped like a dunce's cap; others resemble thatched roof cottages in parts of England. There is ample evidence that ancient civilizations found the area attractive. Although the Caspian littoral itself has not yielded much in the way of 'tepes', ancient earth mounds, the ' Yeylagh' or summer quarters on the slopes of the Alborz and Tales ranges are rich in archaeological finds.

As we travelled east we found the land had risen above the swamps. Stubbled rice paddies were replaced by green wheat fields. There were dried brown cotton plants and the remains of sunflowers. There were chickens and turkeys amongst the geese and ducks. Pack-horses still came down from the mountain forests with firewood but there were more high-wheeled carts drawn by tall, slim horses. The average horse in the Amol region had been a stocky fourteen hand animal. These horses were fully fifteen hands and the conformation was more that of a racehorse than a draft animal. We did not see any ponies.

There was a subtle change in the smells. We were happy to leave the heavy odour of rotting vegetation behind. Rice paddies which had been left for the winter with animals grazing in them have a characteristic smell, rather like a swamp, with gas bubbles popping to the surface and bursting with rank decay.

Further east we noticed that the orange trees had just begun to blossom and the smell mingled pleasantly with the barnyard smells of the wattle and mud villages. Oxen and horses hitched to crude wooden ploughs were turning over the rich black loam for spring planting. Flocks of sheep were grazing green barley, and the first lambs were chasing each other around the ewes. There were fields of lettuce being harvested by women and children. Tall fava bean plants were a different, lighter colour. As we drove east the Alborz mountains ran parallel to the road on our right, their forests of oak and beech and lime trees bright green with spring foliage. On the left rolling fields of wheat and barley led to the Caspian Sea. The Sea itself was not visible until we had passed the town of Behshahr where the summer palace of Shah Abbas of the Safavid dynasty dominates the town from an olive clad hill. Shortly after it is possible to see the Bay of Gorgan formed by the peninsula, Mian Kola, which juts out into the Caspian Sea and provides shelter to geese and ducks that winter there.

The road was both the main highway from Gorgan to Teheran and an extension of the barnyards on both sides. There were trucks loaded with baled cotton from the gins on the Turkoman steppe. They lumbered slowly around chickens, ducks, geese, turkeys, donkeys, cows and horses. Fortunately the sheep were driven in flocks and kept out of the road. Physical evidence of the unequal battle lined both sides; corpses of all kinds lay in various stages of decomposition. It was a salad of olfactory sensations; manure, orange blossom and decaying animal matter.

We reached the small Turkoman town of Gorgan, at the beginning of the Turkoman steppe, just as the sun was setting. Men were strolling in the dusk along sidewalks, dignified in their astrakhan hats. Many of them carried hand- woven carpets for sale. An occasional rider passed on his felt-draped horse. There were few women but those that we saw made a bright splash of colour with their silk or woollen scarves, bright orange and red, their slanted eyes and bronze skins and a relief from the shapeless black chadors of the Gilaki.

We asked for some place to spend the night and were directed to a hostel off a small alley behind the town's main square. It was the only one, we were told. The scent of blossoming orange trees in the garden camouflaged the aura of centuries of travellers and, desperate to wash off the dust of the long day travelling, we were directed to the washbasin in an outdoor corridor. We rounded the corner only to discover that we were last in line. Ahead of us were a number of truck drivers stripped to their shorts, displaying strong, hairy arms and chests, their ablutions sending sprays of water over the walls and the floor. Puddles of water, mixed with dust, cigarette butts and spittle, were forming around their feet. Food was served in the courtyard near the unsanitary wash basin so we found a man selling kebab on a sidewalk where we squatted on wooden benches, picking pieces of meat from a communal dish.

Pahlavi-Dej, eighteen kilometres north of Gorgan, was famous for its Thursday bazaar. Although not planned in advance, the next day was Thursday and we were up at five o'clock, two hours after we had been woken up with morning prayers, impatient cows and stamping horses. Long before we could actually see Pahlavi-Dej we knew we were heading in the right direction. Fur-hatted Turkoman men on tall, felt draped horses, high-wheeled carts with the horses backed half way under the cart, herds of sheep and cattle were all heading in the same direction that we were, and competing for space over an ancient hump-backed narrow bridge. We plunged into the middle of the bazaar where men and women, their orange and black silk scarves billowing around them, crouched by the edge of the dirt road selling everything from camel bone knives, silver and garnet Turkoman jewellery, felt carpets, bright red knotted wool carpets and hand embroidered trouser sleeves.

Further down the road was an open field crowded with horses, camels, sheep and cattle all brought from kilometres away to be sold. The 'raison d'etre' for Pahlavi-Dej was clearly this bazaar, as the entire town consisted of a crossroads with a few shops and some round, felt covered, huts called 'alachekhs' (erroneously referred to in most books as 'yurts'), parked on the outskirts. The streets were given over to the serious business of bargaining. Horses, pedestrians and herds of sheep threaded their way through the merchandise. Everybody must have been up at least as early as we were because they were all hungry. Samovars in the dust were doing a brisk business as glasses of tea were sold. Chunks of meat were being cooked over charcoal braziers, the menu obvious from the skin and head of the butchered animal which lay near the fire. Camel and sheep featured prominently that day. Pahlavi-Dej is not far from the eastern end of the Caspian Sea so there was also kebabed sturgeon. There was something that looked like a hot-dog-shaped hamburger that we did not try because it was impossible to tell what it might have contained.

The Turkomans themselves were Oriental-looking people with round, olive- skinned faces and slant eyes. They were certainly not ethnic Persians and spoke a form of Turkish. They looked exactly what they were - children of the open spaces of Central Asia.

The Persians of the central plateau of Iran have European features with black hair, brown oval eyes and the women swaddle themselves in shapeless black shrouds when they scurry about their tasks outside of their houses. Persian men wear a European type of clothing: trousers, shirt and countless sweaters even when the temperature is over forty degrees centigrade.

The Turkoman women wore an ankle length tunic dress (often red, crude silk) with a brightly coloured silk scarf. The men wore trousers and a long shirt that hung out over the trousers down to the knees. Over this they sometimes wore a striped red silk coat and to complete the picture a tall, lambskin hat.

Many years later, when Narcy and I bought a small piece of land near a village called Ghara Tepe Sheikh, far off on the Turkoman Steppes, we grew to know the Turkomen people very well.

We had a good look that day at all the wares for sale on the street. We also sampled most of the varieties of kebab before we went into the field where animals were being held for inspection and sale. There were many animals and, except for the sheep, they were milling around restlessly.

Stallions tethered on long ropes attached to a stake driven into the ground had soon discovered the limits the rope imposed and immediately claimed their territory. What ventured inside that sacred circle, within range of those hoofs and teeth was obviously considered fair game. The camels were hobbled and had a plug of wood in the nostril, rather like the ring in a bull's nose, for additional control .The camels were both one-humped and two- humped, Dromedary and Bactrian, and paid no attention until you strayed carelessly close and could either be bitten or spat upon.

Azizeh Azodi, the new owner of the pony, Hawk, became very interested in a large gray Turkoman stallion being held by a Turkoman in an astrakan hat and a red silk coat. They were a handsome pair and well worth admiring and what we did not at first appreciate was Azizeh's more serious interest. She was thinking of buying the stallion.

"Azizeh," we said, "are you sure you want to do this?"

'Why not', she answered. "After all I've bought a pony for my nephew. I might as well buy a horse for myself."

This time we negotiated the price ourselves and it was definitely cheaper than paying a commission. Ata Ullah, the owner of the horse, was a considerate man and did not leave us holding the stallion kilometres from nowhere. He agreed to ride the horse to Gorgan and find a caravanserai where he could be stabled for the night. We paid him and forgot to ask just where this caravanserai might be in Gorgan. Our naïve trust in all of these horse dealings was never betrayed. Whether this was due to the unusual sight of foreign women travelling alone and buying horses, or part of the code of honour, I have never discovered. Logic dictates that since I probably pay far over the going price, as bargaining was not part of my early education, it is to everyone's benefit to keep me alive and trusting.

The holding area for animals brought for sale was flanked on three sides by 'alachekhs'. The fourth side was exposed to open steppe. It seemed that there were kilometres and kilometres of gently rolling steppe stretching out before us. We asked what was there apart from green grass and flowers bending in the breeze.

"Nothing", was the reply, " just a few alachekhs, some animals and, of course the Russian border.'"

The road leading from Pahlavi-Dej to the Russian border had once been paved with brick and elevated above the level of the steppe but it was in such a deplorable condition that we abandoned it and drove on the grassy steppe that was much smoother. We passed the remains of an ancient fort that was part of Alexander's Wall, a Parthian structure from the third century B.C. that must have resembled the Great Wall of China before most of its bricks were removed to build modern houses. It was originally built for the same reason the Chinese built theirs - to keep out exactly the steppe horsemen who were living there now.

Our informant in Pahlavi Dej had said it was sixty kilometres to the border and sign posted so we were not worried about straying into Russia and drove into a small river that we reached, without hesitating. Accustomed to the rocky rivers of the previous days in Amol we were not prepared for the mud and sand of the Atrak and were sucked in and immobilized. A Turkoman who had crossed the river just in front of us with his horse watched with curiosity.

"You are stuck,' he said.

"You noticed," we replied.

The Turkoman tethered his horse and helped us push the Jeep out of the river. Then, looking us over more carefully he said

"You were going to Russia."

It was not a question. It was a statement of fact.

"No we were not," we replied, "we're going just as far as the border."

"But this is the border," he replied, puzzled that we could miss something so obvious.

We were grateful to the Turkoman for saving us the trouble of having to escape from Russia. But, at that moment, we saw agitated soldiers clad only in pyjama bottoms pouring out of a crenellated fort to the south of our position on the Persian side of the border. We realised that we were between the Russian fort to the north and the Persian fort to the south. We were caught in the middle and we were also caught because the unprofessionally clothed soldiers carried guns and made their demands quite clear. We were to return to the fort where we would be questioned. Unlike the concrete structure on the Russian side, which looked like a Second World War bunker, the Persian fort looked as if it had been built several centuries previously and had all the defences for horsemen carrying bows and arrows. There did not seem to be anyone in charge of this group of soldiers but finally the soldiers admitted that their Captain was planting cotton in no man's land.

We were offered tea by the soldiers' wives who did not disguise their delight in seeing us. Not many people dropped by for tea in that area.

As the Captain was taking his time we were offered lunch, by far the best meal we had had since starting the trip, the rice and khoresht (meat sauce) hot and spicy. The Captain returned after lunch and treated his visitors, or prisoners, with courtesy. It seemed the border sign had blown down in a recent storm and no one had replaced it.

"There is no need for a sign really," he said. "Everyone is illiterate and everyone knows the border is the Atrak River," he said looking dubiously at us.

We admitted that we did know and that we also didn't know that the Atrak was a creek. We were released and invited to return for a meal any time we were passing by although by common consent we agreed this would not be soon.

We returned to our hotel in Gorgan and the next morning began to look for Ata Ullah, the grey Turkoman stallion having assumed his previous owner's name. We found him in the fifth caravanserai and also found a truck driver who agreed to drive him to Teheran, probably more out of curiosity than profit.

The truck driver agreed to meet us at the caravanserai in Amol where the ponies were stabled while we went ahead with the Jeep. When we decided we were enough ahead of the truck driver we stopped in a likely village near Babol and, instead of spending a whole day looking for just one pony, we found a mare almost immediately. She was beautiful, but thin and covered with parasites. Her place in the history of Caspian horses glitters because, not only was she the first foundation mare, she was also the dam of Momtaz-e-Mahal who eventually became Prince Philip's and lived, for a while, at Windsor Castle.

Long past midnight we arrived at Norouzabad where Narcy, was waiting impatiently to greet us. The little bay pony mare we called Alamara and she became our first Caspian. The two pony stallions left almost immediately; one to a stable near Teheran and Azizeh's to Shahrud, three hundred kilometres east on the edge of the Kavir desert where Azizeh had farms.

Louise with Alamara, her first Caspian mare

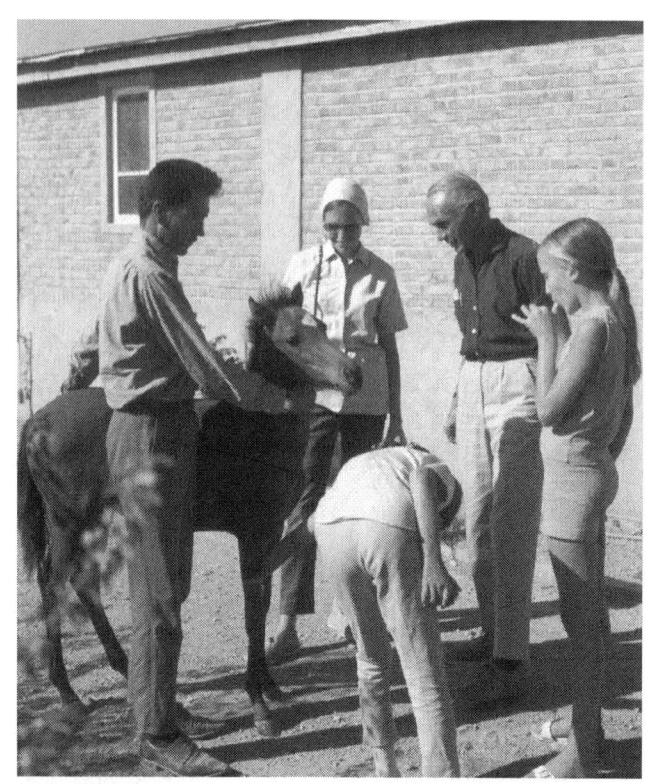

Louise introduces Rostam to the German Ambassador,

Louise and Narcy teaching Caspian foals to be handled

Chapter 4

<u>Establishing a herd of Caspian Horses</u>

Alamara was an instant success with the children. She aroused some curiosity amongst the omniscient horsemen of Teheran who were clearly convinced that she did not exist and to this day the Iranian Horse Society does not recognize the International Caspian Stud Book so brilliantly compiled, first by Lawrence Alderson of The Rare Breeds Survival Trust, then by Brenda Dalton in England. Some years later an eminent German archaeozoologist told me something similar after I had given a paper on the horse at a conference in Budapest." Mrs. Firouz, you showed us some pretty pictures. But, I must tell you, there is no such thing as a miniature horse."

Indeed its height indicated that it was a pony, which is what we called it in the early days, but its structure and gaits and, eventually, research showed clearly that it was a horse.

The horse dealer, Mahmad Ali, had come down with the horses. He impressed our Kurdish grooms with his gold ear-ring and blue eyes. He, in turn, was impressed with the possibilities. He lost little time assessing the situation and offered his services for the further acquisition of what he obviously considered of scant value on its native heath. Although, at this stage, I was not interested in owning more than one pony, Mahmad Ali persuaded me to trade a mule we had been unable to train for three more ponies. As the mule disappeared down the road dragging Mahmad Ali I was convinced we would never see either of them again. But, true to his word, Mahmad Ali returned a week later with three small stallions crowded into a 'vanette' truck.

The first pony out of the truck was a noisy chestnut stallion. Jehan, as he became known, was to become an outstanding stud in the United States. He leapt to the ground and greeted the curious watching horses with a peculiarly high, shrill neigh. We soon realised that this was one of the 'hallmarks' of these little horses. Not shy or bashful or frightened by his dwarfed stature, this horse from the Caspian threw a challenge to the horses of Fars. Following Jehan there came two bay stallions that we soon sold to what was turning out to be a waiting list of children. It began to seem the experiment might succeed.

Mahmad Ali suggested we might make this a profitable small business. The idea had merit but I did not want to ask Narcy to invest in such a problematical venture when he was so stretched with his business and the development of Norouzabad. I told Mahmad Ali to go back to Babol and I would think about it.

The Shiraz grooms had abandoned us when we moved north but we soon found that we had been adopted by a protean Kurdish mafia. Omid Ali, Mohamad Ali, Mahmad and Arab came from Ahjean and Jaffarabad near Assadabad in Persian Kurdistan. This was an area that had once also belonged to Narcy's grandfather, Farmanfarma, so the feudal connection was already there. It seemed to me, however, to have shifted one hundred and eighty degrees. They took over, gradually sorting out class distinctions without recourse to advice from anyone nominally in charge. Omid Ali, by virtue of native charm and an admirable urge to better his lot from day labourer to anything else, emerged as the leader. Tall, with a handsome, even-featured face, he was an attractive man. He had a great deal of dignity and some years later, showing ponies in Virginia, he turned the heads of many young female riders. He bungled his first job at Norouzabad. He had been told to take the sheep to graze the grass lining the irrigation canals but they must have strayed into the fresh green alfalfa with predictable results. Omid Ali burst through the kitchen door demanding a knife. Five minutes later the knife had converted fifty kilos of pregnant ewe into so much dead meat. He was warned that everyone was entitled to one mistake and he had made his. He accepted the reproof with good grace and went on to become a competent, dynamic head groom. He had a shrewd eye for Caspian ponies amongst the ubiquitous scrub stock in the swamps. Mohamad Ali was a good friend of Omid Ali's. He was also the only one to stay with the Caspians through the Turkoman experience to the end. Like Arab he seldom ventured an opinion but, unlike Arab, whose patrician looks concealed an impoverished intellect, he had a knack for getting things done. Mahmad went down in history as having bested the Master of the Shah's Horse in one of the friendly jumping competitions we used to hold but he will be best remembered amongst admirers of the Caspian for his trip to England. He accompanied three ponies and spent three months with the British Caspian Stud in Claverley near Wolverhampton. Despite the warmth and kindness of the Jenveys and their groom, Fred, nothing could dent his horror of English weather and the isolation of an alien land. "Bloody British weather" was about the only English he learned. This heartfelt sentiment summed up the experience, obscuring any novelty the west might have to offer.

Roshan and Ateshe were eight and six respectively and soon learned a basic, minimal control of the ponies. Caren was only three but he was learning on a lead rein. I was encouraged by the initial success of selling the two bay stallions and by the Caspians' performance as children's mounts. I decided it was time to return to the same area around Amol-Babol for a more intensive search for horses. There was still the question of money. It seemed to me that some of the jewellery given to me by Narcy's parents at the time of our marriage could be put to better use in a business than hanging around my neck. So I sold some of it and put the proceeds in a money belt strapped around my waist.

In early June, Roshan, Ateshe, Omid Ali and I left Teheran in the same Jeep. In the pre-dawn quiet the streets were deserted except for a few stray dogs rooting in garbage. We arrived in Amol at six a.m. just as the sun was appearing through the mists that rose from steaming rice paddies. Mahmad Ali was easily found. He was drinking tea from an estikan (tea glass) with the samovar bubbling nearby in his small orange grove. We accepted glasses of the strong tea and reached for fresh warm bread and white goat's cheese. Then we discussed our strategy for the day.

The shortest route from Amol to Babol was the excellent, newly constructed asphalt surface laid over virgin rice paddies. There was the old road that we had taken on the previous trip, which followed the solid ground of the higher elevations of the forested foothills of the Alborz Mountains where villagers had their small huts perched on the drainage slopes. Mahmad Ali still thought this road would take us through greater concentrations of horses. He said that the fields would be drier and we would not be knee-deep in swamps. He directed us south of Amol across an old brick bridge and through neat orange groves. The gravel road started on the outskirts of town and wandered in the vague direction of Babol, weaving through villages randomly strewn on both sides.

After a few kilometres we left the gravel road and took a barely discernible path that led towards the mountains. There was a river to cross. It was swollen with water from snow melting high up on the peaks of the Alborz. Beyond, the track was overgrown with Christ-thorn bushes that shrieked along the sides of the Jeep. After sliding down the side of a steep hill we discovered that the track blended again with the river. The water was white where it played around large boulders. The Jeep somehow made it through and coughed to a stop. We had emerged in a clearing in the woods with a number of small wooden huts. The arrival of a white Jeep caused panic amongst the children that proved that we were not the first people to have travelled with a car to this spot. The Red Lion and Sun (Iranian Red Cross), which uses white Jeeps in its inoculation programs, had obviously made a lasting, if painful, impression. There were a lot of adults around, mainly male, seemingly unemployed for the day. They were oblivious of their fleeing offspring.

When we said that we were there to buy horses there was a change in the atmosphere. Men who had been hanging over bamboo fences sucking on cigarettes or pieces of straw ran to the backs of their huts or disappeared into the surrounding fields. They returned dragging mud covered horses, their manes tangled with burrs. As each tired and depressed Mongol type pony was persuaded near the Jeep we tried to explain what it was we were looking for.

"No," I said, "we're looking for a small horse about this size", pointing to a level at my waist, which, as it happens, is eleven hands.

"Baleh (yes)", they replied, "You want a colt." Almost immediately somebody produced a colt.

"No," I repeated, "no colts. We are looking for a full grown horse this size." "Khanum (Lady), there isn't any such thing. Horses grow, you know. Born small, grow big!" There were many hand gestures and giggles to explain the obvious.

"That's right," said Mahmad Ali, "these are the best and the smallest that there are."

Mahmad Ali seemed to have forgotten that he had recently delivered three fine specimens of the animals for which we were looking. And they had not looked anything at all like these. He remembered this in time to suggest that we adjourn to fresher fields. There was a chorus of angry cries from the villagers who claimed compensation for their time.

There were similar reactions in the next village. There was also a frustrating absence of anything remotely resembling the fineness and quality that we had come to associate with the little Caspian ponies we had seen before. Not daunted, Mahmad Ali suggested further and even more inaccessible places. We became lost in a maze of converging stream, recently cleared patches of virgin forest and roughly constructed, crude log cabins with shingles perched carelessly on the slopes of the roofs. A gray-bearded man in a smoky, airless den sold us a lunch of mast (yogurt) and bread washed down with tea. Our spirits revived but we decided that luck was not with us on this trip. We had better try to find our way back.

We passed large herds of stocky, Mongol type ponies in shades of bay, chestnut, palomino and pinto. New-born foals slithered through the mud at their dams' feet. There were stallions snaking around each other in an initial, vicious mating dance. Although we looked very carefully there was no sign of anything remotely like a Caspian.

Somewhere near a village called Darunkola, at a junction of river and track, we saw a young boy herding a group of nine horses. There was one horse in this group that stood out. He had the tiny ears and bold head of what we were calling the Caspian pony. We asked the boy to stop. He wheeled his mount around his charges while we inspected the elegant grey more closely. Although he was slightly larger than the others we had bought previously I felt he was prime material for a riding pony. We bought him.

Mahmad Ali leapt on his back and, with only a rope around the pony's nose, led the way to a village on the gravel road from Amol to Babol. We handed over Barfie to someone who happened to be going to Babol anyway and agreed to ride the horse in for a fee.

Well, we had one horse. Maybe we could find another. But we had no luck and reached Babol hot, thirsty and limp. Mahmad Ali went off to find horse dealer friends to see if they had any promising leads. We went looking for fruit.

Mahmad Ali returned with a small, stocky man wearing a dirty, wool cap. Apparently he knew of a tiny horse and agreed to come with us. We got back in the Jeep.

"Where are we going?" I asked as I steered the car around a cart loaded with lettuce, narrowly avoiding a woman whose black 'chador' was covering her face and vision.

"Back the way we came," said Mahmad Ali smug with righteousness. Silence seemed too good for him but further speech was impossible.

The two horse dealers were firm. If we wanted to find ponies we would have to go back. I only hoped that the friend's pony inhabited more solid ground than some of the other places that we had visited that day.

We returned to the familiar gravel road and retraced our steps until we were approximately half way between Babol and Amol. We turned off the road through a flock of protesting grey and white geese. We were on a slimy track and sliding between deep drainage ditches. Ten minutes later the track ended at a group of small, sagging mud huts. Their thatched roofs sprouted a fresh crop of bright green grass. Behind one hut there was a pile of manure that partially hid the door to a stable. Chickens were scratching through the rich harvest.

My eyes were glued to the domestic scene and I didn't notice a narrow, deep ditch that ran across the path. Too late, Mahmad Ali yelled "Eest!" (stop) and we hit the ditch. The force of the impact dislodged the back seat. Omid Ali, Mahmad Ali and his friend pitched forward onto the front seat landing on the children. The heavy thud of the spare tyre, broken loose from its mooring mixed with the subsiding tinkle of shattered Canada Dry bottles.

The owner of the hut in front of us emerged through his door at the sound of the crash. We got out of the Jeep and decided to see if there were any ponies before coping with the damage. We asked the man whose ditch this was if he had any small horses. He disappeared around a pile of manure and soon returned with a tiny grey skeleton of a stallion. The most prominent feature of this emaciated creature was an abundant mane that obscured his eyes and face. He had a long thick tail that he carried proudly, swishing clouds of flies. We had found Aseman (Persian for sky/heaven).

We bought him and made arrangements for him to join Barfie in Babol. Then we assembled the curious onlookers into a human bulldozer and pushed the Jeep out of the ditch. An hour later we met at a gas station on the outskirts of Babol where we found a truck to take the horses to Teheran.

While we were avoiding the carts, pack horses and pedestrians of Amol on our way back to Teheran, Omid Ali and I spotted a little bay horse pulling a crude wooden cart with amazing speed. He was a brief vision of elegance before he disappeared down an alley of the bazaar. Omid Ali and I glanced at each other. We parked the car, gave instructions to the truck driver to wait for us on the edge of town, reassured the children and ran down the narrow, dark alley of the bazaar in pursuit.

We were tired from the long day and we were out of breath; past the spice bazaar, past the beaters of copper, we dodged a donkey staggering under bales of cloth. Around another corner we were followed by shouts from two women wrapped like mummies in their chadors. We thought we would never catch more than fleeting glimpses of a tail turning yet another corner when, there he was, standing beside a merchant's stall.

Approaching the owner of the cart I asked whether his horse was for sale. Since no one seemed to have much regard for these small horses I didn't think we would have much trouble. To my dismay the answer was an emphatic "Na," (no)

"But why "? I asked.

"I have been working the bazaar for fifteen years," the man replied, "and I have never before owned a horse like this one."

Having seen us pant up in pursuit we could hardly deny that we, too, had been impressed.

The horse was too beautiful to dismiss. Fortunately the urge to bargain triumphed over sentiment or reason and we were soon negotiating. The owner of the horse had many good points but the most irrefutable was that he could not leave his cart full of materials without a way to move it. At that point another horse appeared around the corner and we bought it and handed it to the owner of the bay; a further cash exchange and we owned Ostad (Professor).

Omid Ali gathered up Ostad's ropes and we ran back through the bazaar, the pony trotting briskly behind us. We reached the Jeep just in time to rescue Roshan and Ateshe from the throngs of children who were crowding around them. Leaving Omid Ali to lead the pony through Amol to the rendezvous with the truck we shoved our way through the crowd and joined the impatient truck driver.

The sun was setting and this last loading was done in the early evening gloom. There was a chorus of frogs from the rice paddies and an instant crowd of children and men who seemed to spring from nowhere whenever we stopped.

"Look at that. They bought some 'yaboos' (nags)," said one man.

"What do you suppose they want them for?" asked another.

"Must be for sausage meat. I've heard foreigners will eat anything, even if it's 'haram' (forbidden)."

"Buy bigger ones, they've got more meat!" yelled a helpful third.

"Don't be stupid. These people know what they are doing. The little ones are cheaper."

What haunting words these are now.

We said goodbye to the curious crowd and got back into the Jeep for the three hour drive back to Teheran. The truck followed us. Roshan, Ateshe and Omid Ali promptly fell asleep.

The road gradually veered away from the rice paddies and passed briefly through dense forest before reaching the cliffs of the narrow pass climbing through the Alborz Mountains. Moonlight played on the snow-covered peaks and occasional jackals darted across the road in the glow thrown by the headlights. There was the twinkle of scattered kerosene lamps across the river where sheep herders enjoyed a last glass of tea before wrapping themselves in their thick felt coats for the night.

Narcy was waiting for us at Norouzabad.

"I hope you haven't bought a load of junk," he said encouragingly. He hopped over the side of the truck and a voice could be faintly heard.

"They're beautiful"

"Well, they will be when they're full grown" said Hassan, his round Kurdish face expressing surprise and disapproval.

Ostad, Aseman and Barfie (snow) settled well into their stalls at No-rouzabad. They seemed reassured at meeting Jehan the next day in the primitive beginnings of a pasture. We had had reservations about releasing four strange stallions together because this sort of thing is not done in civilized parts of the world. But, we reasoned, if they were to be children's mounts, the time for aggressive or excessively lively behaviour was before they were saddled. Our faith in the inherently kind temperament of the Caspian pony was justified. In the next nine years at Norouzabad only one stallion was injured by exuberant spirits in the pasture. This was a new stallion that thought a concerted charge by old timers was a serious threat. He tried to bail out between the pipe railings of the fence and bloodied his nose.

Ostad was found pulling a cart in Amol, a Caspian coastal town

A stallion falls from a bridge on a trip to find Caspians

Searching for Caspians at Alag
in the background is a Caravanserai built into the rock

(Photo courtesy of Farshad Maloufi)
Ateshe and Caren galloping through the Nahr
on the upper boundary of Norouzabad

Chapter 5

<u>Steeplechase and Sunshine days</u>

In 1965, three years after we had started working on Norouzabad, we felt we could live there and that Narcy and the children could commute to Teheran for the Construction Company and school every day.

The house at No. 10 Damghan Avenue was turned into an office for the Firouz Construction Company. The hay store at Norouzabad became a living room with a small kitchen walled off in the north corner. The two rooms that we had built for ourselves when we first settled in Norouzabad were turned into bedrooms. We built an extra bedroom, two baths and a study. We optimistically put in pipes and taps but the well that we had dug was connected only to plenty of buckets. Neither did we have electricity and didn't expect to have it for some time. We installed gas pipes and wall lamps that were fuelled by cylinder gas. There were two open fireplaces that burned twenty-four hours day and night in the winter.

The move was so popular that when it came time for our son, Caren, to start school he refused to go. His point was that he could not afford to waste his time playing around in school when there was real work to be done on the farm.

So far, breeding the Caspians had proved successful but it was more in the nature of random experiments. I established a studbook with the foundation herd of the horses which we had so far collected and bred. Although the Sumerians and Achamaenians must have selectively bred the small horses in addition to just catching them wild in the Zagros Mountains I doubted that anyone had consciously bred these horses since the Medes had experimented with selective breeding using both the small Zagros horse and the imported Central Asian breeds more than two thousand years before.

Our five stallions and six mares were a small nucleus. Audacity was the word applied by local horsemen. "You haven't discovered this animal, you have invented it!" But we did re-establish what turned out to be an ancient breed, set up a Stud Book, initiate exports and help form an International Caspian Stud Book with studs in England, Australia, New Zealand, the U.S, Canada, Scandinavia and Europe. Until we sold Norouzabad and the Caspians to the Royal Horse Society in 1974, we were able to breed without resorting to crossing back into the same parental lines but we were worried by the pathetically small numbers of the horses we were able to find.

From 1965, until 1974, when we sold our herd of Caspians to the Royal Horse Society, we produced twenty three foals. One foundation stallion, Jehan, was bought by a consortium headed by Kathleen Mc-Cormick and exported to the United States. One stallion and one mare were bought by Mrs. Joan Taplin and sent to Bermuda. A stallion and mare were presented to Prince Philip when he attended the celebration of two thousand five hundred years of Monarchy in Iran in 1972. Norouzabad, by this time, was beginning to look like a farm. The early 'yaghouti' (ruby) grapes were fetching a good price in the fruit bazaars; the strawberries were plump and the asparagus was much sought after in Teheran's supermarkets. Bluegrass and clover pastures, with seed imported from Buck Warner's Country Store in Great Falls, Virginia, were thick and green, kept in that precarious state by almost constant overhead irrigation, to the delight of the ponies who grazed happily in an iridescent haze. Narcy had become a good farmer, while still dash-ing to distant towns building water and sewage systems.

After we had moved into Norouzabad, we celebrated the 'house-warm-ing' with a steeplechase. Riders were invited from all of the stables in Teheran and Shemran as well as from the surrounding countryside. There were twelve men and six women starters, each competing in their own race. The course was over four kilometres of undulating wasteland interspersed with 1.20 metre high thorn jumps we had erected. Over one hundred guests had been invited to watch the great race and the betting was brisk.

On the morning of the race gleaming stallions were polished to a coppery shine; cooks were assembling their ingredients beside large cast-iron pots and open fires and guests began arriving in a line of dust along our dirt track. The hay barn had been swept clean and card tables were set up for the guests to eat their lunch in some semblance of comfort.

As I led my mount, Poobah, out of his stall one of his hind feet stepped into a huge cauldron of steaming 'Ash' (a thick soup), one of a row bubbling over pits dug by his stable. No harm was done to Poobah who went on to win his race with a comfortable margin. I declined 'Ash' for lunch and avoided giving the recipe to guests who were consuming the soup with relish.

The races had been divided into 'Ladies' and 'Gentlemen'. Sexual discrimination was not the determining factor, neither for horse nor human; there were simply too many entrants for one race so we divided by human sex and most people rode stallions anyway. Poobah, my splendid little Shirazi stallion, beat Penny Williams on her Turkoman stallion, Windsor, with Mrs. Shaki and three others riding Kurdish horses, trailing not far behind. The "Gentleman's' race was won by Colonel Shaki with his son, Babak, a close second. Narcy, Joe Williams, Narcy's cousin Sharokh and other distinguished amateurs rode well and drew warm applause from foot-stomping spectators for their sportsmanlike approach to some small infractions of rules by others.

The prizes were later given by my father, John G. Laylin, who happened to be in Iran dealing with a dispute on the Shatt-al-Arab River. His attitude towards a wayward daughter had softened since the wedding and the arrival of three grandchildren. We had been welcomed back into the fold, albeit at a distance.

One of the spectators at the steeplechase was the British Ambassador, Sir Dennis Wright. After conferring with his long time friend, Lev Tamp, he suggested that this most successful of events be followed by one in which they could all join: a fox-hunt with Lev's Saluki dogs. Fired by the success of the steeplechase we agreed to host this event the next year.

We practised with Lev and his Salukis for several months in the countryside around Norouzabad. The closest village to us was eight kilometres away. Firouz Bahram was an old Zoroastrian village with a disused fire temple and the remains of a tepe surrounded by a few alfalfa fields and patches for growing melons and vegetables. Between Norouzabad and Firouz Bahram was flat to undulating brown earth bisected with old, disused irrigation canals and 'qanat' mounds (ancient underground irrigation system). There were kangaroo rats, jack rabbits, foxes and jackals in abundance.

Lev and his wife, Margaret, raised Salukis and hunted them as a hobby. Their house and stable were in Shemran, high up at the base of the Tochal range of the Alborz Mountains, with gardens and great open spaces around them. Lev was originally from the Caucasus in Russia but escaped during the Russian Revolution to Iran. He studied engineering in Germany and returned to Iran to help build the great railway system that Reza Shah initiated. When Lev moved to Baghdad, in addition to his engineering work, he became Master of Fox Hounds to King Faisal. After the Revolution there in 1957 and the massacre of the King, he escaped, riding to Teheran on his Arab stallion.

The Salukis were all from Iran although the breed is known widely throughout the Middle East. The Tamp dogs were tall, slim and came in colours of fawn, brown, black and grey. They were friendly to a fault, revealing that their kennel was the furniture in the Tamps house. They were also sight hounds as opposed to smell hounds. If they saw a fox or hare they chased it. If the quarry was smart and hid in an irrigation ditch, they lost it. The quarry was one hundred percent canny but we had some splendid runs and reached territory that we would not normally have explored, leaving the local wildlife to reproduce another day.

All was ready for the great fox-hunt of Teheran. A field of sixty riders was invited and they all came mounted on their stallions. There were Arab, Kurd and Turkoman horses prancing over the dusty plain. There was much neighing, rearing, kicking and biting until it was established that this was work and not some Afghan fighting pit. Fortunately no one was riding a mare.

Lev Tamp cast his Saluki's and we waited for the sight of a bushy tail speeding through the thorn bushes. A few crows flew overhead, some pigeons scurried out of 'qanat' holes and a distant herd of goats grazed peacefully on the sides of an irrigation ditch watched by two shaggy dogs and a boy holding a staff. The air was crisp with low-lying clouds moving slowly over the plain towards the high mountains. Apart from sixty stallions milling angrily around each other, their riders cheering them on in a most non-English-hunt fashion, nothing moved.

Lev was visibly anxious. His dogs were moving out of his control and he was searching for new directions. Lev was looking north when his dogs looked south and spotted the goats. They were streaks of light moving over the brown plain. Narcy, Agha Khan Bakhtiar, riding a magnificent golden Turkoman stallion, and I watched goats, boy, sheep dogs and Salukis blend in a whirlwind of dust. The field of riders, sensing something was happening, took off after Lev who was charging north with a 'tally ho' after the one dog who had not mistaken a goat for a fox. Narcy, Agha Khan and I cantered the one kilometre to the milling goat herd, paid for the goat which had been mistaken for a fox and managed to persuade the Salukis to return with us to Lev who had genuinely been chasing a fox.

The foxes must have sensed something was amiss and put out an alert. Nothing moved, not even another goat and we returned to Norouzabad for the Hunt Breakfast. Sir Dennis Wright led the chorus of thanks to Lev Tamp for a wonderful day in the field.

"Fine day, Lev," he said, "thank you for putting on this hunt."

"I enjoyed the day also, Sir Dennis", he said, "but it was a pity that the dogs were not blooded."

"But of course they were."

"No, they were not and that is a pity for the attitude of the dogs."

"What about the goat?"

"Vat goat!" burst Lev, his Russian-German accent exploding.

There had been many followers on foot who echoed Sir Dennis' rally call for an event that all could follow. This time we thought we could not go wrong with a paper chase and the next year we staged one; emphasis on one.

Our children and their friends laid a cunning trail twisting amongst qanat mounds, tepes, and high dirt walls in Firouz Bahram and eventually back to Norouzabad. During the night a strong wind rose from the west scattered the carefully laid pieces of paper. Roshan was the first to notice that there was no longer a trail to follow. She rallied her friends, who had spent the night with us, and they mounted their Caspians with sacks full of tin foil attached to their saddles. The enthusiastic field of paper-followers was not long in arriving and anxious to begin. We could still see the children in the distance with our binoculars.

Under starter's orders, the first casualty of the day flew to the ground; a Samaritan from the watching crowd was kicked in the stomach while pulling the casualty from under stamping hooves and they were off. In full gallop with no possible opportunity to look for the strips of tin foil the children were laying, the entire field of eighty riders, on stallions seldom offered the opportunity to gallop free out of a riding ring, took off. They passed the children within the first twenty minutes and disappeared in the maze of Firouz Bahram's mud wall alleys. Out on the other side they swept into vineyards, cattle yards, herds of sheep, a brick quarry and then open countryside broken by wide ditches, which claimed a fair share of the field.

Although most of the riders returned for lunch, each claiming to be the winner, it was late at night before the last rider-less horse was found and stabled. The last rider hitched a ride home in a car, never claiming his horse.

Narcy's mother, Safiyeh Khanum, had agreed that her cook would prepare some of the dishes for the lunch. She had not arrived to see the riders start but, according to the Kurdish grooms, was unhappy that we had not waited for her. A young British Third Secretary, who had come with Sir Denis Wright, told me he thought Safiyeh Khanum was locked in the bathroom and refusing to come out.

"Safiyeh Khanum, is that you in there," I asked, my ear glued to the bathroom door. Some muffled sobs were the only answer.

"Please. Come out"

"You started without me," the disembodied voice said, "I was all ready to ride."

Safiyeh Khanum had apparently been a good rider in her youth but I had not seen her near a horse in the ten years I had been living in Iran. The idea that she might have wanted to join the others on horseback never occurred to me. When she finally emerged from the bathroom her riding clothes, a bit tight around the waist and bottom, clearly showed that she had seriously entertained the notion that she would join the riders.

"Safiyeh Khanum, I do not think this is a good idea," I said, "We do not have any quiet horses."

"What makes you think I need a quiet horse," she thundered, "I am perfectly capable of managing anything you have."

She marched out of the house with great determination and I stayed to check on lunch.

"Mrs. Firouz, you had better come at once," the same third Secretary from the British Embassy cried looking distraught. Your Mother-in-law has gotten on one of the stallions and he is bolting around the front pasture out of control."

Safiyeh Khanum was clinging to the mane of a large black stallion, the reins flapping as he charged around at full gallop. The Kurdish grooms were trying to grab the swinging ends of the reins as he thundered past making little impression on the ever-increasing forward velocity. Eventually the stallion grew tired of pursuing the same track and slowed sufficiently for the grooms to catch him. Safiyeh Khanum slid off, looking triumphant.

"I told you I could ride!" she crowed.

The children had returned from laying the useless trail and were watching the performance.

"Granny sure can ride fast," they sighed with awe.

There was Iran and there was Persia. Iran was the cocktail and Embassy parties where Spiro Agnew and Jackie Onassis held court. Teheran was a favourite watering hole for myriad Hollywood stars following the money. Once it was fashionable to say 'rich as an Argentine'. Now the accolade was bestowed on rich Iranians who thought nothing of flying to Nice for the weekend.

There were dinners at Embassy residences and private houses; black tie and long dress. Caviar was heaped in piles of gleaming grey eggs. There were imported cheeses and snipe and woodcock from the Caspian. Cocktails were offered before dinner, a different wine for each course of the meal, and liqueurs after dinner. There was dancing and charades and often the last guests left after three a.m.

In the summer there were lunch parties around swimming pools set in great sweeps of smooth green lawn and shaded by giant plane trees. The latest bikinis barely covered bodies conditioned by tennis and aerobics, massage and much time in the Caspian Sea. The men, arriving at these lunch parties in their Mercedes Benz, Jaguar and BMWs, shed their business suits and ties and put on scant bathing suits before beginning to push the ladies into the pool to the accompaniment of much squealing. White coated waiters moved amongst the brown bodies offering vodka tonics, beer, iced tea and cold watermelon juice. Iran was the glitter and the money, boats and water skiing on the Caspian and skiing at Dizin. Persia was the little mud villages with a green necklace of cultivation; oases in vast brown plains. Here donkeys and horses were the transportation. Women worked, stooped over, hoeing the fields of watermelon, and cattle were used to plough the small plots. Cooking was done over wood fires or small kerosene stoves. Bread was baked in round, dried mud ovens from wheat they had grown and ground on water-driven mill stones. There was no electricity and no piped water.

Trying to establish a bridge between the dichotomies, some American teachers from the Iran Zamin International School, which our children now attended, and I, started the Teheran Gymkhana Association in 1972. This organization benefited greatly from the help given by the Riding and Polo Federation, whose President, General Zamani, seemed to instinctively understand the need to remove children from the destructive influences of so much easy money and how important it was to instruct children early in good sportsmanship. Officials in the riding world welcomed our initiative and placed no obstacles in the path. On the contrary, they did everything possible to encourage us.

They were sunshine days. We had found the solution to making money, though not much, established a breed of horse and were enjoying giving children the feeling of zest and accomplishment that comes with partnership in sport. What we had not anticipated was the oil boom of 1973 and the crazy euphoria, then despair, that tore Iran apart and it became a kind of Persia again in a giant swoop.

Louise waiting to take part in the Ladies Race in Teheran

Albert – Narcy's twenty one year old Fars stallion

Louise winning the Steeplechase at Norouzabad on her Shirazi stallion,
Poobah

"Sunshine Days" – Narcy (second left) and Louise (centre) Her brother,
David Laylin, is on the right

"The prizes were given by my father" –
John G. Laylin with the Firouz family at Norouzabad

Racing in Teheran – Ateshe (left) on Ostad and Roshan (right) on Shahrya. .Roshan and Shahrya accompanied H.R.H. Princess Anne on a ride during her visit to Iran with Prince Philip

Ateshe jumping Ostad at Norouzabad

Chapter 6

<u>The Lure of Ancient History and Archaeology</u>

The ancient Greeks were impressed with Persian horses, writing about their unusual size and praising the lush pastures of the Zagros mountainous regions of what would be the modern equivalent of Kurdistan, parts of west Azerbaijan and Luristan. Timotheus of Gaza, writing in the sixth century B.C, described two different breeds of horses raised in the area around modern Kermanshah in western Iran. He wrote: "The horses of the Medes are of moderate size with small ears and heads unlike those of a horse: they are courageous but tire easily in the heat through difficulty in breathing. The Nisaean horses are remarkable for their great size and feet that shake the earth."

Today's breeds of horses are descendents of those ancient types: a mixture of the Indo-European imports in the second and first millennium B.C. and the tiny indigenous horse. This form of Oriental horse is now collectively called Plateau Persian in Iran to differentiate it from the Turkoman which, while geographically in Iran, is a completely different breed and from an area that has no connection with the Zagros.

The Plateau Persian is further subdivided by the tribes, or areas, that breed them. There are clearly distinct differences in the types. The modern Kurd, a direct descendent of the Nisaean of the Achamaenians, is a stocky horse with strong bone and a short neck and back. Quite often the head is reminiscent of the larger horses on the friezes at Persepolis; a vaulting of the forehead from the occiput to the nasal bones.

By now I had been in Iran for ten years and, spurred on by my fascination with the archaic forms of horses I saw around me, had read many of the books on Persia's history that were in Shahzadeh's and Narcy's libraries. Shahzadeh and Safiyeh Khanum were also ardent collectors of ancient artefacts dug up by amateur archaeologists, better known as grave robbers. The market for these items was international and the prices for the better objects were spectacular. Legitimate archaeologists were regular guests at dinner and tales were told of strange finds and lost civilizations. My fascination with bones was dismissed although I gradually found myself consulted on Luristan horse bits and the identity of animals in carvings and seals.

The archaeologists were from Harvard, the Universities of Pennsylvania, Oxford and Toronto, or resident now in their Institutes like David Stronach or Ghirshman. It was hard to imagine the rigors of their lives 'on site' as they sat at Safiyeh Khanum's candle lit table, spooning golden caviar onto their plates.

Intrigued by the other side of these archaeologists lives, Azizeh Azodi, Jean Engel and I left Teheran in May 1967 for a trip through Azerbaijan and Kurdistan to visit some of the sites which David Stronach and Carl Lamberg-Karlovsky had described and which were contributing so much to my knowledge of Iran's ancient horse breeders and their horses. I was also curious to see if any of the various breeds of horses we might now find resembled the horses the ancient Greeks described.

Azizeh had translated books on Iranian history, from French, German and Russian, into Persian and was a scholar in her own right. Her delight in walking on ground where ancient people had lived was catching. "Whose pot do you suppose this was?" she said, nudging a shard by her feet in Marlik.

The piece of unglazed pottery was lying by a thorn and when she picked it up we could see the piece was at least two thousand years old and probably older. Parthian, Median, Achamaenian? Where Azizeh had her farms in Shahrud there were sites even older and she was not too impressed by anything so modern, since the Japanese team which had been digging there had come upon pre-historic sites dating back more than ten thousand years.

Marlik, a second to first Millennium B.C. royal necropolis, excavated by Dr. Fatullah Neghaban for the Iranian Archaeological service in 1961-2, was somewhere north of Rudbar below the Sefid Rud dam, on the way to Rasht in Gilan, but apparently the local name for the site was Cheragh Ali (Ali's Lamp). The farmers had never heard of 'Marlik' so we covered miles of olive orchards clinging to the mountains before this became clear. With the help of some horses from a nearby village to climb the steep slopes to the top of the mountain we navigated carpets of slow worms (glass snakes) which, by any name, look like one metre long brown-grey snakes but, we discovered later, are actually legless lizards. The horses did not object to the tiresome habit that the village children had of snatching the snakes up and tossing them in the general direction of strangers but these reptiles were a significant factor in our hasty review of the site.

The mound of Marlik looked like a natural hill on top of the mountains with olive trees as well as cypress growing on it. The tombs had been looted by antique hunters but what was to be seen in the Teheran Archaeological Museum showed an advanced culture of goldsmiths and potters who used motifs such as the Tree of Life, winged bulls and mountain goats with great sweeping horns. The impression was of a strong sense of living and supernatural imposed on the natural local beauty of the land which stretched over the hills and down into the Sefid Rud valley where the river tumbles in shades of white and blue; where the olive trees blend a soft moss green colour with a sky that mirrors the river and one feels an atavistic pleasure that living in such a place must have induced. The Marlik people left gradually, around the beginning of the first millennium B.C., probably from pressure of other groups coming down from the Asian Steppes. Today it is deserted. There is only a small village with a few cows and goats and children whose only toys appeared to be the snakes.

The Grand Hotel in the Caspian port town of Bandar Pahlavi (since reverted to its original name, Bandar Anzali) under the shadow of the Iranian Navy and the Shilat caviar factory, provided one of the last comfortable nights we were to have and we were off on the road to Astara on the Russian border by early morning. The road was tolerable until the village of Hasht Par but, thereafter, did not seem to have received any attention since the Russians 'built' it during the Second World War. At a certain speed it was possible to hit only the tops of the deeply indented 'corduroy' surface. Inevitably, just as cruising speed was reached, a cow, a pack horse, a flock of geese or a naked child would appear in the dust of the road. Our progress was erratic and jolting. Azizeh, who was not driving that stretch and could concentrate on the scenery, reported that the horses were of a uniform cast - undistinguished descendents of millennia of Mongol pack animals. There were scrub forests, a few patches of rice cultivation and isolated villages with crudely built huts.

When we reached the town of Astara the first thing we noticed were the prominently displayed and fully manned guard towers of the Russians. One of these, in the middle of town, straddled the border line that divides Astara into a Persian and Russian town.

Since our experience on the Turkoman steppe, we had a healthy respect for anyone's border post and took our picnic on the beach where we were promptly arrested anyway. The Russian border guards, ever alert in their towers, had called the Persian border guards who were drinking tea, and warned them that we were suspiciously close. Lazily indifferent to us, we were released and soon moved on.

My brother David, who had come to Iran to be a professional hunter, once used the telescopic sight of his hunting rifle to get a better look at the towers and reported leaving rapidly when a rifle swerved around to look back at him.

The security precautions continued as we turned towards the Talish mountains on the western edge of the Alborz range, the strong wire border fence built by the Russians running along beside us to within twenty kilometres of the top of the pass before it veered off to the right taking the dense forest with it. The denuded slopes on the Iranian side were in bleak contrast to the prolific growth on the Russian side and reflected a typically sad disregard for this valuable natural resource. There was a mass of dark purple, almost black, iris against a background of tall, green spring grass at the top of the pass and a view of the wide Ardabil valley and Kuh-E-Savalon, the mountain where Zoroaster was supposed to have been born.

The town of Ardabil is in the province of west Azerbaijan and the people who live there now are Azeri Turks, but it is built on Sassanian foundations, by a dynasty founded in 224 A.D. by Ardeshir 1 who claimed to be descended from the Achamaenians. The Sassanians lasted for four hundred years after they had defeated the Parthians, whose empire had stretched from Afghanistan to the Mediterranean, an empire which the Sassanians proceeded to enlarge, capturing the Roman emperor Valerian and taking him back to Iran along with thousands of other Roman prisoners. As a result some Christian communities were established but the main religion was still that of Zoroaster; the worship of Ahura Mazda, Mithras and Anahita, the goddess of water and fertility.

Ardabil stands in the shadow of the highest peak in Azerbaijan. Kuh-E-Savalon is four thousand eight hundred and eleven metres and dominates the green plain with its white peaks .The valley was full of sheep, cows and water buffalo grazing the pastures and Azizeh was soon eyeing the sheep with an expression which I recognised from our trip to Pahlavi Dej. Archaeology and the quest for horses were temporarily lost in her admiration for a ram she saw grazing with a flock on the slopes of Kuh-E-Savalon. Azizeh made a comfortable place for her purchase amongst the suitcases in the back of the Land Rover.

The innkeeper that night in Sarab showed no surprise when the sheep followed us into the bedroom and after we inspected the room we were not surprised either. There were two wooden 'takhts' with a filthy brown blanket on each and a dirt floor with wisps of straw and sheep dung. We hoped that other forms of life had been discouraged by the unsanitary conditions but this hope, on examination the next morning, proved futile.

There were yoked oxen, dragging crude wooden ploughs or ancient looking 'arabehs' (carts) and creating their own version of peak time traffic on the road when we left Sarab for Tabriz.

Tabriz is the capital of west Azerbaijan and is surrounded by high mountains and, although it was probably founded in Sassanian times or earlier, it flourished during the Saljuqs who rose to power in 1040 A.D. They were a Turkish-speaking tribe from Turkistan and were themselves defeated by Chengis Khan in 1218 A.D. The Saljuqs were well known for their architectural monuments, particularly the ornate brickwork of their tomb towers and under them, literature, the sciences and ceramics flourished but the Mongols did not tread lightly when they invaded Iran and the destruction was devastating. Many old cities were destroyed but the Mongols apparently had a change of heart later when the II Khanid Mongol dynasty made Tabriz its capital in the thirteenth century and it became the main intellectual centre of their empire. They built splendid mosques of which mainly ruins now remain. We did stumble across a modern museum which housed photographs taken by a French couple of the 1906 constitutional revolution against the Kadjars. The photographs were graphic and, looking at it now, prophetic, showing bodies hanged from trees and very young children struggling with oversized muzzle-loading guns.

Our next destination was Rezaiyieh, on the west side of the large salt lake then called by that name. In ancient times it was famous as Urumia and has reverted to that name since the 1979 revolution when many names changed with the disappearance of the Pahlavi dynasty. The dirt road wound past the green pastures of Khoy and through rolling, grassy hills bordering the salt lake which, with its flocks of pink flamingos, looked like gaudy jewellery. We were now driving in ancient Urartu, where exceptionally fine horses were reputed to have been bred in the ninth century B.C. Although we did notice some fine, strong specimens pulling carts, the enthusiasm for good horses would have appeared to have diminished since the days of the Urartians and the plunder parties of the Assyrians whose 'razzias' (raids) into Urartian territory two thousand eight hundred years earlier supplied them with cavalry remounts.

The Urartian kingdom centred round Lake Vann in Turkey and was important from the ninth to the sixth centuries B.C. They were probably indigenous peoples as they were non-Indo-European speakers, their language described by scholars as being close to Hurrian, the major non-Indo-European language of eastern Anatolia and northern Mesopotamia. The Armenians may well be their descendents as they borrowed much from their language and rose to power in the Armenian mountains after the collapse of the Urartian state in the last half of the first millennium B.C. The Urartians clashed constantly with the Assyrians over control of the horse rearing regions south of Lake Urmia and the devastation which remains from some of these battles were our destination the following day.

We spent the night in Rezaiyieh in a real hotel while the sheep slept in the car and in the early dawn made a quick visit to the two Saljuq towers in the middle of town or the Church of St.Mary's where one of the three wise men who went to Bethlehem is reputed to be buried. Turning onto the track which led to Professor Robert Dyson's site of Hasanlu, somewhere near the lower end of the lake, we passed through vineyards and Chaldean Christian villages and found a sign that said Hasanlu was just off to the left.

This first millennium B.C. site was being excavated by the University of Pennsylvania and was of particular interest because of the remarkable preservation of many of its structures and streets.

The walls of cut stone blocks clearly indicated the original configuration of the town and palace destroyed in a violent battle. There was a vivid contrast to the modern mud village of Hasanlu; an eerie feeling of travelling backwards in time in terms of cultural achievement. It had been attacked and devastated by Urartians and Assyrians in the Early Iron Age and, for all its impressive fortifications, had never been duplicated in succeeding ages.

Chapter 7

<u>A Hunting Trip, a Fallen Horse and a Stolen Gun</u>

Fascinating as our travels were, definitive evidence of a small horse eluded us.

Excavations at Hasanlu had yielded fragments of bones belonging to very small horses measuring about ten hands but the only equids in evidence with such small stature on that day were donkeys.

Maragheh, our next stop, had been the site of the discovery of a very small, pre-historic horse by a nineteenth century archaeozoologist named Wilkens. 'Equus fossilus persicus', the name Wilkens gave to the fragments of bones he unearthed, was subsequently questioned by other researchers who, for lack of contemporary evidence of a minia-ture horse in the Near East, insisted that any small equids must have belonged to the species Equus hemionus (onager or wild ass). Wilkens was eventually vindicated after an intensive study of skeletal remains from archaeological sites (aided by the presence of a modern Caspian skeleton). I was curious to see the area that had featured so strongly in arguments amongst researchers of equine lineage and there was also some reason to believe that Maragheh might have been the site of one of the seasonal pastures of the famous Nisaean horses of the Achamae-nians so admired by Herodotus. He had claimed breeding herds which ran to as many as fifty thousand mares. It was also reputed to be the pasturage for Mongol horses in the thirteenth century A.D. However, no particular type of horse was evident, although the Saljuq tomb tow-ers were striking; the brick work a tribute to the genius of man working with such a mundane source of construction material.

We knew we had arrived in Kurdistan when we passed some Kurdish women carrying water on their heads in old earthenware jars in the town of Saqqiz. They were not swaddled in black, but looked as if they were dressed to go to a wedding with layers of skirts, each a different colour and shimmering with gold or silver thread. Their head dresses flowed out behind them and their feet were bare.

Forty kilometres later we reached the turn off for Ziwiye, an archae-ological site located on the top of a steep hill, probably built by the Assyrians at a slightly later date than Hasanlu, although the presence of seventh century B.C. Scythian arrow heads found there indicated that settled civilization was in danger and empires were going to be tram-pled under the hooves of steppe hordes.

We were told that the track to Ziwiyeh was 'not good' but we judged the prospect worth the potential damage to the Land Rover and found a young man as a guide before turning off the main road into the hills. The phrase ' not good' was probably meant for horses because it was impassable. By using rocks under the wheels of the Land Rover to gain traction each time we found ourselves stuck (which was often), we eventually reached the village of Ziwiyeh and. abandoning the Land Rover, climbed over the remains of huge terracotta storage jars littering the near vertical slopes of the hill and arrived at the excavation on the top. There were remains of a fortress constructed by the Assyrians (or possibly by the Mannaeans, allies of the Assyrians), those bold plunderers of Median horseflesh.

We were easily persuaded to take an alternate return route which, we were assured, was shorter and, with the possible exception of the absence of any bridge across the river, much easier. Our authority proved to be correct on all counts. Due to lack of four-wheeled and hoofed traffic, the track was virgin. Once we were committed to the wide river we realised why no one had used the track. The wheels of the Land Rover left solid ground and we were washed down to a mud bank past what appeared to be an exit on the other side.

The timely arrival of a Red Lion and Sun Society truck saved us. While the crew applied shovels and force to the Land Rover we admired an old Kurdish hunter who was hitching a ride with the truck. He was cradling an old muzzle loader which was obviously a proud possession and proudly offered to show us how it worked. We made a good audience: we were intrigued. After the gun had been stuffed with black powder and rags the hunter politely offered it to me to shoot but some sixth sense warned me off. Not, however, our young guide, who was anxious to make up for his obvious lack of guiding abilities. Nuzzling the stock into his shoulder with his cheek snug against the polished old wood, he aimed into empty space and pulled the trigger. When nothing happened he pulled the gun down in disgust and a loud explosion followed, charge and rags escaping from the wrong end. Undaunted, the hunter reloaded and this time showed us how it was done. Holding the gun at waist level, far away from his eyes, he braced and let fly with a magnificent barrage. He added, somewhat unnecessarily, "You have to creep close to the game!"

Thanking the helpful Red Lion and Sun personnel for rescuing us from the mud we continued to Bijar for the night. There was a 'mehman sahra' (guest house) reached only by penetrating the bowels of the bazaar so we had to leave the Land Rover parked on a street and walk past closed shops, carrying our bags and followed by the sheep. Bijar had recently been equipped with a piped water system installed by the Firouz Construction Company. Confident of the well washed freshness of the local sabzi, or greens, we gorged on kebab, sabzi and freshly baked flat bread before bedding down for the night with the sheep curled loyally at Azizeh's feet.

The next day we visited the early fourteenth century Mausoleum of Oljeitu in which Sultaniyeh Oljeitu of the II Khanids lived in the fourteenth century A.D. and, having added to the splendours of architecture in Tabriz, built a new town on the Zanjan plain and called it Sultaniyeh. He made this his capital and built himself a mausoleum. Its egg-shaped dome of many-hued tiles rose over the flat mud roofs of the surrounding village. The interior, which was reached though a cramped wooden door, echoed emptily to the flutter of pigeon wings. The cavernous interior, supported by massive buttresses, resembled an aircraft hangar.

Oljeitu was a convert to Islam and the process was not without confusion. He was baptized with the Christian name of Nicholas, converted to Buddhism and then Sunni (Hanafi) Muslim. A violent thunderstorm, during which some of his companions are said to have been killed by lightning, stirred trouble amongst his advisors. Instead of reverting to shamanism (altaic-mongol), which appeared to have been the recommended course, or remaining Sunni, he surprised everyone by becoming a Shiite in 1309, thus maintaining his popularity to this day.

We climbed the steep spiral stairway to the balcony surrounding the top for a closer inspection of the tiled dome. The wide valley was green with growing wheat. Flocks of sheep were grazing the lower reaches of the mountains. There were donkeys being ridden by men with baggy pants and carrying shovels on their shoulders. They were on their way to irrigate the wheat with water which was flowing in irrigation ditches along the paths where women were kneeling washing clothes.

We reached Norouzabad that evening and, having told Narcy of our adventures in great detail, he dismissed such luxurious explorations and suggested a trip to find small horses that would really test our stamina. Once again, Azizeh's intrepid spirit was equal to the occasion. She even went so far as to introduce her eight year old nephew, Mahmad Reza, to the rigours of mountain travel on foot and horseback. Roshan, Ateshe and Caren, aged ten, eight and five respectively, accompanied us. Several days later five year old Jamie Williams, part owner of the pony Napoleon, was brought up by Narcy.

Narcy and I had decided that our children would not be left behind when we took trips unless it interfered with school. We had seen new born babies carried on tribal migrations and toddlers strapped on donkeys along with puppies and chickens. If they could survive this so could our children. Most of my friends in Teheran did not subscribe to this attitude and found the 'rough and tumble' atmosphere of Norouzabad a bit barbaric. Azizeh occasionally rescued Mahmad Reza from his sanitary surroundings and gave him a taste of 'real' life.

My brother, David Laylin, had grown weary of life in a bank in Washington, D.C. At the suggestion of one of Narcy's many uncles, Tari Farmanfarmaian, he had come to Iran to help set up a professional hunting business. David's previous experience had mainly been chasing squirrels on our father's farm in Great Falls, Virginia, but neither he nor Tari seemed to think this limited C.V. a deterrent. We decided to combine our Caspian foray with an exploratory hunting trip for David. He offered his fledgling services for setting up base camp in a likely place, which turned out to be a five hour drive from Teheran along the Firouz Kuh road to Alasht, birthplace of Reza Shah. There was a further hike of ten hours by foot and horseback. Not surprisingly we did not reach our destination that evening. We spent the night huddled in a shepherd's hut along the path with nothing to eat and only a bottle of cognac. Welcome as we found this, it was little solace to the children who were exhausted enough to sleep without dinner.

Early next morning Bayard Fox, an American businessman and a good friend of the Williams' who had joined the expedition, left in advance to warn David that he was about to be host to an unfriendly horde. We forgave him, after we finally found him. He gave us an excellent lunch and we had to agree that, from the huntsman's point of view at least, the terrain could not have been surpassed. Our tents were pitched on the banks of a snow-fed stream in a large green valley surrounded by rocky mountains. As David was not intending to take children on safari for wild game, his concern for their welfare was most conspicuous by its absence. We were also beginning to appreciate the basic skills of our guides from Alasht - a refined ability to steal anything not securely lashed down or buttoned up. By this time Azizeh had lost her camera and Caren his only pair of shoes.

The next morning, after breakfast, David, Narcy and Bayard went after wild goats that we could see in the distance with binoculars, skipping amongst the boulders in the mountains. Azizeh, Roshan, a guide and I walked up the folds in the valley, noting and photographing the horse population. There were many herds of mares, foals and stallions, which were traditionally moved from the Caspian littoral in spring to these summer pastures. The scene must have been similar to recurrent waves of steppe peoples pushing down from the north and the conformation of the horses was such that any one of them could have served as a model for the stocky Scythian horses that have survived the centuries on gold and silver bowls preserved under mounds of dirt. There was nothing resembling a Caspian but we were rewarded by the appearance of eight barrow graves on a promontory overlooking the valley, which looked distinctly Scythian. A further steep three-hour climb led to the top of a range of mountains that separated us from the heavy cloud cover of the Caspian coast. Our guide told us that the small hamlet poking out of the mists below was inhabited by cannibals.

Obviously the people in that village were not related to the Gilaki Alasht folk and not friendly with them either.

On our return to camp we were delighted to find that the men had had a successful hunt and kebabed goat was the main feature on the menu for dinner. Narcy and Bayard both had business in Teheran, leaving early the next morning while we spent the day making jerky out of the remains of the goat by smoking it over a fire. The next day we assembled the pack horses and loaded our gear and the dried goat and moved south into the forested upper slopes of the mountains. Caren, by virtue of being shoeless, rode perched on one of the bulky packs. The rest of us alternated between riding and walking. When the vegetation became thicker and Caren was in danger of being swept off his perch he was forced to walk barefoot until we could find a path without low lying branches. Although he complained, and with justice as there were sharp pebbles on the ground, he was soon watching with awe as the pack horse on which he had been riding lost his footing on a rock ledge bordering a perpendicular drop. The horse scrambled wildly but was unable to get a purchase with his smooth shoes and dropped out of sight with a sickening crash. The fall, however, had been cushioned by his pack. When we peered over the edge, the horse was quietly grazing; the burst pack in a shambles around his feet. The drop had been more than thirty metres but the horse suffered only minor scratches and we were soon able to retrieve him, reassemble the pack and continue on our way.

It was not until we had arrived at a likely camping spot near a clear spring that we discovered the theft of one of Narcy's guns, part of the ill-fated pack. We argued and threatened with no result. The drivers looked sullen and uncooperative. That night most of them left for their village taking their horses with them. We sent a midnight delegation to the village with the message that we would go to the authorities the next day and report the theft unless the gun was returned that night. Stealing a gun was a serious offence which would involve many months in prison. At five o'clock the next morning there was a concerted howling and barking from a nearby shepherd's camp. By seven o'clock we discovered the gun leaning against a rock by the spring. During the night we also discovered that we were surrounded by what appeared to be a strange new form of wildlife. By day it was apparent that the source of the mournful, nocturnal trumpeting was that of half feral cows, their scanty milk production being used for making butter at the crude log and mud habitation up the hill. The scrub forest was practically impenetrable and seemed home to creatures for which domestication would be as novel an experience as it sometimes seemed to the cows.

Azizeh and I tactfully refrained from reminding David that game, welcome as it was for the pot, was not the sole object of this exercise in mountaineering. Although Caspian ponies had many of the attributes of forest animals we doubted that we would find any in the company of wild boar, bear and leopards, whose sign was ubiquitous around the spring. David, had he wished to make it, did have a point. We were rapidly running out of provisions, the result of further pilferage. Azizeh and I joined David looking for dinner. We each took a shotgun and went after the cabk (partridge) that were calling on the slopes of nearby hills while David went after more serious game. We flushed covey after covey of cabk but they flew off with no more serious damage than a missing tail feather and we decided that we should abandon the sporting convention of waiting for the birds to be airborne. We crawled under low lying Christ thorn bushes and over sharp rocks to a spot from which small chuckle sounds could be heard. They were there, directly in front of us, their sharp brown eyes looking directly into ours. All predatory intentions dissolved and we returned to camp empty-handed. Fortunately for all of us David had been luckier, or more business-like, and dinner that night was a fat hare. Since there was only one we hoped the children wouldn't like it, but they did.

Narcy returned that night with Jamie Williams. They had ridden for six hours in the dark over rivers and boulders and through thick forest. They had a good guide. The next day we organised the children into beaters and tried driving wild boar towards Narcy and David. There were no wild boar but we did scare up a bear. Fortunately for the beaters the bear was more frightened than we were and fortunately for the bear he ran off in the opposite direction of the guns.

By now we were reduced to eating cold boiled potatoes. There was nothing else left. We packed up and started the long trek back to Teheran.

Chapter 8

<u>Showing in Virginia and on to Bermuda</u>

In the autumn of 1965, I had taken a short trip to the United States to visit my family. While in Virginia I met Kathleen McCormick. She was managing a stable for my brother, John Laylin, on a stud farm that he and my father had bought for land development. Although the stable no longer functioned as a stud, Kathleen became interested in the possibilities of the Caspian for cross breeding with local ponies to introduce a fineness and quality lacking in the imported Celtic stock. Narcy and I agreed that exporting some Caspians would give a much-needed impetus to the breeding programme in Iran. We 'press-ganged' a number of friends into supporting the venture financially.

By April 1966, we were able to send the chestnut stallion, Jehan, to the U.S.

Dr. William Santoro of Upperville, Virginia, arrived in Teheran to supervise the transport. The route was via a catholic assortment of airlines from Teheran to Beirut, Madrid to London and, finally, the quarantine station in Clifton, New Jersey.   On the day that he was to be collected by Kathleen, her car broke down she was hopelessly late to collect him. The station had closed by the time she arrived, horrified to find Jehan tied to a tree outside the quarantine compound. It was now night time and, as the problem was electrical, Kathleen was forced to complete the journey back to Virginia with torches tied to the vehicle in place of headlights.

Jehan was an instant success in the United States. He attracted visitors from some distance, all anxious to view the possibilities of using him as a stud stallion. Unfortunately neither Kathleen nor we were able to support the financial burden of providing Jehan with purebred Caspian mares in the United States, although it was already obvious that the market for riding ponies of this type was in the western world. Pony clubs, horse shows, backyards and a rural or suburban way of life were more conducive to children having ponies than our rigid Riding Club system. Moreover, the breeding and marketing of ponies and horses was a 'business' in the west, not an accidental adjunct to tribal or village living, as it was in Iran. Kathleen loyally supported the ideal and formed the first national Caspian Society, which is still in existence, and produced some excellent half bred Caspian show animals. As far as I know Jehan's stock were so valued by their owners that none were ever sold. Jehan remained with Kathleen until his death.

In 1970, Joan Taplin, who had been involved with the finding of some of the foundation Caspians, and whose husband was retiring from Shell Oil Company in Iran to settle in Joan's native Bermuda, suggested that she take a stallion and mare with her to use and breed near Hamilton. Joan had been one of the organisers of the Teheran Gymkhana Association along with Frederica Lincoln and me. While working with all of the native Persian breeds of horses she became as impressed with the potential of the Caspian as we were. Her daughter, Kay, was a similar age to our children and she had learned to ride on the Caspians. Joan felt that the Bermuda Pony Club would benefit greatly by the addition of Caspian blood.

She bought the grey stallion, Daria Nour, which Helen Kemp had left at Norouzabad when she was leaving for the United States. Helen was struggling to transport a sixteen hand, Palomino stallion she had brought from the U.S. and was not interested in adding Caspians to her equine baggage. Also from Norouzabad, Joan acquired the bay mare, Mitra, and, at the last minute, we threw in Momtaz-e-Mahal. This last profligate gesture was prompted by a decision to have the ponies make a two-month tour of the Virginia show circuit after they had completed the obligatory quarantine for Bermuda in New Jersey. Roshan and Ateshe would both be riding but, Virginians frowning on stallions cavorting in their elegant show rings, we felt that two mares would forestall arguments and present a better showing than one.

There was a tedious quarantine procedure involving many sheaves of forms and unco-operative officials in Iran but it was all completed and the crates were built. We made arrangements with Pan American Airways to ship the ponies in the luggage compartment of a regular passenger flight. At the last minute Pan American developed a case of 'cold feet', citing lack of precedent for sending horses unaccompanied, like dogs, with the suitcases. Although we sympathised with the airline, all arrangements were in such an advanced state that we felt we could not possibly abandon the project. Frantic pleas to the Foreign Office culminated in IranAir's reluctant agreement to take the three Caspians as far as Istanbul, where they could be transferred to a Pan American cargo flight bound for New York.

Dr. Santoro had reported that Jehan had travelled so quietly that he had not required the use of tranquilizers. So Joan and I arrived at Mehrabad airport at nine a.m. on the day of departure with the ponies, crates, quarantine papers and no tranquilisers. True to Dr. Santoro's observation, no opiate was required as the ponies were asked to jump on and off the scales at Customs. They waited outside the Pan American cargo office in milling airport traffic while the waybill was prepared and trotted quietly past the whine of 707 jets to their aeroplane. After they had been put inside their crates waiting by the IranAir cargo door, a train of little cargo carts pulled alongside to wait its turn for loading. As one pony after the other struggled to leap out, Mitra's box moving on the tarmac like a Mexican jumping bean, we realised that they were terrified by the intense cold of the barrels of caviar on the carts. The loading superintendent, sceptical from the beginning, now found the excuse for which he had been groping to refuse the load; "No tranquiliser: no ponies".

The closest source of tranquiliser was the Large Animal Veterinary Clinic of the University of Teheran at Se rah Azari, a half hour's drive at the best of times. As the time was now twelve noon, this was not the best of times. Grabbing the keys to Joan's car, I ran off the tarmac, wasting precious time trying to find the right key for the ignition. The car finally started and I rushed off with squealing tyres and blaring horn to try to beat the traffic, the closing hours of the clinic and the departure time of the aircraft. Arriving at the clinic, I found it preparing to shut down operations for the day. There were still students ambling round the halls with syringes and the pharmacy was open. I grabbed two syringes from an astonished student. I also made a quick raid of the shelves of the pharmacy and, promising to return to pay, sped back to the airport.

Joan was nervously pleading with airline officials to wait, while passengers could be seen peering from their windows above, obviously annoyed at the delay in departure. We quickly knocked off the tops of the glass vials and, drawing the fluid, injected each of the three ponies. The loading superintendent was satisfied and the ponies were loaded into the forward luggage compartment, far from the caviar. We watched with relief as the doors were closed, the engines started, and the aircraft rolled away for takeoff. On April 6th, 1970, they had left.

On his return to Norouzabad for lunch, Narcy was surprised to find that Joan and I were sitting numbly over two glasses of strong vodka and tonic. Only we knew that the full effect of the tranquilisers would probably not be felt until the ponies were half way to Istanbul. To our relief, word reached Narcy's office the following day that the ponies had arrived safely in New York and were on their way to the quarantine station in New Jersey.

On June 6th, Roshan, Ateshe, Omid Ali and I left for New York to meet the ponies at the quarantine station. On our way we stopped for four days with the Littauers' in Long Island. Mary was a leading authority on ancient domesticated horses upon which she wrote several authoritative works which are now in the International Museum of the Horse at the Kentucky Horse Park. They were old friends and had helped with many aspects of the Caspian project from the beginning. The meticulous neatness of their farm was in some contrast to the usual shambles at Norouzabad and we hoped it would help prepare us for occidental order as opposed to Oriental chaos.

Kathleen McCormick arrived with a truck and car from Virginia for the journey from Clifton and we all travelled back together to a farm in Virginia. The ponies were unloaded by the light of fireflies and the scent of honeysuckle. The latter was an acceptable alien experience but the former was not. Ponies flew blindly in all directions to escape what must have seemed like thousands of giant sparks. We eventually extricated them from hiding places under bushes and dense hedges and guaranteed them safe refuge in a barn for the night. The following day they were moved to my father's farm, Hidden Springs. They spent the rest of the summer there, knee deep in clover and blue grass when they were not on the show circuit or at various establishments learning how to behave on the show circuit.

Kathleen had arranged for a personable young man, Ronny Beard, to help with the complex arrangements surrounding the mysterious process of launching ourselves and our animals into Virginia's show circuit. Ronny's active participation was essential as we had only two weeks to prepare for the Warrenton Horse and Pony Show. This was one of Virginia's most prestigious shows and would be attended by the very best ponies.

Mitra and Momtaz-e-Mahal were broken in but had never been properly schooled. One of the first objects was to use those two weeks to good advantage for training. Thanks to a co-operative nature on the part of the ponies and their above-average intelligence and sheer perseverance on the part of the two young riders we made good progress. By the time of the show the two mares were fairly adept at keeping to a walk, trot or canter. Their jumping was spectacular, if erratic. We were definitely not ready to compete with the clockwork ponies we would find at Warrenton but we felt that if we were committed to a season of showing it was best to start and practise as we went along. I shudder now to think of all the good friends, professionals in the field, who kindly guided us and, when we floundered against impossible odds, restricted themselves to constructive criticism.

Faith is no substitute for homework and all we demonstrated at Warrenton was several acts of sublime courage, the most notable being simply going. The mares walked, trotted and cantered, but usually on the wrong lead. When called to line up, they were conspicuous not only for their small, slim lines, but for the large, peering eyes on their curious heads. They stood out amongst the passive indifference of the Virginia aristocracy of ponies.

Just before the pony hunter classes the thunder storms that were to plague us for the entire summer burst forth in a half -hour of rain and cacophony. The deluge turned the ring and outside course into a sea of mud that rendered the 'going' useless to the ponies' tiny hooves. It is a tribute to the ponies and the children that they tried. The Warrenton show officials have probably still not forgiven the performance over the chicken coop. When faced with the slippery mud and an unfamiliar obstacle, Mitra hesitated, and then climbed over the coop leaving a trail of muddy hoof marks on the gleaming white surface. She completed the course.

We emerged from Warrenton with the dismal feeling that our precarious financial investment was not going to bring the desired results. We were unfamiliar with show procedure and our horses were untrained. We were facing a very competent group of experts who also had a considerable investment in their breeds. We had two months in which to demonstrate the abilities of our breed. We also had that limited time in which to convince breeders that a judicious mixture of Caspian blood with the native British breeds would produce a type of 'miniature Thoroughbred' which would be more suitable for children's needs. The judges were sympathetic to the problem. But they maintained that even if a Caspian were to put in a flawless performance they would find it difficult to award prizes to a breed that had only two specimens showing over the many typically Celtic types so popular at the time.

Nevertheless, we still had six weeks left to prove a point. Although we fell far short of accomplishing anything concrete, the Caspian achieved certain notoriety for sheer perseverance. Every weekend we were at another show, slightly more competent but always out-classed. The time was drawing close for our departure to Bermuda as we scrambled through our last shows. These were of a small local variety that were far better suited to our limited experience and we actually won a few ribbons. We ended, in effect, where we should have started.

Omid Ali was putting in some good performances of his own. We persuaded show officials to let us demonstrate the stallion, Daria Nour. He had a fine brass horse halter from Kurdistan and Omid Ali was dressed in the baggy pants, sash and turban of his native mountains. When they flashed around the ring they always drew great applause which made up for some of the miseries of being away from Iran and in the United States. By this time Omid Ali was dreaming of the cool springs of Kurdistan, real bread (not cellophane wrapped Wonder bread) and the homely clutter of a tightly packed mud village. He had done a careful calculation, concluding that his standard of living in Iran far exceeded anything he could expect to achieve in the United States. Each added day in western civilization grated on his nerves. Even lunch with the Iranian ambassador at the elegant residence in Washington extracted only the remark; "I don't know how he can stand it!" He promised he would never ask me again why I, an American, lived in the primitive surroundings of the Middle East if only I would take him home.

Pan American Airways had assured me that they could not fly the ponies to Bermuda from New York but that Boston had flights which would serve the purpose. We booked the ponies and ourselves for a flight. Omid Ali left with the ponies by van for Boston one evening in August taking all the proper veterinary certificates and papers. Roshan, Ateshe and I followed the next morning by air. On arrival at Logan airport we found that Pan American claimed total ignorance of the shipping order. Omid Ali was distraught. He threw himself spread eagled on the pavement in front of the horse van.

"I'm not going back!" roared Omid Ali in distress.

"Of course not. We're going to Bermuda."

"That's what I keep telling them," Said Omid Ali, on the verge of tears, "but they won't listen. YOU tell them."

The problem was easily solved when Pan American looked at the shipping papers from Teheran. They saw that they had, indeed, completed the manifest. Their point had been that they had never shipped horses in the luggage compartment of their aeroplanes and felt that Boston was no place to start. (Unknowingly this was their first experience. Although Pan American had completed the manifest in Teheran, it was IranAir that had flown the 'luggage compartment leg', Pan American, the cargo). Some years later Pan American flew a Caspian from Teheran to Venezuela in the luggage compartment, which must have set some sort of record. The problem resolved, we took the ponies by truck to the aeroplane and loaded them in with our luggage. Rushing down from the truck and through the Pan American check-in counter and back up to the aeroplane, we barely made it in time to travel with the animals.

A very welcome drink and lunch saw us over the varying shades of blue Atlantic that denote the approach to Bermuda. By this time the injudicious choice of a new pair of shoes had made itself apparent. My feet were swollen and a blister had burst. I took the shoes off and carried them in my hand as we left the aeroplane.

As a gesture of courtesy I slipped under the fuselage to offer help to the cargo manager should he be upset by the idea of unloading the horses. My bare feet did not impress him.

"Madam," he said, "we will take care of the cargo."

"I'm sure of that," I replied, "but you might need help with the horses."

"This is a passenger flight. The cargo hold contains suitcases, not horses."

"It also carries three horses," I persisted.

Losing his aplomb; "then wait for your horses at the luggage claim!"

Having collected our luggage, but no horses, we were directed to where we were told the heavy cargo was released. There we saw Mr. Taplin. He was standing in for his wife, who was in England. Together we waited for the first of the horses to appear. We were delighted when the small, grey head of Daria Nour appeared over his crate, carried along on a small cart. Beside that head was one of ruddy tinge which belonged to the cargo manager who had so promptly dismissed my offer of help.

"Madam, I'm sorry," he said, "but I could hardly believe it when I opened the door and found three horses in the hold!"

The only problem remaining was that of payment of customs on the three crates, wood being a dutiable item. As I did not want the crates, the Taplins did not want the crates and Customs did not want the crates, we paid the Customs duty and burned them.

We spent a delightful evening with Mr. Taplin and some of his friends at their house on the waterfront of Hamilton. The next morning we went riding with the owner of the stables where the Caspians were being kept. In the afternoon we went sailing on the bay.

The BOAC officials at Bermuda airport maintained a stoic silence at the sight of the many little satchels of riding and grooming equipment that Roshan and Ateshe considered indispensable hand luggage. They drew the line at Omid Ali's heavy booty; enough pairs of blue jeans to outfit all his male relatives in Ahjean, Kurdistan.

The rest of the trip went smoothly except for Lod airport in Tel Aviv. All transit passengers were asked to leave the plane for forty minutes. As we stepped out onto the stairs Omid Ali looked around and asked; "is this Palestine?" "Omid Ali," I hissed, "shut up!" Jehan, crated for his flight to

Jehan, crated for his flight to New York –
photo: courtesy of Kathleen McCormick

An artist's impression of the Seal of Darius the Great (500 BC), currently in the British Museum, showing a pair of Caspian type equines pulling the chariot of Darius in the hunting arena - drawing by Lez Harvey

An artist's impression of a gold chariot from the Oxus Treasure –
5th to 4th century BC (British Museum) - drawing by Judith Dalton

A team of Caspians owned and driven
by Dick Kearley, Florida, USA. Photo: courtesy of Dick Kearley

Chapter 9

Racing with Royal Patronage

When we limped back to Iran in late August we found that any fame that might have accrued to us on the trip had preceded us. We had impressed no-one in the U.S. with anything more than audacity. We discovered that Ambassador Aslan Afshar had written progress reports on the Caspians to the Foreign Office. This had stimulated interest in the breed in Iran. It was strange that we had to go all the way to the United States to make Iranians aware of their own native horse.

The first official visitor to appear at Norouzabad was a Colonel in the Army Veterinarian Corps. He had orders to find out everything there was to know about the Caspian. As the research was still in an infantile stage, this was not much. After a further meeting together with Kambiz Atabai, Master of the Imperial Stables, the Colonel was seen no more. (I have since learned that the Army maintained a small breeding group of Caspians at their stud in Jallilabad, but I have not been invited to see it, nor has the Army expressed an interest in being included in the Stud Book.)

Troubles with United States Customs were causing letters to fly back and forth between the two countries. According to the forwarding agent in New York, the problem was caused by an article in the social section of the Washington Post. An alert Customs official was either bored or had social aspirations. He had read that the Caspian was so rare its value would soon exceed ten thousand dollars. As I had declared the ponies at the local market value (which was the price Joan Taplin had paid), plus air-freight, I was being held liable for gross misrepresentation. Would that that had been the case! The only escape from a charge of felony was to have the Ministry of Agriculture verify the Norouzabad pedigree papers as coming from a recognized stud. This was supposed to be sufficient to mollify Customs. Only unregistered animals are liable for Customs duty.

I telephoned the Ministry of Agriculture to ask for an appointment. They gave me a seven a.m. spot with an undersecretary in charge of Animal Husbandry. He listened to my story sympathetically and, at the conclusion, sadly shook his head.

"I wish I could do something for you, Mrs. Firouz, but unfortunately my hands are tied," he said.

"I don't understand why," I persisted, "after all, most countries have societies or agencies within the government which recognize the validity of pure breeding."

"You fail to understand the basic point. You see, we have in this country cows, sheep, water buffalo and even camels. But we do not have any horses:' we are mechanised!"

This sounded quite impressive in Persian but translated into English in my head it did not make much sense.

So much for impressing United States Customs with fancy red ribbon and, unless I could solve the problem, so much for visiting the U.S. in the near future.

Before leaving for the U.S. that summer, Kambiz Atabai and I had had a few discussions about establishing a horse society. The aim was to recognize and register Iran's unique range of native breeds. Stimulated by the customs troubles I approached Kambiz again. With the added impetus of the 'success' of the Caspians in Virginia that summer, Kambiz and I pleaded our case to form the society.

Kambiz Atabai was a graduate of Sandhurst in England and had attained the rank of captain in the Iranian Army when he was transferred to the Imperial Court. Like the Shah, whose similar physical resemblance was uncanny, he was a good rider and hunter. He attended to his duties as Master of the Imperial Stables and Game Reserve at Farahabad with genuine dedication. He was a slim, handsome man and also the adopted son of one of the Shah's most trusted adjutants. He was in a unique position to petition the Shah for permission to form such a society. The enterprise received royal sanction. An impressive array of generals, ministers, elder statesmen and a few horsemen and women were invited to be founder members of the Royal Horse Society. The first meeting was held in the autumn of 1970, in the presence of the Minister of Court, H.E. Assadollah Allam, at the Saadabad Palace in Shemran. Among those voted in as the Board of Directors were the Minister of Court, the Minister of War, the heads of the gendarmerie and G2, Military Intelligence. Kambiz Atabai was voted a member of the Board of Directors and, later, Managing Director. A Mr. Arab-Sheibani and I were made Inspectors. This was a position I never did understand although it gave me a seat at the board table for two years.

We met all winter in interminable and tiresome meetings to decide the wording of the charter. By the summer of 1971 the Royal Horse Society was ready to begin work. It was decided to start with the Turkoman horses. The Turkomans were more organized in their breeding and racing than any of the other breeds. They did not keep pedigrees as such but, since certain lines won better than others, they had a good grasp of who was breeding what to which. Even those betting at the race- tracks could reel off sires and dams to many generations back. There was not much point in cheating since a couple of races would find you out. With the later introduction of Thoroughbreds this changed.

As far as the Royal Horse Society was concerned the Turkoman horses whose names appeared in the Turkoman registry could best be described as 'observed'. The Turkomans themselves were more puzzled than enlightened by the process. They concluded that if the government thought fit to issue them with a piece of paper declaring their horses to be purebred for the paltry sum of a hundred and twenty toumans (at that time about twenty dollars) who, indeed, were they to argue. Besides, unheard of sums of prize money were promised for future races sponsored by the Royal Horse Society. There was a racing organization but, in true Persian fashion, the Royal Horse Society ignored them. Eventually the old became an imperceptible part of the new.

The first of such races was held in the autumn of 1971 on forty hectares of open steppe belonging to Air Taxi, a private company, and the Gendarmerie near Gonbad-e-Qabus in north eastern Iran. Mina Sheriker and I, having been the staunchest members of the registration committee, were rewarded with the task of organizing and running the race. Mina was the secretary of the Royal Horse Society and, although not a rider, was as enthusiastic about making a 'go' of the society as anyone else. She was also a good organizer and was not daunted by what seemed to be impossible tasks.

For one week we ploughed through ever deepening mud in attempts to register enough horses to fill the card. We had tee shirts made for the young jockeys. We thought we were clever to have a different colour for each race but we discovered this was highly impractical when one little fellow stumbled over to us with seven shirts on, although all in the correct order. We composed and arranged to have printed enough banners waving in support of enough organizations and sponsors to appease all factions. The Turkomans were a big help. They had been running races up there for centuries and did not mind that the 'foreigners' (Fars) were attempting to take over. Anyway, we were not, we were only running one set of races and they would be winning the prizes.

Mary Gharagozlou, a friend of long standing, appeared out of the gloom one drenching evening having driven from Teheran. She had come to offer her help with levelling what appeared to be a track. We rented a bulldozer and filled up the obvious holes. If we had done nothing else to win the respect of the Turkomans this did it. They had sad tales of the numbers of horses and jockeys sacrificed to the caverns of the mud Gods.

As the day approached it seemed we might be ready on time. The one thing about which we could do nothing was the weather. It could not have been worse. Horses from tens of kilometres away were pouring in through the mud and still the rain fell in ever increasing sheets. The Turkomans seemed unperturbed by the weather. They assured us that Friday would dawn bright and warm. The track would be dry in plenty of time for the races. By Thursday night it was still raining and it was difficult to make myself sound cheerful over the bad telephone connection with Kambiz in Teheran. Whatever optimism the Turkomans had been able to instil in us was not 'rubbing off'. Kambiz insisted that the races for the following day should be cancelled. The thought of all those little Turkoman jockeys sleeping huddled under the horses' feet, protected by the medievally draped felt horse blankets was enough to cause us to break the connection. "Can't seem to hear you. We'll see you tomorrow!"

The Turkomans were right and we did have our brilliant sunshine. The mountains to the south were a green barrier of dense forest and the steppe to the north an unbroken expanse of smooth, even grass. The horses to be raced were 'sweated' in the morning. They cantered twice slowly around the track and then galloped once. They were rushed back to the trainer for an addition of heavy, sheepskin blanket on top of the seven felts under which they had galloped. All this was tied around the legs to conserve the heat and steam (a practice that has puzzled not a few western trainers who have since visited Gorbad-e-Qabus). Horses that had arrived the night before were registered (one by the name of Bist Solleh was twenty years old and registered in the two thousand metre race). The details for the programme were rushed to the printers and somehow returned no later than half way through the races. Members of the Board of Directors and guests arrived from Teheran in seven small aeroplanes, landing on the track. The Governor General of Mazanderan and the Governor of Gonbad-e-Qabus (Gonbad) produced a feast for the guests in the Governor's house in Gonbad. Turkomans, the men wearing vibrant red silk robes and fuzzy astrakhan hats, and the women wearing long, bright printed dresses with orange and black scarves over small caps, all converged on the track.

We were ready to start the first race ... but wait, where was Prince Gholam Reza? Neither Mina nor I knew that he was supposed to be coming, although a banner in his honour as President of the Racing Federation floated over the approach to the small grandstand. Generals, ministers and senators sat quietly at first, enjoying the view, digesting lunch and waiting for the Prince. Soon they grew restive and could be seen giving their watches covert glances. Eventually they left the grandstand and began pacing the ground in front. An hour and a half passed before word arrived from the Prince's hunting lodge on the edge of the Mohammad Reza Shah wildlife park that he would not be attending the races. As if shot from guns, spectators returned to their seats and Turkomans prepared to cheer. The first race was off in a melee of flying hooves and dust. Two starters were knocked to the ground when they were slow to get out of the way. Passing the last bend the racing horses were greeted with the ululating cry of the Turkomans. The first of seven winners was presented to the Minister of War, General Azimi, for his prize.

As the afternoon wore on I noticed the pilots of the air planes were giving their watches the same treatment that the guests had focused on theirs while waiting for Prince Gholam Reza. When the distinguished guests had officiated at the final race they left in somewhat unseemly haste for the planes but the pilots said it was getting dark and it was too late to leave. They would have to wait until the following morning. The consternation with which this information was received seemed out of proportion to the gravity of the situation. A little later we realised that, with the exception of General Oveissi, head of the gendarmerie, none of the guests had ever been in Turkoman country before. Certainly none of them had spent the night in such an outpost of civilization. The Turkomans had a well-deserved reputation for disliking Persians, as for years they had raided south to plunder and capture slaves. The Persians were still afraid of the Turkomans, although they had been discouraged from taking slaves for over fifty years. Perhaps the guests were unaware of the new protocol. Most Iranians adapt better to the climates of Paris and London than their own provinces and this was an alien experience. The Shah had given specific orders that they were to attend this first race meeting of the Royal Horse Society. One or two decided to return to Gorgan, an hour's drive to the west, to try their luck on the overnight train to Teheran. The others actually found they enjoyed the unique opportunity to tour the streets of Gonbad-e-Qabus. They ate steaming beans from sidewalk barrows and shopped for bargains in old Turkoman jewellery: heavy silver and garnet pieces of tribal work. The next morning they left for Teheran unmolested by the Turkomans. We gathered together the paraphernalia of race track management and left by Land Rover and Jeep barely ploughing our way through the drifts of snow on the high Alborz pass.

The next breed to receive the attentions of the Royal Horse Society was the 'Arab'. This was a sticky subject when one considers the war of words (until that time limited to invective) waged over the question of 'Persian vs. Arabian Gulf'. This was a tradition of rivalry centring on the body of water that touches the shores of Saudi Arabia, the Emirates, Qatar, Kuwait, Bahrain and Iran. The problem was solved to the satisfaction of most by designating the term 'Persian Arab' to describe examples of the breed extant within the limits of Iran's border. There was little regard to the fact that, by calling the animal an Arab at all, it automatically was not Persian. Iran's quite legitimate claim to have fostered the antecedents of the Arab was abrogated. In addition, Iran would be subject to the same internationally accepted standards for the Arab horse as all other non Arabian breeders (i.e. not within Saudi Arabia or other Arab countries as opposed to Europe or the U.S.). Since then an organization called the World Arabian Horse Organization has subjected everybody to international standards set mainly by the United States.

Although the name was eventually changed to 'Asil' (meaning purebred in Arabic), the subtleties of semantics were temporarily ignored. A committee was formed to travel to Khuzestan, the province bordering the Shatt-el-Arab River which produces both Arabs (equine and human) and oil. With the co-operation of the local sheikhs, animals that were considered pure were to be noted for future registration.

The committee consisted of three people; Mary Gharagozlou, an Army veterinary colonel and myself. Mary's credentials as technical expert on the Arab horse were impeccable. She was married for many years to Madjid Bakhtiar, one of the Bakhtiari Khans who ruled over the Bakhtiari tribes in the lower Zagros and Khuzestan. Her father had been a large landowner around Hamadan and married an American when he was studying medicine in the United States. He died in his thirties and his two daughters, Mary and Tuti, became competent at managing their affairs at an early age. They were both athletic and educated women. Tuti married an Italian diplomat and left Iran but Mary stayed and managed their properties. After her marriage to Madjid she joined him to help farm his large tracts of land in Khuzestan and together they ran a stud of over one hundred Arab mares and stallions. Later, she spent six years with the Bakhtiari tribes in the Zagros Mountains managing a project for the government. She only agreed to this initial registration program as a temporary measure to help the Royal Horse Society (she was in charge of an agricultural development program in Baluchistan at the time).

I had heard much about Mary and was anxious to meet her. I ran into her one day at lunch at my parents-in-law and was impressed. We became friends and fiddled with a few enterprises together; not the least of which was a beef -fattening project for feeding American oil-men in Khuzestan. Most of what I remember of that was that my hands went numb after cutting up seven steers in one day with a blunt knife. Fortunately I thought, for me, the slaughter house we were using was confiscated by the government and our business collapsed. We started a few others after that and they all had the same flavour, slightly unsuccessful. She later directed the entire Royal Horse Society Arab Stud and registration program on a full time basis. The army veterinary colonel seemed to be there in an advisory capacity. He was remarkably silent, no doubt cowed by being junior to two women.

We approached the quagmire of the Arab problem via three tickets on IranAir. Mary was suffering from bad nose-bleeds and I with a head cold. The colonel suffered embarrassment from his attachment to a female contingent along with confusion over his orders. Our instructions from the Royal Horse Society were, I thought, explicit; contact the local Sheikhs in Ahwaz and obtain particulars of the horses they wished to register. After a review by the board of directors, certificates of registration would be issued.

We saw our first Sheikh that same afternoon and also inspected his horses. Intimations of trouble loomed as one goose-rumped, shaggy fetlocked and coarse headed animal followed another. Further trouble loomed that night when the Sheikh included sheep's eyes in the lavish dinner, a delicacy I left Mary to enjoy. The following days were repetitions of the first, with the exception of the sheep's eyes.

The countryside was green with the early spring of a Khuzestan February. Khuzestan is a flat alluvial plain that, according to archaeologists, was probably one of the first sites to be cultivated by man. Irrigation channels dating back three thousand years can still be seen as shallow indentations in the land and the flood that carried Noah's ark swept over this region. The remains of the ark remain hidden despite serious attempts to trace its resting place. In the summer it is blistering hot and in the winter it is mild and wet. Bakhtiari tribes winter in this region and then trek over the snow passes of the Zagros to their summer pastures. Originally called Susianna, it is said that the name of Khuzestan comes from the Khuz tribe that occupied the area when the Achamaenians conquered it. The population was mainly Arab and Bakhtiari and, at that time, American oil-men. Lines of zigzagging pipes carried oil from the drilling areas to the refinery in Abadan and the whole area carried a faint aroma of oil. Iraq is right across the Shatt-al-Arab and both sides of the river had groves of tall date palms.

The steadily deepening mud was a challenge to the two Russian built Jeeps that belonged to the gendarmerie and had been put at our disposal. Their heaters were an integral part of the workings: some Siberian engineer seemed not to have foreseen the need for a cut-off switch. There were no bridges over the branches of the Shatt River so we stood on the flimsy wooden ferry rafts and took bets on the probable fate of the Russian Jeeps.

A stable at Shohebieh had belonged to Mary and her late husband, Madjid. The horses that we saw there were the finest examples of the Arab we had seen: a tribute to the breeding stock they had acquired. Inheritance tangles (Mary and Madjid had been divorced for some years at the time of his death) had dissipated some of the stock and the katkhoda (headman) after their separation claimed a share in everything they had had. This was an unforeseen complication to the registration procedure. We had neglected to anticipate the possibility of misuse of registration as proof of ownership. The reluctance of the Board of Directors to have registrations issued before a thorough review, proved wise.

Having covered as much territory as we felt able on this first trip we returned to the Ahwaz Hotel to correlate our information and prepare to return to Teheran. It was not until then that I realised that Mary and the colonel were unaware of the Board of Director's instructions and their suggestion that Certificates of Registration be issued forthwith were in direct contradiction to our orders. The resulting misunderstandings with the Royal Horse Society were the source of much confusion and Orwellian machinations. They eventually led to a fragmentation of effort and intent that irrevocably split the Royal Horse Society. It was inevitable, I suppose, that an organisation such as the Royal Horse Society should become a hotbed of intrigue. It had all the ingredients; royal patronage, status, horses and, apparently, power. Kambiz Atabai once told me that he could not understand why embassies were always after him to attend dinners. "But I'm only a groom at the Royal Stables" he would say. He was also manager of the Royal Stables and game reserve, managing director of the Royal Horse Society and adjutant to the Shah.

The main aim of the society had been the registration of Persian breeds of horses. This was slowly forgotten in a swell of enthusiasm for show jumping. At first Turkoman horses were mainly used and did very well but they took a bit of skill and good riding. It soon occurred to those who could afford it that trained European show jumpers would be more suitable. The Royal Stables and wealthy individuals imported large numbers of horses from Ireland, England and Germany. They also invited famous riders to help them learn to jump and build courses. Thoroughbred stallions were imported by the Royal Stables and bred with local mares. The imports of both European show jumpers and Thoroughbred race horses discouraged efforts to register our own breeds since somewhere in all of this it had been decided that Persian breeds were not up to an international standard and therefore worthless. While we were exporting Caspians to England to 'upgrade' their pony stock it was suggested we import New Forest ponies to Iran to 'upgrade' the Caspian!

In the meantime the Royal Horse Society slowly began to take on the outward appearance of many similar organisations in Iran. There were many tea boys and many chiefs but few in between. A Department of Registration was established and the haphazard bits of flimsy paper were replaced by an up to date cardex file. Range Rovers, Jeeps and Toyotas formed a fleet for registering officials. Kurdistan and Fars were added to the territories in which horses were to be registered. As only the Arab and Turkoman registries were ever published, information with regard to the populations or principle breeders of the remaining breeds was never made public.

By 1999 only the Arab had an official stud book and that was kept by Mary Gharagozlou. The Caspian has an international stud book (International Caspian Stud Book - ICSB) compiled in England. The Caspian continued for several years at Norouzabad. Although registrations of Caspians are maintained, the Royal Horse Society never officially recognized the stud book and U.S. Customs lost interest, dropping the case.

Chapter 10

Establishing Norouzabad as a Major Equestrian Centre and Smuggling

Operating a riding school had never occupied a high priority on my list of preferences. So it came as a not too pleasant surprise one morning in early June of 1971, when I discovered myself with two young instructors from Virginia, a stable-full of boarders and rings full of students.

The Norouzabad Equestrian Centre (NEC) was the result of pressure put on us by enthusiastic young riders and the sudden reluctance on the part of the Royal Horse Society to continue the 'Pony Club' activities that had been initiated at the Royal Stables.

In late autumn, 1970, I asked Kambiz Atabai if he had any idea how we could organize a centre for the many children who were enthusiastic about riding. Most of the children I knew attended the Iran Zamin International School in Teheran. They were a mixed lot of Iranian and half-Iranian: some were children of diplomats and several were children of American military personnel. They had asked me about forming a pony club. Narcy had made it clear that he did not want Norouzabad turned into a 'circus' so Kambiz asked the Shah for permission to use an old empty stable on the outskirts of the Royal Stables property at Farahabad for their use as a Pony Club Centre. The Shah gave his permission and, in the late autumn of 1970, the children attacked the stable with pitchforks, brooms and white wash. They transformed the quaint old building from a recent sheep shed into elegant accommodation for eighteen horses. The stable had been built during the reign of the Kadjars and was in the Old Persian style with domed arches. It would be warm in the winter and cool in summer.

The children moved their horses into the stable and spent the winter and spring exploring the outer limits of the Royal Game Reserve where there were large herds of wild sheep grazing in the hills. Narcy and I spent most weekends at Farahabad giving riding classes and generally helping the children. Gradually, other parents also became involved and this started an unusual, for Iran, family atmosphere. Even the royal children became involved and joined the classes with the Shah and Empress Farah occasionally looking on.

Kambiz was justifiably proud of this project and it certainly proved to the Shah that the idea behind the Royal Horse Society was sound. The Pony Club members were ecstatic and I suspect the attendance at discotheques on Thursday evenings dropped. (Friday is the Moslem Sabbath).

The popularity of the Pony Club meant that we soon ran out of space in the stable. Narcy was talking with Empress Farah during one of the classes and mentioned that we were going to have to build another stable and would she help. She immediately agreed and provided all the funding for the new stable.

Narcy was an engineer, not an architect, but he designed a stable for thirty horses that had lovely high arches and an Old Persian flavor. It was constructed next to the original Kadjar stable at Farahabad and its own set of rings and jumping courses were built beside it. Work on construction was started in the late winter but in late spring, without any warning, Kambiz Atabai rescinded permission for the children and closed the Pony Club on one week's notice.

We had an uncomfortable lunch with some members of the Royal Horse Society at the French Club in the centre of Teheran where it became clear that something was brewing under the surface but, apart from the fact that these gentlemen had been delegated to tell us that we were no longer running the Farahabad Pony Club it was difficult to find out exactly what was going on. There was obviously an element of jealousy; most activities associated with the Court being afflicted by this malaise. Someone had apparently decided that Narcy and I were straying too close to the sources of power and decided to take over. Kambiz Atabai stayed in the background while all this was going on but, as soon as the children moved their horses out, a new lot moved their horses in. Most of these were not children but generals and colonels and members of the Imperial Court. Narcy finished the new building as he had promised and courtly hangers-on got themselves a free stable. There were two young instructors, graduates of the Madeira School in Virginia, who had already been signed on by the Royal Horse Society to come to Iran for a year to assist with the proper organization of the Pony Club. They were also to teach riding classes for Pony Club members and the Royal children. But the Royal Horse Society rescinded the contract and we had no choice but to open Norouzabad to the children, their horses and the instructors. There was a wattle construction hay barn which we turned into an extra stable and within two weeks the instructors had arrived. Frederika Lincoln, who had been one of the organizers of the Teheran Gymkhana Organization and a good friend, had left her teaching job at Iran Zamin and was working in Colorado but she responded to an urgent SOS and flew from Colorado to help for the summer. The Norouzabad Equestrian Centre was a going concern.

Every able bodied horse, regardless of sex or breed, was pressed into service as a school horse. Even the Caspians were required to join in the classes.

There was some doubt about the wisdom of mixing stallions and mares in the same class but, as we lacked sufficient numbers of either sex to keep them separate, they went in together and to the best of my knowledge, no mare became pregnant during class hours.

Although the Norouzabad Equestrian Centre was originally designed as a 'stop gap' measure for the Pony Club children, it grew to a full time undertaking. There were foreign instructors, grooms, our children and other people's children all pressed into service to help with the teaching. Norouzabad began to reflect the international atmosphere of the northern suburbs of Teheran with Iranians and many other nationalities in a polyglot mixture.

There was definitely a need for such a facility. We were soon staggering under the load of over two hundred students a week. We were also running once weekly horse shows. In Karadj, forty kilometres west of Norouzabad, Ali Reza Soudovar and Fereidun Elganian built stables and rings and began training horses and riders. Soon they started hosting horse shows and the small, circumscribed world of horses expanded. In the three years that the NEC existed, it initiated dressage tests, cross-country events, trail riding and trekking in the provinces.

There was still the farm to run. We had a large peach orchard, grapevines, strawberries and asparagus, all of which we marketed in Teheran. There was also a flock of about sixty sheep. We had thought ourselves clever when we selected for twinning and tripleting twice a year but we kept running out of space. Norouzabad catered to everyone's special interests. It was overrun with chickens and turkeys that were Caren's chosen project. These were not commercial ventures, they were all pets, as was Billy-Jean, the female goat the children said they had found as a kid out riding (I suspect they paid for her), which was raised with the Fox Terriers and could dig a mouse hole, swim in the pool and sleep on the furniture like any dog.

We were almost self sufficient as we raised and butchered our own beef and lamb, and grew and froze all our vegetables. By this time we had a generator for electricity and piped water. We never had a television set, out of choice.

In addition to the Caspian, Darshuri and Fars breeds of horse, the success of the NEC depended on a plentiful supply of sound, good natured riding stock at a reasonable price. We tried the local horse dealers with some success but the prices had a way of rising as their products did well in the local shows.

They were also not above selling opium addicts as safe children's mounts. The practice of eating, smoking and drinking opium is fairly common in Iran and I suppose the extension of 'what is good for me is good for my dog' to a horse is not unreasonable. A horse that was 'ass-abi' or nervous was soon soothed with a bit of extract of the poppy. The trouble was that you were seldom told that the horse required a certain number of grams of opium a day or that his barley had to be soaked in beer. The result was that we often bought a calm horse at the horse dealers to wake up the next morning and find a horse with frightening withdrawal symptoms.

We were discouraged after scouting Kurdistan with doubtful results and returning from the Turkoman Steppes with one magnificent an-imal instead of the four average types which we had intended to buy. Where were the horse dealers finding all their horses?

When he was young, one of my grooms had briefly joined the Kurdish smugglers' guild which operated a major slice of the busy commercial traffic on the Iran-Iraq border. For obvious reasons they avoided the normal roads and used horses to carry the goods from some point in Iraq to some point in Iran. Did he know where they found their horses? Not necessarily, but he knew where to find the smugglers. Feeling op-timistic about our change in approach to purchasing horses, we drove ten hours to the town of Qasr-e Shirine on the Iran-Iraq border.

Qasr-e Shirine, named after a palace built by King Khusrow for his wife, Shirine, in the seventh century, was a small town full of palm trees. There was an INTO (Iran Tourist) hotel instead of the usual teahouse with wooden 'takhts' (beds) for the comfort of travellers. The groom went off to find a horse dealer. After agreeing to meet at five thirty the next morning I had tea and went to bed exhausted after driv-ing for ten hours.

The next morning was misty and warm as the Jeep bounced gently over the desert to a location that promised a fine view of the smugglers re-turning from their rendezvous in Iraq. I did not believe it was possible to sit on a hillock looking along the old Royal road to ancient Ctesi-phon and Baghdad viewing prospective purchases charging past loaded with contraband. But soon horses began to appear in the distance mov-ing fast. As they passed in front of us at a gallop we saw that they were loaded with cases of tea, glassware and blue jeans stacked high on their bulky pack- saddles. The word had been broadcast that customers for their horses were waiting as soon as the horses were unloaded so, while horses were still coming in at a fast pace others had been rubbed down and were being presented for our inspection.

During that day, in three different locations, we tried out sixty horses and bought fourteen. At last we had discovered where the horse dealers were finding all their horses.

Our return to Teheran was triumphant. Quite a few people knew we were going and buyers for the horses were waiting when we arrived at Norouz-abad. All but two of the horses were sold within twenty-four hours. This did much to keep the NEC solvent but meant another trip almost immediately. We simply turned around and went back to the border.

This time the weather was ominous. There were thunder-storms that chased us along the Kermanshah valley and up the pass to Mahi Dasht. At the top of the pass, the full violence of the weather, produced by warm winds from the Baghdad desert meeting the cool of the Zagros mountain range, erupted in a frenzied encounter. Lightning streaked horizontally across the windscreen, thunder shook the car and hail stones the size of walnuts forced us to stop. We covered our ears to block out the crackling noise of the car being shelled by ice and thunder exploding all around us. When we were able to see again, a ghostly flock of sheep passed by with two inches of hail clinging to their wool. The shepherd, huddled in his felt coat, barely lifted his head in acknowledgment of our greeting. We found the horse dealer, delighted to see us back after such a short time and most willing to repeat what had evidently been a profitable day. We watched the paces of horses returning from the arduous twelve-hour trip to pick up contraband near Baghdad and again repeated the painful process of trying out horses bareback or with their pack-saddles. I was wondering why anyone intending to ride horses would choose to wear a business suit but it seemed that the groom's sartorial choice precluded any contact with a pack saddle. As a result he was still able to walk at the end of the day while I was feeling worn and had blisters on all the parts that had made contact.

This time we bought two stallions from a Gendarme post on the border. These horses were of a different calibre from the ordinary smugglers' horses that were strong, sound but kind tempered. Riding perched on top of a bulky pack with a prancing, rearing stallion would be uncomfortable. As befitting Gendarmes, whose sources and methods of acquiring horses differed from ours, their horses were more 'blooded', or perhaps less ex-ercised and a fine, spirited sight to see. We called the first one, a beautiful white stallion, Alexander the Great.

Once more word had gone out that we were on a 'trip' and buyers were waiting for us on our return. We were too exhausted to undertake the same trip immediately so we limited the sales to what we could spare from the school.

Two weeks later, on our third and last trip, we expanded our horizons and, as we were trying out horses, landed in the middle of a battle. Relations between the Iraqi's and Iranians were never cordial but recent manipulation of Kurdish sympathies had further strained the fragile peace. Border inhabitants were mobilized and issued with ancient Berno rifles to protect the borders. The antiquity of the guns restricted the temptation to escalate the skirmishes to any serious level but, as the Iraqi-Kurds, who were actively fighting the Baghdad government, continued to receive friendly 'rest and recuperation' facilities in Hamadan, courtesy of the Iranian government, the situation remained volatile. Women on lookout on the flat, mud roofs leapt to the ground and, running barefoot over the earth, thrust gun belts at their men. Half of the men stayed to horse deal and the other half charged to the nearby river which, as it turned out, was the border. Bullets were smacking into the sides of the mud huts when we decided that the khaki coloured Jeep was too tempting a target and we fled. Further, having inspected a number of horses that would have made fine school mounts had it not been for their suppurating bullet wounds, I was in no mood to stop any stray ammunition myself.

Leaving that village, we dropped in on a wedding a safe two kilometres from the border and bought five horses. No one seemed to mind interrupting the wedding to sell horses. We were treated to a meal of rice and kebab washed down with the local brew.

Shortly after this, military operations on the border became more serious as Mullah Mustafa Barzani's Kurdish troops intensified their battle with the Iraqi army and the role Iran was playing as an Iraqi Kurdish retreat was threatening to turn the battle into something more in line with twentieth century armaments. This coincided with the summer heat descending on the border desert and we abandoned our efforts to find more horses.

Chapter 11

<u>Thoughts on Trekking to Ancient Civilisations</u>

Norouzabad now bore little resemblance to 'home'. It seemed more like a centre for farm -starved orphans and a number of adults who seemed to prefer the primitive, rural eccentricity to the congestion of a developing Teheran. Narcy had added a master bedroom and large living room while we were extolling the virtues of the Caspian in the U.S. in 1970. Even these additions seemed cramped when each weekday lunch saw us marching hamburgers out of the minute kitchen, like eager conscripts. Friday (the Moslem Sabbath) lunch usually numbered over forty people, whether invited or not. Although the company was amusing and welcome, we occasionally announced that we were disappearing for the weekend to swim in the Caspian or hunt in the mountains. Then we would hide at Norouzabad catching up on work or lying exhausted on the uncluttered lawn. Omid Ali's attitude was more practical; "You think you're running a business," he said, "but you're not. You're running a non-profit hotel!"

I had to agree that there should be a separation between business and family. Feeding the 'five thousand' certainly depleted any profit that we may have made. Despite this, we thought the murky line could perhaps be clarified by the addition of a new barn with living and entertaining facilities incorporated within the structure.

In early 1973, Narcy and I designed what we thought would be a solution and we were soon digging the foundations, ordering bricks and assembling workmen. The barn was to have thirty box stalls for the use of the boarders exclusively. There was a large living room with fireplace. There was also a small kitchen, bathroom and laboratory in addition to tack room and storage. Overhead we allowed ample space for a year's supply of alfalfa and straw. There was an apartment for the instructors portioned off from the hay- loft over the living room. It was decided that, once the barn was completed, we would move all socializing from the house and that a nominal charge would be made for the rustic cafeteria facilities. As far as I was concerned, the children, all of them, were more than welcome to run this. If they could make a profit they were more astute businessmen than I, which, under the circumstances, would not be difficult. Teheran, with its very urban population and structured riding clubs, did not lend itself to the relaxed participation of small horse shows, gymkhanas, fox hunts, point-to-points and small three-day events that are usual

in parts of the west. As our growing group of riders became more so-
phisticated, and more literate, they realised that tramping around rings,
or scampering haphazardly around the countryside was only a part of
the joys of riding. They wanted more. Because we used mares for riding
at Norouzabad, we were gelding the stallions we bought from Kurdistan as a precautionary measure. This practice enhanced my macho
reputation but did not make me popular with local horsemen although
the grooms at Norouzabad were relieved by the safety measure. The
events we staged were also attended by my deprecators, whose stallions
found that the heady atmosphere of a stud farm did much for their
libidos. Inevitably their enthusiasm for mares inhibited the variety of
competitions we could hold. Our first event had been the steeplechase
over nine kilometres of thorn jumps, held as a house warming for Norouzabad when we first moved in. Lev Tamp, a self-exiled Russian from
the general exodus period of the 1920's and, at one time, Master of Fox
Hounds to the late King Faisal of Iraq, introduced fox hunting with
his Saluki's the following year. A paper chase which ended with more
riders on foot than mounted succeeded these two events. We began to
organize a variety of events that would encourage our students to better, and safer, efforts and still afford a release to riding adults from the
tensions of a frenetic week in the business world of Teheran.
When Ali Reza Soudovar opened his elegant stables in Karadj and
offered to host half of the events, we were relieved. Although Ali Reza's
place was too small for one-day events or steeple chases, he maintained
a large grass ring which was admirably suited for show jumping. He
was also as anxious as we were to give beginners, both horses and
riders, a chance to compete. For the one year that this lasted we felt we
were living in an equine Camelot.
Towards the closing days of Norouzabad we introduced 'trekking' in
the provinces. It was a bizarre idea and certainly without precedent.
Subsequent experience ensured that this was not going to be a permanent feature of our programme. The brusque comment of a prominent
oilman summed it up;
"Mrs. Firouz, I admire your courage, but not your common sense."
This accolade was offered one evening in my brother's Safari Lodge on
the edge of the Mordab Lake in Bandar Pahlavi on the Caspian. We had
crashed in there with ten horses and seven children after being chased
around Kurdistan by Kurds, bees, thirst and hunger for one week.
We survived primarily through the efforts of the Drakes, a U.S. military
family whose daughter, Shelley was a summer instructor. They had a

large black Pontiac which was thoroughly unsuitable for the rough dirt back roads but it followed the riders where it could and picked up the strays and provided comfort for the saddle sore.

Omid Ali had suggested that we use his home town, Ahjean, in Kurdistan as a first site for trekking. He said the advantage was that members of the village would be able to provide food and we would not have to carry camping equipment. When we settled on to the banks of a stream under old walnut trees with a vineyard nearby and the horses grazing in the shade we had to agree that Omid Ali had had a fine idea. That evening members of his family came along the path carrying trays of rice and meat on their heads. We enjoyed a Kurdish meal under the stars.

The next morning Omid Ali was able to find some tea and bread. Soon after, the children saddled their horses and we all went exploring the valleys around Ahjean and Jaffarabad. For lunch we had some dry bread and drank water from the stream. For dinner there was nothing. The reason there was nothing, said Omid Ali, was because we had eaten everything in the village the previous evening.

"So what are we going to do?" I asked. "I don't know," was the answer. The nearest town, Assadabad, was about an hour's drive away. Kathy Ford, Shelley Drake and I got into my Jeep and we drove to Assadabad to find a kebabi where we could order dinner for everyone, including the village. We were so hungry that we had dinner there while the food for the rest was being prepared. We ordered enough so that there would be cold leftovers for the next day. But the next day we found that the food attracted swarms of bees which were otherwise harvesting the ripe grapes. They were tenacious and would hang onto a piece of meat even while it was disappearing into a mouth.

Omid Ali suggested that we make our base camp closer to a steady supply of food. Kangavar was only four hours away by horseback and we could be there by early evening. He and the other riders left while the Drakes and I packed the few items left behind. We followed as best we could; taking dirt tracks that looked as if they were going in the right direction. Occasionally we caught glimpses of the riders silhouetted on the horizon or crossing a ridge. We caught up with them at a spring with a deep pond in front of it. The horses were knee deep in water with their muzzles buried deep. The small children were lying on their stomachs with their faces submerged. Kathy Ford was completely underwater and later said she was trying to see if she could swim and drink at the same time. Shelly Drake was sitting a little way up the hill nursing her foot. She had started to run for the water, had tripped, and broken a toe. The heat, the unrelieved sun and the dust were taking a toll.

We could not stay there. It was imperative that we make Kangavar by evening. Putting Shelley in my Jeep, the Drakes and I left to look for a garden on the outskirts of Kangavar where we might camp. We found one and drove back to encourage the riders.

The denizens of Kangavar were excessively curious but not all that friendly. The first thing I noticed was that my Pentax camera was no longer on the front seat of the Jeep. The women were more discrete and simply looked at us as they passed by with jugs of water balanced on their heads. But the men and children not only looked; they mingled around us and poked into belongings, not a few of which disappeared. We had a good dinner of chicken kebab from a local tea-house and, since it was night, the bees were asleep.

The next day convinced us that Kurdistan was not ready for trekking. The local Gendarmerie threatened to arrest us for disturbing the peace and the chicken kebab at lunch-time was so covered with bees it was difficult to decide whether you had picked a leg or a wing. Omid Ali and I went to the trucking syndicate and ordered a truck for the next day. We decided we would go to the Caspian where my brother had a Safari Club and plenty of land around it to graze the horses.

We were loading the horses the next day when we discovered that the truck sent for us had a defective floor. It was rotted right through. We unloaded the horses and put them into a caravanserai until a proper truck could be found. Omid Ali stayed to take the horses to the Caspian. The Drakes took most of the children to the Safari Lodge and Cathy and I took a sick American child back to Teheran.

We waited for Omid Ali for three days at the Caspian and we were getting worried. There were no horses appearing and no word from Omid Ali. When he finally arrived he looked both haggard and triumphant. "I made it," he said. "So we see." "What happened? "

It seemed that he had gotten into a fight at the trucker's syndicate and had hit a driver. For this he was put into the Kangavar jail and told he would have to pay compensation. This he refused to do. After two days one of the guards gave him some money and told him to go buy cigarettes. Omid Ali took the money and left. He found a truck not connected with the syndicate, retrieved the horses from the caravanserai, loaded them and came to the Safari Lodge.

We spent a week swimming the horses in the Caspian Sea and galloping along the beaches. There were jackals darting out to pick up fish washed onto the shore and occasional wild boar in the forests, which we chased until they plunged into swamps.

Our second and last trek was to the Mohammad Reza Shah Wildlife Park in northeastern Iran. This time we had the sense to take the children only into the part that permitted returning to the hunting lodge each evening. We sent them home to Norouzabad after a week, along with a truckload of horses. There were large herds of wild goat and sheep in mountains that were covered with juniper trees. The needles that were crushed by the horses' feet gave off a rich pine aroma which, warmed by the sun, surrounded you with a pungent smell. There were fleeting glimpses of dappled leopards, grunting wild boar and loping bears. Cantering over the brow of a hill we would startle herds of two to three hundred mouflon (wild sheep) and watch them flow over the next crest like fields of wheat bending with the wind. Cabk (partridge) called from every canyon and maral (red deer), their antlers seeming ponderous on their graceful heads, would watch warily from the edge of oak forests.

The children left unwillingly after seven days but I was not about to repeat the Kurdish experience and we were going into unknown territory. The instructors, Cathy Ford and Anne Freligh, Omid Ali and a friend, Hushang Bakhtiar, Narcy and I left the confines of the large reserve to explore Persian Turkmenistan. We stayed another eight days, spending the nights in Turkoman villages as we came across them, exhausted and hungry at the end of the day. We were not prepared for the virgin forests of oak and beech trees that still grew outside the game reserve. We had been led to believe that the villagers had cut down everything not under protection. But, if anything, the forests north of Lowendore, which is the north boundary of the reserve, held even older and more massive trees. We rode in shade along narrow winding tracks all morning until we reached Gholli Dagh at noon. We were joined along the way by Turkomans travelling on horse-back from one village to another. Mostly they were riding fast pacers and invariably challenged us to a race. We were out of control for considerable bits of the ride. The Turkomans were curious about our reasons for being on this trail. They were not belligerent. It was just that they normally did not run into this form of traffic. When we explained that we were exploring, they accepted this as perfectly natural. Unlike the ubiquitous penchant for harassment that so characterised the Kurds, the Turkomans accepted our presence as natural, probably because they had never been subjected to the idiosyncrasies of foreigners and could not believe their eyes. We did run into trouble outside a large radar station above Yek-e-Chenar that overlooks the Russian border. We were lost and trying to find out from an old U.S. air force topographical map where we were. The engineers who made the map seemed fond of indicating nomad camps but had little love for sedentary villages. We were looking for Agh Imam when a busload of blue clad air force personnel stopped by us on a dirt road. They were out of the bus and had us surrounded with their guns at the ready before we quite realised that this bus was belligerent. Their leader insisted we turn back. When he admitted that this was one way of reaching Agh Imam, we insisted we continue. He finally agreed but only after he'd lent us a tiny Turkoman as guide.

A bit further down the road we understood his reluctance to let us continue. There was a huge installation of radar dishes and buildings; all very modern. Scrawled into the dirt bank was a message from Dante's Inferno, translated into English: "Abandon hope all ye who enter here." It seems American personnel were running this unlikely outpost. We did not stop to socialize and were hurried past it as fast as our guide could make us go.

Agh Imam was a typical Gouklan Turkoman village in the middle of the forest. They did not have much to eat as their chickens had all died of a plague the previous year and they had not bothered to replace them. I found that the bottle of vodka I had put in the saddle pack with my underwear had all leaked out. We found a bottle of cognac in another saddlebag and drank this while chewing hard wild sheep jerky we'd made while in the park. We slept on the porch of the katkhoda's hut and I used the gunny sack with the jerky as a pillow. The next morning my neck was stiff and I discovered that the gunny had deflated. The village curs had eaten it all out from under my head without my waking up.

After Agh Imam the countryside opened up and there were no more trees. We met a group of men and women returning from spending the night in their sunflower fields protecting them from wild boar. They were surrounded by large dogs that were all looking proud of themselves.

A Turkoman friend from Gonbad-e-Qabus was with us on this part of the trip. He had many friends in the area and had thought this a fine way to visit them all. This meant stopping in villages all the way to Maraveh Tepe which was our target for the night. Hadji Avaz Safai was a minor landowner but mainly he was a race-horse trainer and his list of acquaintances was legend. He was a tall man with the slant eyes of the Turkoman and a long white beard. He had no trouble talking all day, whether he was at the top of the line or the bottom. He could also spend much time talking to his friends in their mud huts or alachekhs. We sat and listened to him, although we did not understand his Turkish, and drank pot after pot of tea.

In the middle of the day down on this dry plain the heat was intense and we urged Hadji to let us reach Maraveh Tepe before we too turned to jerky.

Hadji's friend in Maraveh Tepe had a large compound with a house and several alachekhs in it. There was also a 'talar' (raised platform) which we were told we could use. We tethered and fed the horses and joined the family for a lunch of bread and mast. After lunch, Hushang Bakhtiar and I saddled our horses and rode down to the Gendarme post to introduce ourselves. Since this was a border post they would be suspicious of any strangers. They were, but they were nice about it and did not object to our spending the night. Narcy arrived by car about midnight. He had had to leave us at Lowendore as he had business in Teheran and we had led his horse for two days.

We rode for three more days slowly making our way back to the edge of the wildlife park where we could find a truck to take the horses back to Norouzabad.

The hills and the forests were in such contrast to the desert oasis villages and towns of central Iran that we knew we were on the fringes of a completely different civilization. As indeed we were. We were skirting the beginnings of Central Asia. To the east was the Tejend River and then Samarkhand and Bokhara. There was also Afghanistan so tantalizingly near. The compulsion of early travellers on horseback to cross the next mountain and see the next civilization was all too clear.

This would have to wait for another time.

Chapter 12

The Peacock Throne, Hungary and the Grand National

In October 1971, Mohammad Reza Pahlavi, Shahanshah of Iran, celebrated two thousand five hundred years of Royal Dynasty. He gave a party to mark what was called an unbroken line of monarchs from the Median to Pahlavi reigns. Royalty and statesmen from all over the world were invited to attend the festivities which were to be held at Persepolis the most famous of the Achamaenian palaces. Most of the guests flew directly to Shiraz where they were driven to Persepolis. Prince Philip and Princess Anne remained in Teheran for a day. A member of the British Parliament had seen the Caspian ponies at Norouzabad the previous autumn and, knowing of the British royal family's interest in horses, thought they would be interested in this unusual breed. With the Shah's permission, Kambiz Atabai arranged for Prince Philip and Princess Anne to visit the Royal Stables at Farahabad. Princess Anne was invited to ride in the mountains of the Royal Game Reserve on one of the Shah's horses. Three Caspian stallions were brought by van for Prince Philip to inspect.

Princess Anne was accompanied on the ride by the Caspian, Shahryar, ridden by our daughter, Roshan. There were other official outriders, including Narcy. At the conclusion of a strenuous twenty kilometre ride over rocky mountains and through surprised herds of wild sheep, the group pulled in to the Royal Stables at a smart hand gallop. Princess Anne dismounted and, approaching Roshan, complimented her on her pony's superb performance in keeping up. As Roshan had been detailed to ride abreast of Princess Anne there was little chance that anyone would have been foolish enough to pass, but the praise was a fitting crown to Shahryar's illustrious gymkhana, racing and jumping career. While Princess Anne was in the mountains, Prince Philip looked over the Caspian stallions that had been brought to the Royal Stables in Farahabad from Norouzabad. He made some astute comments about the wisdom of keeping such a rare herd all in the same place. I was happy to hear this because I was hoping he would accept the gift of a mare and a stallion having had similar misgivings myself. When the stallion Rostam was presented to him he kindly accepted the gift and laughingly agreed to the mare, Khorshid Kola, sight unseen. As it turned out, this generous gesture of Prince Philip was, indeed, what did save the Caspian.

Kambiz Atabai showed some of the Shah's horses and presented Princess Anne with a Pahlavan stallion. The Pahlavan was a breed developed by Mr. Atabai using Plateau Persian stallions on Thoroughbred mares. Atesh, as his name implies (fire) was a splendid spirited chestnut. The subsequent transfer of the two Caspians and Atesh presented the usual difficulties. Iran had suffered an epidemic of African Horse Sickness in 1959 that had resulted in a ban on equine imports to most European countries from Iran and other countries where the disease had also occurred. As a result, a direct flight from Iran to England was impossible and an interim solution had to be found. When Prince Philip stopped off in Budapest on his way back from the celebrations, he mentioned the problem to the Hungarians who graciously agreed to keep the three horses for two years quarantine.

Arrangements were then made by the Imperial Court for the horses to fly to Budapest on an Imperial Iranian Air Force Hercules freighter.

In March, 1972, Ateshe, three 'Jelodars' (attendants and outriders for the Shah) from the Royal Stables and I left from Doshan Tepe military airfield in Teheran for Hungary with the three securely crated horses. Someone had neglected to arrange over-flight permission for Rumania and our flight was delayed for several hours. Someone else had neglected to arrange visas for Hungary but we did not know that yet.

The flight was noisy and cold and the seats, such as they were in the hold, were hard. I decided to visit the cockpit to pass time with the pilots and see how we were doing. Underneath the plane was a thick carpet of dark grey cloud.

"Have you ever been to Budapest," I asked.

"No, but we're looking forward to it," the pilot replied.

"If you've never been there, how are you going to find it?" I continued.

"We have a map," he said, pointing to his lap.

Indeed he did have a map and I could see the lines of rivers and positions of mountains. I looked out the window again and all I could see was the thick blanket of cloud.

"Well, I hope you're right," was all I could say.

I did not say anything to Ateshe or the three Jelodars about how we were going to find Budapest. The Jelodars were discussing what they were going to do in Budapest which sounded distinctly different from what Kambiz Atabai had told us to do and Ateshe was doing homework. All of a sudden the aeroplane lurched to the left and the horses scrambled in their crates to stay upright. No sooner had they regained balance than the aeroplane lurched to the right. The Jelodars rushed to Atesh to calm him and Ateshe and I held on to the Caspians. The lurching motion continued for another fifteen minutes and then we seemed to straighten out. When all was calm I went back to the cockpit to see what was wrong. We were in a vise between two MIG's. They were so close you could see the pilots' heads.

"What's going on," I asked our pilot.

"I guess that Iran still hasn't got over-flight permission," he said, " or else, maybe we're lost."

We did find Budapest and landed at the airport. Nobody seemed to be expecting us. We sat forlornly on the edge of the tarmac looking vaguely for someone who seemed to be looking for horses. Soon the aircraft was inundated by Russian pilots and technicians from nearby Soviet aeroplanes. They took the opportunity to poke and pull at the inner workings of an American made military aircraft. Eventually a van arrived with a cargo lift in tow and the precarious job of moving the crates from the aeroplane directly to the van was accomplished. There was some heart stopping moments as Atesh's crate teetered on its way to the van.

After the horses left we were taken to immigration where we discovered that there were no visas for Hungary in our special 'Service' passports. As the three Jelodars were in khaki Royal Stables uniforms and we had arrived in a camouflaged military transport aeroplane, our chances of slipping quietly through the arrivals lounge and filling in temporary visa forms was slim. Our escort took us to a special room and called the Foreign Office. I am told he said:"There is an invasion from Persia. What do we do"? After considerable delay we were given special pieces of paper, which evidently made us legitimate visitors to the country, and we left. We followed the route taken by the horse van to see that the horses were comfortably bedded down in their new stables.

We found them in one of the elegant stables at Alag where they were reveling in the attentions of the grooms. We returned to Budapest and the Marienzeit Hotel on the island of the same name situated in the middle of the Danube. It was beautifully decadent with all of the old-world splendor of large rooms, spacious bathtubs and a dining room with sparkling white linen, and unlimited supplies of Hungarian wine. The wine was probably not a good idea. It inspired the Jelodars to greater flights of imagination that resulted in their late arrival for breakfast the next morning. First one showed up looking as if he had slept in his clothes. He grunted 'good morning' and attacked a cup of coffee as if it had some property that would save his life. The second showed up also looking as if he had slept in his clothes. They were both quiet.

"So where is the third?" I asked.

"He must still be out," they answered.

"Oh yes, out where?'

"You see, we decided to see Budapest last night,' was the answer.

"We went to some bars and had a few drinks and met some people," they said.

"Then it got late and we couldn't find our way back to the hotel. We were in a park and there were some benches so we decided to sit down for awhile and sleep. Then we woke up but Reza was still asleep so we thought it would be a good joke if we left him there."

Kambiz Atabai had given specific instruction about what we were to do with our one week in Hungary and these instructions did not include painting Budapest red. Fortunately the hangovers were such that the idea of repeating their experience had no immediate appeal. When Reza finally showed up we were ready to meet with Dr. Feher, President of Horse Operations in Hungary.

Arrangements had to be made for the official transfer of the horses to the Hungarian government. Dr. Sandor Bokonyi, the archaeozoologist whose work with faunal remains at the British Institute of Persian Studies established the existence of miniature horses in ancient Persia, had kindly agreed to take time off from his busy schedule at the National Museum. As his English was excellent he was able to translate procedures which, however, were beyond my understanding in any language.

Without any official duties for a week we rented a minibus and visited as many studs as we could around the countryside. We were accompanied by a government guide and translator who was knowledgeable not only about the studs and the complex horse organization but was also a student of history, art, agriculture and seemingly, of every subject on which we questioned him. The communists had confiscated his family studs and farms in the past.

We started with the Thoroughbred Stud at St. Tomas, which was one of the newer studs and was breeding very attractive race horses. The next day we went to the old Esterhazy Stud which was attractively laid out around a large lake. The stable was the ultimate in elegance; spacious standing stalls with old prints hanging on each of the arches separating the stalls which surrounded an open space with a massive stone fireplace. There was a dining table covered with a checkered cloth and a large bowl of flowers. Coffee and apricot brandy were served as we sat listening to the swishing of horses' tails, the occasional stamp of a hoof and the quiet munching of hay. From there we drove to Babolna where the Jelodars rode in an indoor ring, dramatically lit by crystal chandeliers. Kambiz Atabai was interested in an independent judgment of the Jelodars riding skills so, after they had warmed up their horses, they took a few fences for the riding master to see. He would have been more impressed had he not seen them on the morning after.

Afterwards the Babolna groom trainees gave an exhibition of musical chairs on newly imported Egyptian Arab mares. We were given a tour of the archives where the earliest records of Arab imports from Syria and other parts of the Near East are kept. They showed us the harness rooms with gleaming brass and the immaculate stables. There was a room with a welcome wood stove glowing in the middle and the ritual three thimbles of coffee to three thimbles of Barraks, absolute essence of apricot. Ateshe was learning to drink since the Hungarians distill everything that comes off a fruit tree.

Ateshe and I gave the Jelodars a reprieve one morning while we visited museums with Sandor Bokonyi. They spent the time shopping for girl friends and wives. Towards the end of our stay we spent an afternoon at the trotting track which impressed the Jelodars who thought the trot was simply a gear between walk and canter not a pace which could be used for a purpose. We were given a special afternoon at the 'Gallop' track. The racing officials invited us to join them in their special section. They gave us lunch and a warm speech to conclude the afternoon. Unfortunately my training in these official events did not include knowing that I had to give a return speech and I simply smiled my appreciation and thanked the officials individually instead of collectively. When we went to Alag to say 'good bye' to the horses they had a special treat for us. They mounted us on fine steeplechase horses and took us out to the training fields. Ateshe and the Jelodars were ready to head immediately for the advanced fences and my heart stopped. Ever since ploughing through a fence when I was training a horse at Cornell University and breaking my back I've been careful to go around fences, not through them or over them. Fortunately the riding master took us over the lower jumps and reprimanded the Jelodars for angling over in the direction of the larger barriers.

We had decided to take a bus to Vienna to catch a Sabena flight from there as no proper connection to Teheran via Malev Airlines could be found from Budapest. There was one flight that involved an overnight in Athens but the minute one of the Jelodars said he had a friend there

I vetoed the idea. Losing them amongst strangers in Budapest was one thing. Collecting them where they knew people spelled trouble.

The bus station was cold and grey in the early dawn. We were unable to decipher which bus was going where in the gloom and were beginning to panic when we met an English-speaking Hungarian whose destination was also Vienna. We joined forces to find our bus and eventually reached the Austro-Hungarian border where we detected consternation on the faces of the officials checking papers. Apparently our 'visas' stated Budapest airport as our port of entry and exit and we had no right to be sneaking out the back door, so to speak. The border officials held up the bus and telephoned to the Foreign Office to say that we appeared to be escaping into Austria.

Foreign Office patience with Persian disregard for formalities was sorely tried and they ordered a curt; "Let them go!" We were just in time. We made the Sabena flight with ten minutes to spare.

Rostam, Khorshid Kola and Atesh remained in Hungary for the prescribed two years, after which time they were sent to England. While the Caspians were in Hungary Khorshid Kola gave birth to a filly foal, which Prince Philip named Ateshe after my daughter, who had accompanied them on their flight to Hungary.

As the months went by, the NEC was able to break even financially, though Narcy would not corroborate this statement, but the Caspians were a luxury that were becoming increasingly difficult to justify.

After we compiled the First International Caspian Stud Book (with a preface kindly written by H.R.H. Prince Philip) for publication, in the spring of 1973, the herd of twenty three Caspians was sold to the Royal Horse Society. This was done with the proviso that they should remain at Norouzabad where we could continue the research and breeding programs. The arrangement should have been ideal as the Royal Horse Society received credit for the work without doing any and we continued to enjoy the presence of the animals and the stimulation of the research. The aim, still, was to have the Caspians eventually finance themselves so we were delighted when the Caspian Stud (UK) decided to purchase a mare and a stallion in the spring of 1974.

The Caspian Stud (UK) had been founded the same year by Elizabeth Haden, (now Webster) her mother, Stephanie ('Jaffa') Jenvey and Arthur ('Griff') Griffin, with a nucleus of Joan Taplin's Caspians from Bermuda. Momtaz-e-Mahal went to Prince Philip's Caspian Stud, then at Windsor Castle. Daria Nour, Mitra and two foals born in Bermuda were bought by Elizabeth Haden. Joan had been loath to part with the Caspians but the oil crisis of 1974 had pushed the price of feed imported from the U.S.to astronomical levels and she could no longer afford to keep them.

Mrs. Haden was aware that starting a new breed with so few animals was an impossible task. She formed the Caspian Stud (UK) in order to finance the import of a further mare and stallion to augment their existing herd and formed The British Caspian Society. Another member of what was later to become The Caspian Horse Society, Muriel Harris, was also interested in a stallion.

The Royal Horse Society gave permission for Taliyeh, her colt foal, Maroun, and the stallions, Mehran and Karoun, to be sent. The horses were to be the guests again of an IIAF on a flight to Lyneham airport in England. We went through the usual time consuming export formalities and were on time with the horses, crates and papers at Mehrabad airport. There was a delay while the officer in charge of IIAF cargo flights was located but we eventually made contact with the pilot, attendants and aeroplane and loaded our cargo. With admirable foresight Narcy drove the car around to the other side of the runway to wait for us to complete customs formalities. He was still there when it was discovered that the pilot had mislaid his passport. We would be unable to leave until he found it. The horses would have to remain in the aircraft for the night since they had already cleared customs.

Narcy drove me into Teheran for lunch and an attempt to contact the British Embassy to have them alert Elizabeth Haden in England about the change of arrival time. Luckily, just as we were being seated in Ray's Pizza No. 2 on Villa Avenue in the middle of commercial Teheran, the man in charge of the Caspian transfer at the British Embassy leaned across from a nearby table. He said he was surprised to see me having a pizza at Ray's instead of a sandwich at thirty thousand feet. I explained the problem and he agreed to telegraph immediately, tactfully suggesting 'technical difficulties' to cover the delay.

The next morning dawn and I collided at the steps to the aircraft. I fed the horses and awkwardly milked Taliyeh from the back of her crate. Maroun was in a separate box and unable to relieve her; content with a nose-bag of barley instead of his morning milk. When these chores were done I sat down on the steps of the Hercules transport to await the crew. The early sunlight was turning the snow on the peaks of the Tochal from blue to rose and white. Behind me, F4 fighter planes were shattering the morning quiet, practising landing and take-off before the rush hour of international commercial flights.

Once we were airborne the pilot asked me if I would mind if we stopped over for the night in Rome.

"I certainly do mind," I said, "these horses have been in here already twenty four hours."

Later, at Lyneham Airport, I mentioned this to a RAF pilot. He laughed. "They do it all the time," he said. "The Iranian Military pilots drive these birds like taxis."

After the bright sun of Teheran, the dark fog and drizzle at Lyneham was depressing but the smiling faces of Liz, 'Jaffa', 'Griff' and 'Twink', his wife, more than made up for the weather. Miss Muriel Harris was introduced and we began unloading what should have been our exhausted charges. The attending Ministry veterinarian assured us that, although the horses would be stiff and run a slight temperature as a result of the time they had been confined, we would find that by the next day ... and Karoun was away. He had slipped his rope and was performing slaloms around the fighter planes parked in the hanger with anxious Air Force personnel in hot pursuit. Our combined efforts soon corralled the spirited Karoun and he was led with the rest into the waiting horse-box where none of the horses showed signs of suffering from exhaustion. Miss Harris later reported a total reluctance on Karoun's part to take instructions from any woman.

I had first met the three members of the British Caspian Stud in 1971. After presenting a paper on the Caspian miniature horse at the 3rd International Congress of Agricultural Museums in Budapest, I had gone on to England. Mrs. Jenvey had invited me to their comfortable and elegant house, Hopstone Lea, Claverley, Shropshire. She spoiled my Spartan life style with an excellent pheasant cooked with cherries. The two other members of the Caspian Stud were also present. I had climbed out of the Hercules with a flask of tea and a piece of dry 'barbari' bread and could not understand why they were laughing until I found they never travelled without champagne and smoked salmon.

Mahmad, one of the grooms from Norouzabad who had come with me, went off with the horse box ahead of us bound for Claverley. 'Griff' took my arm and led me to his Rolls Royce. 'Griff', his wife, Twink', Liz, 'Jaffa' and I went several miles down the road before 'Griff' pulled over into a by-pass. They unloaded a wicker hamper from the back of the car and produced - champagne and smoked salmon.

'Jaffa' and her husband, Charles, were going to Liverpool that weekend for the Grand National. This was a yearly jaunt in the company of their friends the Le Mare's who owned the famous two time winner of that race, Red Rum. As Mahmad was to stay for two months to help with the initial working in of the Stud's Caspians, there was no urgent need to attend to the day to day chores and we left.

'Jaffa' was a striking looking woman. Although her given name was Stephanie, she was called 'Jaffa' because of her natural bright red hair. She was always stylishly dressed even when dealing with the less fastidious aspects of horses. Her husband Charles was an easy going man whose hobby was pheasant shooting and, as far as I could see, enjoying 'Jaffa' pursuing her bizarre interest in Caspians.

I had only read about the Grand National but on the drive to Southport, where we were to spend the night, the Jenveys told me what I should expect. This was the night before the race and there was a spontaneous party each year where owners, trainers and the more intrepid jockeys celebrated before the event. Later I understood why everyone celebrated before the race instead of after.

The next day, at the race-track, there was row upon row of Rolls Royces, Bentleys, and Rovers. Out of the back of each appeared identical wicker baskets all seemingly packed by Fortnum and Mason. Each contained champagne and smoked salmon. Red Rum won the race, his third victory in the Grand National and, I think, set a record. He had also been runner up on two further occasions and had earned himself a place in racing history.

By this time we had been 'celebrating' this victory since the previous evening and I could think of nothing more tempting than bed. The Jenveys and Le Mares lasted a little longer.

Not for the first time, I was struck by the unqualified enthusiasm the British brought to all aspects of their lives and I was relieved that they were including the Caspian in their impressive list of interests. It is no exaggeration to say that the Caspian was 'saved' as a result of the combined efforts of Mrs. Joan Taplin in Bermuda, Prince Philip, Colonel Sir John Miller (Crown Equiry to the Queen) and the British Caspian Trust (which later became the Caspian Horse Society, founded primarily by the Caspian Stud UK) through their unstinting support of the rare and vanishing representatives of this ancient breed. Without their recognition of the potential for the Caspian we would have had little incentive to augment the pitifully small numbers in our herd. We owe a deep debt to them all for their unswerving efforts and, I have no doubt, their overdraft.

Presented to H.R.H. Prince Philip, Rostam was quarantined with Khorshid Kola, at Alag, Hungary. En route to the U.K. the pair produced the filly, Ateshe

H.R.H. Prince Philip has given unstinting support to the survival of the breed. He is seen here with Brenda Dalton during the making of a documentary film about the life of Louise Firouz in October 2008.

Elizabeth Webster (nee Haden) with Khorshid Kola, the mare given to H.R.H. Prince Philip on the anniversary of 2,500 years of royal dynasty

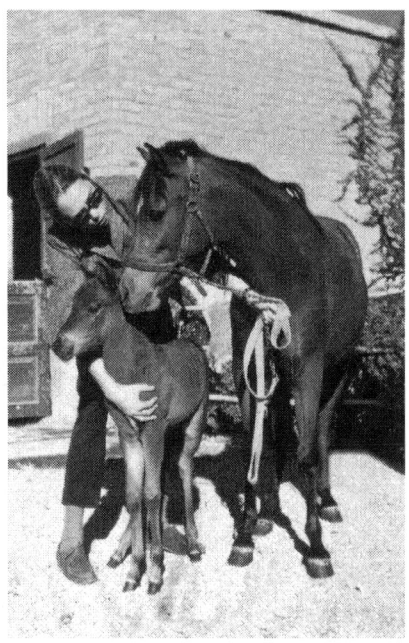

Momtaz-e-Mahal, who was loaned to Joan Taplin in Bermuda and was later given to H.R.H. Prince Philip by Louise Firouz

Chapter 13

Financial Problems, Enforced Sale and a Major Life Change

Financial difficulties forced us to sell our herd of twenty three Caspian horses to the Royal Horse Society in the spring of 1973. Theoretically this was an ideal solution to the problem of preserving them in Iran if we were unable to preserve them ourselves. After all, the complete name of the Royal Horse Society was Anjoman e Saltanat I-e-Parvaresh-e Asb va Behboud-e-Nejad (the Royal Horse Society for Breeding Horses and Preservation of Breeds). Shortly after, we realised that our financial problems were not going to melt away this simply. We would have to sell Norouzabad also if the Firouz Construction Company and thus the Firouz's were to survive.

Some writers maintain that the beginning of the rot in Iran that eventually led to the Revolution in 1978-9 was sparked by a press conference given by Mohammad Reza Pahlavi, Shah of Iran, in December 1973, announcing a dramatic oil price increase. There is some merit in the argument. In less than three months the income of the country quadrupled and Iran's oil revenue went from five billion dollars to nineteen billion dollars in one year. But of course, the prices of everything else took giant leaps too. Contracts for construction signed before December 1973, at fixed prices, became tickets for debtors' prison. There was no escape from the financial bind.

I was unaware of the extent of political and financial pressures and the unhealthy aura of the illusion of power that hung over the whole country. The signs were there for us to see but perhaps we took refuge in ignorance. While the Firouz family was feeling the pinch of poverty and the Firouz Construction Company was accumulating debts in an uncontrollable way, the country was revelling in an orgy of sudden huge oil profits. This sounds a bit dramatic but it was; catastrophically so.

The loss of the Caspians had not been such a bad blow because they were still with us and we had control of the whole project. The idea of selling Norouzabad to cover the debts was a bitter pill to swallow but we had no choice. Norouzabad would have to go and the Caspians with it.

We offered Norouzabad to the Royal Horse Society. They seemed delighted with the idea. It would give them a ready built prestigious stud farm and riding school. This matter was put to the Board of Directors and discussed at some length. Eventually it was Richard Helms, then United States Ambassador to Iran, who told us while we were out riding together that the Minister of Court had agreed to the purchase. The Minister of Court was also President of the Board of Directors of the Royal Horse Society.

Several weeks passed before I had found sufficient courage to make an appointment to see him at his house in Shemran. He was charming and assured me that they were interested in buying Norouzabad, provided we agreed to stay on and run the place exactly as we had been doing. He was nice enough, or honest enough, to say that it was important that a stud farm and riding school of this quality should be preserved. He added that there would be some disgruntled diplomats if they had to move their horses. This all seemed a reasonable solution.

The farm was assessed at thirteen and a half million toumans, which at that stage were seven to the dollar.

There were lengthy negotiations (which I did not attend) which took up most of the summer of 1974. It was not until October that I realised that Narcy apparently had agreed to sign a contract that was in direct contravention to the original agreement. The original stated that the Royal Horse Society would buy Norouzabad at the assessed price of thirteen and a half million toumans and that we would remain in place for four years to run the farm, stud and riding school.

Though I never saw it, the new agreement evidently stated that we would close the school and remove ourselves by November 1st. There would be a fine of five thousand toumans for each day after that date that we remained.

A price of seven million toumans would be paid for Norouzabad. I assume that the only reason we agreed to all this was because we were desperate.

This was a traumatic decision, requiring the closure of the riding school in mid season, repayment of outstanding lessons, finding alternative stabling for approximately one hundred horses and a house for ourselves. In addition to packing furniture, books and possessions, storage-space for all the equipment and paraphernalia of the farming side of the operation had to be found. As usual, this decision was taken just as the Tochal mountain range gave visual proof of the beginning of winter, the powdered summits, glowing softly and rising in the early evening light. When the horses were bedded down for the night and the gentle bleating of sheep was replaced by the crackle of wood in the fireplace we gathered to nurse an evening drink and shattered nerves. The eleven days following our eviction notice were a nightmare. We searched frantically for stabling for the animals, and for some place to put the farm equipment and ourselves. Omid Ali and I rose early each morning to scour the countryside surrounding Norouzabad, searching for any form of shelter for rent. We would return in the evening to report complete failure. On the eleventh day there were six ten-ton trucks idling at the farm while Omid Ali and I looked at each other in despair. We glanced only casually at a white Mercedes that wove its way around the accumulation of effects to be removed. One of the more enthusiastic riding students from the American Women's Club stepped down from the car. She was waving her arms with glee. She had found us a stable.

There was a quick word with the truck drivers, I got into the car, and we broke speed limits going to Karadj, a town forty kilometres West of Teheran. There were some sheep barns belonging to Iradj Chodjania who, it seemed, could not resist an SOS with such a rich blend of disaster and romance. His sheds were adequate and we were in no position to be anything but grateful. We returned immediately to Norouzabad. Anne Freligh, Cathy Ford and I made quick lists of which horses were to go to Karadj and which to be sent to Kurdistan where Omid Ali assured me that something could be done in the area where we had been trekking the summer before. The boarders clearly would prefer to have their horses within commuting distance while the breeding stock would require the space and tranquility of the mountains of Kurdistan.

We cleared all the horses, sheep, cows, feed, farm machinery, household effects and the dogs within twenty-four hours. It would not be fair to say that I managed to pack the house while doing the rest. Full due goes to the ladies from the American Women's Club, to which I did not belong, who substituted packing house-hold effects for their riding lessons. To this day there are things that I still cannot find! Narcy quietly found us a house in Shemran and various kind people offered shelter to the children to spare them the last poignant moments of leaving home.

There were the school horses, the Fars and Darashuri breeding stock and the boarders. There were also the foundation Caspian horses that the Royal Horse Society had insisted we continue to accumulate. They had not paid for them and said they did not want them. When we left there were twenty-three Caspians remaining at Norouzabad; the original herd they had bought and the foals born in the meantime.

Omid Ali did not seem to think it was necessary to inform anyone in Kurdistan of his impending arrival with two truckloads of horses, one of sheep and two of alfalfa and straw. We waved him goodbye. Some fifty boarders and school horses went to Zarrindasht, Iradj Chodjania's farm in Chahr Dongeh outside Karadj.

On November 7th Anne Freligh and I loaded the foundation stallion, Aseman, which the Royal Horse Society had originally rejected, and an orphan Fars foal into our horse trailer at Iradj Chodjania's farm. We turned west towards Kurdistan and drove to Hamadan on our way to deliver them to Jaffarabad for the winter. We stopped for the night in Hamadan, two-thirds of the way to Jaffarabad, as dusk was falling fast and I was not entirely sure I remembered the route well enough to navigate in the dark. We parked the trailer in the Bu Ali Hotel courtyard, and left to find the Wynns, friends whose house was reputed to be off a narrow alley somewhere in the vicinity. We found the small brick house at the end of a cul de sac and knocked on the door inviting ourselves for dinner and a chance to relax in the company of two people whose pursuits were buying carpets for the European market. Horses for them were animals you ride for pleasure. Jane Wynn was intrigued by what she considered a funny story and insisted that she accompany us the following day to experience the 'next chapter'. Anthony Wynn said he would pick her up the next day as he had business in the bazaar.

We left early in the morning and reached the top of the Assadabad pass as the first rays of morning sun hit the valley below us, reflecting off the large dish of the Satellite Communications Centre. At the village of Assadabad we turned off onto a dirt road which the responsible Ministry was 'improving' by cutting through it every two hundred metres to insert drainage ditches. There were bypasses that were seas of mud and I seem to remember that we became mired in all of them. Eventually, however, we reached Ahjean which, I knew from the trek of the previous summer, was the absolute last place that the trailer could reach. The horses were unloaded and Anne and Jane led them up a stony track through the narrow valley to Jaffarabad while I unhooked the trailer and followed them with the Jeep.

We reached Jaffarabad, a tiny village of about fifteen mud huts, housing families of five or more. We found Omid Ali and Mahmad Ali looking happy for the first time in weeks. Not only had they trucked sixty sheep and thirty horses about five hundred kilometres from Norouzabad, but they had also brought two large truckloads of alfalfa and straw, stacking the bales neatly by the barn. They had converted a structure designed for hay storage into a barn with box stalls and fenced a small paddock - all in the space of four days. The sheep were feeding in a courtyard, the yawning hole in the middle being the only sign of the large underground stable that was their winter home. Mares and foals were grazing on late grass and one of the stallions was trying out the space in the small paddock. The mountain air was clear, with a tinge of burning cow dung from the smoldering 'tanours' (oval underground ovens for baking bread). The leaves from the fruit trees were a ripe gold and the swift stream that ran through the village splashed over rocks as it continued through the vineyards towards Ahjean. In the hectic and frustrating days of the close of Norouzabad I had forgotten that places like Jaffarabad existed.

Omid Ali introduced us to our host, his friend and relative, Farzollah. He was a tall, slim man with aquiline features and piercing eyes. Somehow he had become convinced that we were political refugees in need of a place to hide. Farzollah immediately made us welcome and assured us that as long as we were under his protection we were safe. The generosity of the poverty of Kurdistan contrasted to the foreclosure brought about, in part, by sudden wealth and it did not go unnoticed. This feeling was reinforced when Farzollah and his family shared their evening meal with us. We had tea, unleavened bread baked in their tanour, and thin soup with a few beans resting on the bottom of the bowl. Farzollah and his wife, a handsome woman nearly as tall as her husband, had cleared sacks of beans and hanging winter squash from a store room on top of one of the sheds that formed the courtyard of his establishment, and they offered this room to me for the winter. There was an adobe (mud) staircase that climbed steeply to the room. There were windows on two sides that looked out on the surrounding mountains and the valley where sheep were grazing guarded by small children and fierce looking shepherd dogs. The dogs had no ears and their tails were cropped. Farzollah told me they did this as protection against the wolves. As long as the wolves did not have an extremity to grab, the dogs' chances of surviving an attack were improved. On the courtyard walls cow paddies were stuck to dry and large piles, stacked like logs, waited to warm the winter chill. Used also as fuel for the tanours, it gave the bread an earthy taste.

There did not seem much that we could do. The animals were in capable hands. We left the next day to return to the house that Narcy had found in Shemran to try to put it in some sort of order and supervise the unloading of household goods. Narcy suffered the loss of Norouzabad quietly but his despair was obvious. Respect for the prestigious complex from the highest level had kept his spirits high when all else failed. Though the fortunes of the Firouz Construction Company were temporarily saved with the influx of cash from the sale of Norouzabad, its loss devastated him. The future was not bright. Fixed price contracts and inflation are not conducive to profitable enterprises. Those businesses with

Royal contacts and partners were able to manipulate their contracts. Those without were powerless.

During that winter I returned to Jaffarabad every two weeks to check on the animals and breathe the uncluttered air of the mountain valley. This was a relief after the unaccustomed traffic of Teheran crashing through pot holes in the road by the front door and the incessant ringing of two telephones and as many door bells. In its way Jaffarabad became a refuge from more than just unaccustomed city sounds. They were unchanged by the hectic turmoil of oil money that had transformed Teheran into a metropolitan bazaar of international quixotic dealing. I admired the stoic attitude of the Jaffarabadis towards the back-breaking work required to eke out an existence of subsistence level. I suspected they augmented their meager incomes with the odd smuggling jobs that almost came with being a Kurd or of living on the periphery of Kurdish territory. Land reform had been a boon of sorts. The officials in charge of parcelling out the land, however, had arbitrarily decided that one hectare here, one half a hectare three hours by donkey there, and one eighth of a hectare of walnut trees and vines another two hours by donkey, was an equitable division of land. It seemed that donkeys were constantly on the go, their riders drowsing peacefully draped on the donkey packs making up for lost sleep from constant commuting. Omid Ali waived off comments, saying winter was long enough to make up the sleep. His puritanical approach to work precluded any great Western arguments about efficiency.

The piecemeal nature of agricultural work made a mockery of modern technology. The tracts of land were too small to justify buying a tractor or installing water pumps but co-operation between the owners of these minuscule and widely separated plots seemed doomed to failure from the start. Each mistrusted the other and was afraid of starting a blood feud by even suggesting financial partnership. They seemed fated to move around and around on their donkeys, clutching a sickle in hand. I felt a bit snared in the inevitability of it all. But I began to understand why Omid Ali, Hassan, Arab and Mamdali had left to find work in Teheran. Omid Ali's expression as his eyes took in familiar fields and members of his family held both exasperation and pride. As winter continued the snow piled deeper and deeper on the road to Kurdistan and the Jeep was usually in four-wheel drive. The vast expanses of white Savannah were unblemished but for the tracks of wolves crisscrossing each other in undetermined patterns. The mice had snuggled into burrows for the winter forcing the packs of wolves down out of the mountains in search of food. The little room overlooking Farzollah's courtyard was warm with the blaze of a wood fire in the small stove Omid Ali and I had bought in Kermanshah. When the sun set over the crisp peaks of the near mountains a hush descended on the small village, broken only by the firm bolting of heavy wooden doors to prevent the wolves breaking through.

I sat cross-legged on the floor with a book for company and vodka for courage. I would watch the 'crystal' mountains in the moonlight. Soon the first long-drawn out howl that signaled the nightly patrol of wolves would echo through the valley and I would watch their dark shapes as they circled cautiously around the village, advancing and leaping against the shuttered barriers of the courtyard.

The wolves were as much a part of life as the cows the Kurds kept for milk or the sheep that gave wool for clothes and carpets. When I suggested to Farzollah that the shotgun I had could be used against the wolves at night he was shocked.

"God put them on earth and it is a sin to kill them".

This philosophy seemed alien to Judeo-Christian not to mention Islamic pragmatism. When I discovered that there were too few children to have a school in Ahjean, because a number of them had become victims of wolves, I did not argue. I did question why the villagers had hanged one of our dogs.

"That's different," said Farzollah. ` ""Your dog was stealing peoples clothes drying on the thickets. That is damaging personal property. And the dog was eating our salt."

He also told me about a horse that had run amok in the village killing a child. They hanged that horse too. The wolves were only doing what comes naturally whereas the domesticated animals were expected to live up to a certain standard. They were 'eating the salt'; a phrase denoting hospitality over all of Central Asia and the Middle East. If you have eaten someone's salt you are bound to the laws of hospitality. The same applies to domestic animals; if you feed one it is bound to your laws of hospitality. Piddle-face, as the children had named the dog, abused his hosts and was dealt with in the only way they knew. I had to accept their verdict even though I had been fond of the dog.

There was a symbiotic quality about the inter-relationships. Whether this was logically reached or whether it was habit and tradition handed down over generations I was not able to determine. The land on top of mountains that was difficult to reach and plough by oxen, was tilled in a brilliant manner. The villagers would spend the evening cutting up potatoes and the next morning they would carry the sacks to the inaccessible areas with donkeys. They dug small holes at odd intervals and 'planted' the potatoes. Within a few days the entire area would have been cultivated by the wild boar searching out the potatoes. Then they scattered wheat seed over the area and waited for the snow to take it down to germinate. Their soil remained fertile, did not develop a 'plough pan' and had no run-off from erosion. Now that city pleasure hunters, not the Kurds, have decimated the pig population this method is no longer possible.

Pleasant as living with Farzollah and his family was I realised that we had to make a decision about our herd of horses. The Royal Horse Society had acted dishonourably in some aspects with the Caspians. If they were going to make the Caspians a personal vendetta there was little point in our working with them any longer. I wrote them a letter reminding them that we had a certain amount of foundation stock we had picked up while still working for the Royal Horse Society and would they register these animals? They replied that the Royal Horse Society would not actively prevent our participation in the promotion of a new herd of Caspians and assured me that they would by no means interfere with the project as long as our Caspians came up to Royal Horse Society standards!

There seemed no good reason not to start again. Omid Ali and I went to the Caspian to see if we could find a few more mares and, if possible, a good stallion to complement Aseman. The weather was cold and we came close to being frozen into congealing rice paddies. We did manage to find a nice grey mare, Nour, which was later bought by Narcy' cousin, Hassan Nemazee, for his niece and nephew in Venezuela. We also bought a strange coloured, honey-red, mare that flew to England with six other Caspians in 1976 and was later purchased by Brenda Dalton. On our way to find a truck for the two mares, what looked like a bundle of shaggy, black fur trotted down the muddy track past the Jeep. We squeezed into a one hundred and eighty-degree turn and followed the little horse. He turned into a bamboo enclosure that held a small hut on stilts. There was a woman in a chador, kneading dough for bread on the small porch. She broke off long enough to call her husband from a back corner of the yard where he was splitting kindling. When we told him we were interested in buying his little horse he had trouble hiding his surprise. Obviously no one else had ever made him an offer. He recovered though and agreed to the sale. Prince Caspian was ours.

This group was trucked to Iradj Chodjania's farm, Zarrindasht, where Sherri Platt took over the conditioning and training of Prince Caspian. Their combined talents eventually led to Prince Caspian dancing the equine role with the Sadlers Wells Ballet, La Fille Mal Garde', in Rudaki Hall in 1977.

By early March we were tentatively starting up the Caspian business again, but we owned no land and our current shelters were temporary oases under very short-term leases. I was still reeling from the perfidy of the Royal Horse Society, all of whose top officials had been in Paris watching Ruba II win Supreme Pony Champion at the Salon du Cheval while we were evacuating Norouzabad.

I decided to take a short vacation before committing myself to any new ventures in Iran.

Afghanistan had often beckoned. It was almost Norouz (the Vernal Equinox) and spring was pushing back the snow-drifts. There was no reason for a further excuse but this did seem a good opportunity to investigate the horses there and the possibility of any Caspians having 'spilled over' should the situation on our side of the border ever become untenable. Both sides eventually became chaotic at about the same time.

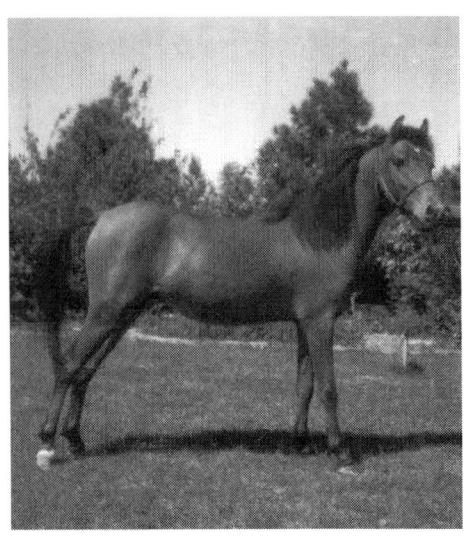

Left: Shirine, "a strange honey-coloured mare" from the 'wolf shipment'

Right: Ruba II, who won the Supreme Pony Championship at the Salon du Cheval, Paris - exported to Australia via the UK

A young groom riding Ostad, Narcy and Ateshe riding Aseman at Norouzabad

Ruba (Foxy) - Caspians are fast, flexible and have extraordinary jumping ability

Taliyeh – part of the first shipment to The Caspian Stud U.K. where she became the dam of seven stallions

Chapter 14

<u>Discovering Afghanistan</u>

I was intrigued by the form the Oriental horse would take in Afghanistan. Although famous for its horses they were far removed from the Arab horse and any influence that the Arab might have had on the development of their breeds. The people who bred them, Turkomans, Uzbeks, Tadjiks and others, had developed strains over the centuries that were said to have unique characteristics. The strong, elegant Buzkashi horses used in Afghanistan's national sport, the swift pacers best immortalized in the Chinese statue known as the 'flying horse of Ferghana' and the slim, long-backed Turkomans similar to the ones in Persian Turkmenistan.

The German archaeozoologist, Duerst, had reported the discovery of a miniature sub-fossil horse from Anau on the fringes of Persian and Russian Turkmenistan in 1904. Would there be horses similar to the Caspian in Afghanistan? There were the four tiny golden Achamaenian chariot horses from the Oxus treasure which are now in the British Museum. Were they early Caspians?

By now I had been studying the history and development of the Oriental horse in Iran for ten years. I had travelled through most of the country observing the different horses and talking with breeders and trainers. My impression was that all of the breeds on the plateau of Iran were basically the same type, developed from similar original sources. The work with faunal remains from the British Institute of Persian Studies archaeological sites had established that there were three basic types to be found from Median, through Parthian excavations. The tallest (one hundred and seventy centimetres at the withers) horse was found near Damghan on the edge of the Kavir desert. There were medium sized horses in most of the sites and the tiny Equs fossilis persicus was found in the most ancient sites but gradually petering out in the later sites. Afghanistan had been part of the various Persian Empires since empire building became fashionable about four thousand years ago. The Achamaenians, Parthians, Sassanians, Seljuks. Mongols, Moghuls and even the more recent Kadjars, to mention a few, considered Persia, Turkmenistan and Afghanistan as one united piece of real estate. There was little reason to believe that crossing the border would take us into an alien atmosphere.

The promise of Herat with its tall minarets, the solid rock barrier of the

Hindu Kush Mountains and the Oxus River plain stretching on the other side into Central Asia were further inducements to leave the immediate worries of what appeared to be a precarious future. The self-indulgent luxury of being a tourist after a winter of the snow and wolves of Kurdistan was too good to miss.

Fortunately most of the school horses had been sold during the winter and Anne and Cathy had agreed to stay on until a more permanent solution could be found.

In March, 1975, I left Teheran with Sherri Platt, whose husband had been aide to the U.S. Ambassador in Kabul before coming to Teheran to take up the same duties with Richard Helms who had become American Ambassador to Iran. Omid Ali was also with us, to protect us from being sold into slavery, should we have proved attractive to the trade. We reached Gonbad-e-Qabus, on the Persian Turkoman Steppes, in Narcy's Peugot the first night.

The next morning we visited the Royal Horse Society Turkoman Stud before driving on to Mashad for the night. On arrival in Mashad we promptly lost Omid Ali who wandered off to have his picture taken in front of the Mosque of Imam Reza, Iran's most holy shrine. As infidels we were not allowed to visit the mosque but the drive to the border was accompanied by hand-waving descriptions of the beauty of the tiles and magnificence of the courtyard and how lucky Omid Ali was to have found us before we left.

There was a reciprocal paranoia at the border. Officials on the Iranian side were searching in modern tile buildings for opium and hashish coming from Afghanistan and officials at the Afghan border were suspiciously eyeing prospective drug customers in their fly-specked mud huts. The officials on the Iranian side could not understand why anyone would want to go to Afghanistan and the officials in Afghanistan knew perfectly well why most people were going; marihuana and hashish attracting 'hippy' long-haired western children by the decrepit bus-load.

Herat was floating on apricot blossoms that provided a frothy, pink base for the minarets sweeping in lonely spires to the sky. The streets were the province of the one and two horse 'ghawdie' (dog cart) instead of a battleground for the internal combustion engine. The men's turbans punctuated the swirl of the women's beehive 'chadris'.

Having arrived early in the day we decided to take a ghawdie and see Herat properly during the afternoon. We had lunch, in a small nook of a kebabi carefully watched by silent men chewing thoughtfully on their pieces of meat while sitting cross legged on the carpet covered takhts (wooden benches). After lunch we rented a ghawdie and rattled along briskly behind a competent grey pacing horse which took us on an extended tour of the town. Ominous black clouds were building up from the Persian border to the west when we returned to the main square but we found ghawdie drivers waiting for fares there and they were enthusiastic at the suggestion of a race we proposed around the square. We wanted to catch the unique pacing action of these compact horses on film and did not mind paying for non-existent passengers to whirl around the square. The competition was fierce and growing when a lone policeman pleaded with us to stop this madness in the city's main square. We left to applause from the crowd that had gathered and was placing bets and returned to the hotel. We were just in time, the deluge hit as we were pulling up to the front door.

Herat was like jumping into a lithograph of eighteenth century Persia. There were horses, donkeys, mules and camels carrying goods and people through the bazaars. There were flocks of sheep and goats being driven down the streets. Everywhere there was the noise of a market town. Hawkers and bargainers were haggling over prices of skeins of wool, kilims, carpets, rough hewn knives and knitted caps. There were round-faced Hezaras from the Peloponnesus, descendents of Ghenghiz Khan's hordes; there were Tadjiks and Turkomans. There were Baluch from the south. Through the men, looking for bargains or selling the merchandise, wove the women, indistinguishable from each other except by the pastel colours of their chadris. An occasional Turkoman woman stood out; her tall red silk headdress identifying her immediately.

Omid Ali was impressed by his ability to speak the language of a foreign country. Most Afghans speak Dari, a pure form of Farsi (Persian). The Turkomans and other northern tribes speak Turkish or Persian so Omid Ali, fluent in both, was completely at home. What surprised him most were the 'backward' aspects of the country. He thought he had hit rock bottom at Ahjean.

Sherri and I were impressed by the elegance of the two-wheeled carts and the very good quality of the horses. They were similar to the best of the Persian Kurdish horses. The height of these animals varied from just over thirteen hands to sixteen hands with an average of fifteen hands. They were in European breast collar and shaft harness. They were shod with long caulks and a solid, Kurdish type of closed shoe. They appeared to come in all colours for a horse: grey, bay, chestnut, pinto, palomino, dun, calico (a rare mixture of colours) and black.

Their gaits were excellent - from a fast working trot to a pace and an occasional running walk. In spite of the hard road conditions on which they worked, we spotted very few splints or signs of lameness. We noticed a few with 'Turkoman' conformation; longer in the back with a 'tucked-up' appearance of the belly, rather like a greyhound, and a slight ewe neck. All of the carriage horses were festooned with bright red pom-poms, silver harness bells attached to the yoke over the saddle pad and a yak's tail suspended under the throat-lash by a string. In response to our enquiries, we discovered that the majority of the horses were raised in the northern part of Afghanistan where grass is plentiful in the winter and spring, on the Oxus plain. During the summer the herds were taken to the heights of the Hindu Kush to graze the mountain grass. South of the Parapamissus range the arid conditions were more favourable for camels and donkeys which led a precarious existence on the periphery of the Dasht-e-Margo (Plain of Death).

We feasted that evening on dishes specially ordered by Sherri, fuelled the hot water heater in the bathroom with wood chips, and tumbled into exhausted sleep after a hot bath to the sounds of thunder and the flicker of lightning on the ceiling.

This should have been fair warning of the road conditions for the next day but I had not studied any road maps, as there were none, and had no idea of the next day's marathon from Herat to Kabul. Promptly at five the next morning we woke to rain hurling against the window-panes. The hotel-keeper muttered grumpily something to the effect of waiting until the weather cleared, but we ignored him, somewhat to our later regret.

A half hour out of Herat the driving rain had turned to snow which increased in depth on the road as we climbed the pass. Towards the top we slewed around the odd truck jack-knifed on the road and forced the Peugot to plough its way through ever-thickening snow. The top of the pass was a welcome relief as the Dasht-e-Margo in front of us had never acquired a reputation for snow storms.

What most travellers describe as a brown waste stretching for miles from the mountain pass near Herat to Kandahar resembled, at this season, a vast golf green dotted with sheep, camels, horses and donkeys. The road was an excellent, unblemished concrete surface with a total of four vehicles for company in five hours.

Lunch in Kandahar, consisting of small pieces of kebab and bread, was eaten only by me. Omid Ali later confessed that what he had seen in the 'kitchen' had turned his insides to jelly, and Sherri had been to Kandahar before. I did not know what Omid Ali had seen so there was nothing to prevent my enjoying lunch.

The five hour drive up the long valley to Ghazni was threatened by an ink-black mass hovering over the eastern edge of the Parapamissus and provided a fitting end to our beginning. From Ghazni to Kabul it snowed. It snowed in three separate layers; hard at the top, hard in the middle and hard at the bottom.

Between each layer we could clearly see the bottom of the storm we had navigated and the top of the one to come. Kabul was a welcome refuge by the time the car entered the narrow, crowded streets. I was slumped over the steering wheel having been the only one to drive, and needed a vodka-and-tonic and a hot bath, simultaneously.

The American Ambassador to Afghanistan and his wife, Ted and Pat Elliot, were old friends from Teheran days and had very kindly invited us to stay with them while we were in Kabul. The Ambassador's residence was unpretentious and comfortable. There was a wood fire burning in the traditional Afghan bronze fireplace in the middle of the room, and a tan and white pointer sprawled on the carpet absorbing fire heat as snowflakes drifted gently past the window. The starkness and vicissitudes of the eleven-hour drive from Herat became a memory.

Narcy and the children, who were to join us in Kabul, were delayed for two days as the snow-storms prevented the Teheran plane from landing. The American Air Attaché offered his sympathy and reassuringly referred to the mountains around Kabul as 'granite cumulus'. When they finally arrived we found that they had flown over Kabul the day before, had landed in Kandahar and then taken off again for Teheran when they found they still could not land in Kabul. All pilots seemed to know about the granite cumulus.

We spent a week exploring the bazaars and sight-seeing which included a trip through the gorge to Jalalabad, made famous by several fatal British expeditions in the past. The bazaars were narrow dark covered lanes with stall after stall selling richly coloured furs; foxes, wolves, leopards, mink and sable. These were either sold by the pelt or fashioned into coats or coverings. There were shops selling old Afghan tribal jewellery; silver, garnet and gold. There were some items in these shops that looked as if they had been fashioned from old Georgian napkin rings, as no doubt they were, considering the number that must have been left behind in the gorge and Khyber Pass at one time or another. There were practically no foreigners in the bazaar. Men, wearing raw silk coats to their knees with long knives stuck in their sashes, jostled, and women in chadris slipped past with fresh vegetables clutched half under the silk. At one point a large man in chavadar's clothes (Buzkashi rider) clutched my arm and pulled me to a stop. I was alarmed as I had strayed from the others. But he showed me a picture I recognized. He was standing next to a handsome grey horse. I had taken the picture that morning at the Buzkashi stadium with a Polaroid camera and he had immediately gone to the bazaar to find a frame for it. This gesture made me feel a part of the bustling Kabul scene and I felt like a friendly native.

We had visited the Buzkashi stadium in the morning with the Elliots. They were looking forward to the contests in the afternoon that were the finals of the national tournament and promised much fast action. The arena was empty, but all around were horses tethered by long ropes. They were watched over by their grooms and being inspected by the chapadars. The horses, all stallions, were pacing in circles at the extreme edges of their ropes and, by their constant pacing about, looked as if they knew what was coming that afternoon. I made the mistake of trying to cross over one of these circles and was thankful that I was in good shape. Without hesitation the horse put his ears back, bared his teeth and charged. His groom indicated he didn't think much of my sense of self-preservation.

Buzkashi is a Central Asian equestrian game that has reached its ultimate violent refinement in Afghanistan. As the name implies, 'pulling a goat', a beheaded animal, in this case a large calf, is placed in the centre of a de-marked circle. Numbers of riders in the teams seem to be variable depending on terrain and available competitors. Riders and horses enter the circle and, at a given signal, the calf is lifted onto the pommel (front) of the saddle by the successful competitor and then raced, in this case, around a circle of the arena. On the open steppe the race is to a distant object, around it and back to the centre of the original circle. The chapadars (literally he who owns four-footed animals) or riders are tough even by Afghan standards and must be heavy enough to be able to lift the animal and defend it against the other riders. In the meantime the other riders are not idly watching the calf disappearing into the horizon but whipping, grabbing, pushing and pulling the encumbered rider to dislodge the calf. Usually successful in this attempt, the next burdened rider makes off at full gallop followed and harassed by the rest. Eventually somebody gets the mangled remains of the animal back into the beginning circle and that team is the winner.

The games started at two o'clock in the afternoon. We were there in time to see the opening ceremonies that included some western gestures like the man in the hard hunting hat and pink coat, riding something that looked like an Arab horse, who led out the various teams.

There were four teams that had reached the finals. The Kunduz and Samangan from the Oxus plain were considered the favourites; Buzkashi having been a sport that originated in the north was generally dominated by teams from that area. The riders from these teams were dressed in sharp contrast to their horse show equivalent up front. They wore furry sheep wool hats, carried whips in their teeth and had long sheep wool coats and loose trousers tucked into soft leather boots that came up over their knees. Their horses were tall with massive chests and they acted as if they didn't care who they were out here to fight.

After a bit of out-of-control parading around, the gentleman in the hard hat gave the signal to start and two teams converged on the dead, headless body of a calf lying in the middle of the arena. The reason that these horses had chests like battering rams became evident. The horses reared up on their hind legs as they reached the circle and, stretching their heads up, surged into the fray, pushing forward with their chests. A few riders were dislodged and disappeared under the horses' hoofs while their loose horses ran rampant around the arena. There was too much dust to see exactly what was happening but one rider emerged from the melee with something draped over the saddle in front of him. As soon as the other riders realised that the prize had been captured they took off in pursuit. The idea seemed to be to circle the arena once and then drop the calf back into the spot where it started. This was not easy. The calf was torn from the original rider, dropped by the second, fought over by all until the third grabbed a fistful of hide and dashed off with most of the body dragging on the ground.

Two riders in hot pursuit lost control of their horses and jumped the concrete barrier into the spectators. An Afghan standing near us said that the game was usually played on the open steppe near the Oxus and they didn't have to worry about stopping. He said he found the way the game was being played here in an arena very tame. I told him I thought it would be interesting to have Afghanistan host the Olympic Games some year and introduce this new sport but he didn't seem to have heard of the Olympic Games.

We drove over the Salang pass of the Hindu Kush to Kunduz hoping to be able to cross the plain and see the Oxus. This pass is credited with having killed more people than the endless battles that have taken place over Afghan territory. Alexander the Great lost camels, horses and men by the thousands. Just the name of the mountain range, Hindu Kush (killer of Hindis) strikes fear into the heart of the traveller. By the time we ventured across the Russians had built over-hang tunnels to protect the road from snowdrifts and the Peugot had no trouble.

We were most anxious to see the Oxus River, the Amu Darya of old, but Gendarmes on the way prevented this as the river was also the border with Soviet Russia. We did see herds of horses, sheep and camels grazing amongst 'alachekhs' (yurts). They were probably the same tribes described by Robert Byron when he also was prevented from seeing the Oxus in 1937. On return to the hotel in the town on the southern edge of the Oxus plain, Kunduz, we broke out a bottle of vodka the Elliots had given us and were having an evening drink when there was a knock on the door. Narcy opened it and let out a whoop of joy. Standing there were Anthony and Jane Wynn from Hamadan and another friend, Anthony Fitzherbert. We hadn't known they were going to Afghanistan but apparently they could sniff a cocktail in a dry country from some distance.

The next day we drove over a dirt track to Mazar-e-Sherif. Owners of Land Rovers had told us that it was not possible to travel this way by anything but horse. It was a challenge but, to be honest, we had to pick up the Peugeot and carry it over irrigation ditches.

Mazar-e-Sherif could have been designed by MGM for Scheherazade or a film featuring Omar Sherif. The mosque was a jewel of rococo, Oriental splendour in many colours and with many domes and arches. The town itself was an endless bazaar selling jewellery, striped silk coats, ropes, saddles, bridles, soft leather riding boots, saddle bags, 'Persian' lamb pelts and fighting animals. Afghans will fight with anything, as the world has cause to know. They seem to prefer fighting with animals if left to their own devices. Depending on the owner's circumstances they fight with camels, rams, dogs, cocks, partridge and sparrows. In the case of the bird, no owner is ever without his animal. He carries it around in a little wicker cage and feeds it out of his hand so a strong protective bond is formed. It is not unusual to see a man bargaining in the bazaar stroking the bird in his hand.

We also went to see the remains of the huge ramparts circling Balkh. In ancient times Balkh was the capital of Bactria and an important commercial and caravan centre for trade between China and the west. Some say Zoroaster was born here; Alexander the Great came through in the third century B.C; Genghis Khan made a lasting impression in the thirteenth century; in 1825, William Moorcroft, the British East India Company's Stud Manager, died here searching for the legendary Turkoman horse. In the little main square a man offered me a large string of lapis lazuli for only a thousand toumans. It was tempting but I only had a thousand toumans for the whole trip.

Sherri and I had insinuated ourselves into a trip with the Elliots and the British Ambassador, John Drinkall, and his family for what they promised was to be an epic example of Anglo-American trekking solidarity. They were proven correct. Even the Afghans were impressed when we finally emerged, mud-splattered, exhausted and in need of much mechanical repair in Herat. We attempted and succeeded the 'impassable' road from Mazar to Herat during the spring floods.

Lest we forget the original purpose of the trip, Sherri and I spent one day in Mazar looking up people involved in breeding horses for Buzkashi. Here we ran into some trouble as Sherri and I, blondes without benefit of male escort, were researching in the province of man. By this time Narcy and the children had returned to Kabul and left the Peugeot with Omid Ali who was to deliver it to Herat along with the Elliot's driver - it being considered not sporting to have a driver on this trip.

In Afghanistan women appear to occupy the same position as the other livestock, their worth possibly equal to that of a horse, although our own position in the hierarchy of things only became clear as we were sitting in an adobe room on the outskirts of Mazar drinking tea.

We were trying to find out how they bred the strong-barreled Buzkashi horse; whether it was a purebred strain with a name or if they bred them haphazardly. Four men were sitting around us, one of them fondling a thrush he was training for the bird fights.

"So you are here alone?" the owner of the thrush asked.

"Not really, we are waiting for friends, but, in the meantime we would like to learn something of how you breed your horses," we said.

"Ah, so you are interested in breeding," a statement, not a question.

"Yes, horses."

"Breeding, now that is an interesting subject."

The thrush attempts to escape and is gently pulled back and fed a crumb of bread.

"You will be spending the night," they ventured.

"No, no, we are staying at the hotel and expecting friends."

"Do you have any horses? We would like to see them," we insisted.

We all trooped out to see some horses, the thrush cradled in the warm prison of the man's hand. Having seen the horses, a large fierce fighting dog, a massive-necked fighting ram and some blossoms, we decided to leave.

"Thank you very much for taking the time to show us your animals.

Now we must leave."

"Oh no, you cannot leave now, it is too soon. You will spend the night. It is the least we can do for you," they said.

"NO," cried Sherri, "we are expecting friends. Seven large men!"

"Seven large men!" they exclaimed, "You are brave women."

Blushing furiously, we made a break for the gate followed at speed by one of the younger men who was restrained by a peremptory word, presumably from his father. We slid through the narrow entrance; beat a hasty retreat down the 'kuche' (narrow alley) and into the road. We hailed the first passing ghawdie and asked to be taken as fast as the horse could go to the hotel. Once back in the cool quiet of the hotel garden with its large, leafy plane trees, we vowed to abstain from situations that did not include the presence of a troop of our own cavalry. The British Ambassador, John Drinkall, appeared that evening in his Land Rover and we shared a dinner of fresh, fried wild spinach before retiring to the tasteful concrete copies of alachekhs in the garden that were the hotel 'rooms'. Next door to us a French couple were tearfully arguing about 'l'amour' which underscored the difference in cultures.

The Elliots and Ambassador Drinkall's family arrived the next morning and we were ready to embark on the trip. The convoy consisted of two Land Rovers and a Chevrolet pickup truck along with what looked like much unnecessary equipment. Before the journey was over, however, I was to discover that only Ted Elliot's far-sightedness was to keep us the necessary number of moons in Turkoman country to wait out the spring floods.

The first night we camped in tents out on the open steppe amongst red tulips, beautiful, black, nauseous smelling lilies and the first turtles to de-hibernate from their beds underground. As the rain began to streak down shortly after one a.m., the lights of a vehicle could be seen circling our camp at a distance of two hundred metres. Sherri, an old hand at Afghan customs, whispered; "Quick, Louise, on with your shoes. This situation looks bad and we may have to make a break for it." Fortunately I could not find my shoes so we were spared having to make a dash for the open steppe sliding through mud and tripping over turtles. The Ambassadors were awake and very much on guard. The next day gave us a true taste of what was to come. The rain was relentless and the track of what yesterday had been dust was now deep, glutinous mud. The mud was not solid mud, but slippery seas of mud which sucked at the cars and thrust them into a crazy dance from side to side not unlike the lurching motion of a camel; but even less predictable than a camel. For five days we fought mud and we fought flooding rivers, winching ourselves across to keep from being swept away. At one point we were forced to open the back doors of the Elliot's Land Rover in order to allow the turbulent water to flow through, the added weight bringing us back to the river-bed. Although the Elliots had learned some Persian while they were in Iran and were taking lessons in Dari with a teacher in Kabul, Sherri and I usually acted as translators. One night we were guests of the leading lights of Bala Murghab who served us a magnificent feast and wine they had made themselves (Afghanistan is dry). After the Ambassadors and their families went to bed, the gentlemen suggested that Sherri and I stay for another glass of wine; they were intrigued by the two blonde American women who spoke their language and were curious about our role in this trip. We pointed out that we did not have a role, we were hitching a ride. We also explained that we were primarily interested in horses and were researching the various breeds. After some discussion about horses they suggested that we would find out much more if we abandoned the Land Rovers and rode with them to Herat on horseback. This sounded most appealing and had honour not intruded we might have made the fatal mistake that we had avoided in its cruder form of invitation in Mazar. As it was, the horses would probably have reached Herat before the Land Rovers.

On the penultimate day we accomplished twenty miles in twelve hours. We winched ourselves over raging torrents nine times. That was the day we were to have reached Herat but, instead, we spent the night in a collection of small adobe huts that supported two 'hotels' for the stranded such as we. We took up residence in the better of the two. This consisted of one room approximately sixteen metres long. Turbaned Pashtu's and Hejara crouched around the three small, wood-burning stoves placed along the middle of the room. Dinner consisted of a thin soup with chunks of fat floating at the top and hard, unleavened bread. After dinner the Mullah called out the prayers and forty turbaned heads made obeisance towards Mecca as forty neat bottoms shot towards the murky ceiling. Shortly afterwards everyone stretched out where they had been sitting and, pushing turbans down more firmly on their heads, drifted off to sleep. Sometime during the night, as I was moving over to escape another drip from the roof, I heard the mewling sound of a small baby and, straining my eyes, caught a glimpse of women crouching there amongst the turbans. Where had they been while we were dining and warming our hands around the stoves? By morning, when we awoke, they were gone.

Looking out of one of the two windows, a hole in the wall covered with burlap, we saw that, during the night, the rain had turned to snow and the mud was deceptively covered with a blanket of the purest white. In addition, more snow was falling gently from leaden skies. We all decided that to spend the day and another night would add nothing but fleas, so we ventured out to the cars and started up the pass to try to reach Herat that night. We did, to the relief of the Governor of Herat whose responsibility it would have been had the Ambassadors disappeared in a snowdrift or down a muddy ravine.

Omid Ali was beaming, basking in the reflected glory of being associated with this notorious party. He was also justifiably proud of producing the Peugeot at the right place in this alien land. He was waiting with government officials in front of the hotel where, suddenly, the servants were dressed in clean white coats and a red carpet had been rolled down to the road. Ambassador Elliot treated everyone to a large dinner of kebab, rice and salad amongst other delicacies (including Coca-Cola). The next day Sherri, Omid Ali and I left Afghanistan to return to Persia. As we drove west, crossing the border, we began to encounter the twentieth century. Omid Ali was not disappointed to find that he belonged to an 'advanced' civilization. Sherri and I were snatched back to all the problems.

A Fars horseman

A ghawdie in Kabul

A Buzkashi horse

Buzkashi - played at Kabul in Afghanistan

Chapter 15

<u>Adopted by the Turkomans</u>

On our return to Teheran we discovered that Iradj Chodjania needed his sheep sheds for his own sheep and Farzollah needed his hay barn, both immediately. I appealed to Mahmad Agha, a horse dealer friend in southern Teheran near Seh Rah Azari, for use of a portion of his caravanserai while we considered what to do next. Unfortunately no place could be found for the sheep and we had to sell them to the slaughter house. This was a great pity as they had been carefully bred, selected for twinning and their hybrid vigour was a credit to both the Rambouillet and the local fat tail.

All of the stallions and the mares without foals were crowded into Mahmad Agha's limited space. No matter how much we sprayed the black cloud of flies stayed the same density. His stables were tucked into the over populated rabbit warrens of southern Teheran. There were small dusty streets winding among one-storey mud brick houses. Stray dogs, chickens, children and donkeys mingled freely in the right of way. Doroshkeh makers spilled wheels out over the jube, and metal workers kept up a steady hammering. Women swathed in black chadors clutched bundles of sabzi which they had bought from barrows wheeled through the streets, the hawkers occasionally stopping to scoop old tin cans full of garbage-soaked jube water over the green herbs to keep them fresh.

Butchers slaughtered sheep in the street, hanging neck stumps over the jube for the blood to join the effluent. The dismembered heads were piled neatly to one side for sale as ' kaleh-pacheh ' (a favourite breakfast dish of whole boiled sheep's head, the eyes, of course, being a prime delicacy). Sheep skins flopped loosely in adjacent piles. A blacksmith plied his trade in the middle of the road, his forge blasting sparks from a mud encased half barrel.

Mahmad Agha and his brothers, Safar and Ali, moved comfortably through the congestion introducing unbroken two year olds and fiery stallions to the clatter of civilization with a relaxed disregard, which we found admirable. The elegance of their transient animals contrasted with the urban filth and spoke volumes for clean desert air, snow peaks in the Bakhtiari country and sparkling springs in some cool Kurdish valley.

Few cars ventured into these congested alleys. Those that did were mainly battered orange taxis. They honked their way in repetitive blasts between the crowds on the street and horse drawn carts laden with produce from the customs warehouses to bazaar storage. There were doroshkehs drawn by teams of emaciated stallions, the poor man's taxi. Our reasonably respectable Jeep stood out alarmingly and was a tempting target for idle young boys. We paid guard fees to these boys which was cheaper than replacing hub caps and windshield wipers.

The mares with foals, fortunately few in number, were quartered in the garden of our rented Shemran house. Here, wide, tree-lined streets wound along between the walled enclosures of large, elegant gardens. Climbing roses bloomed in cascades to further shade the paved sidewalks and potted geraniums overhung balconies in shades of pink, red and scarlet. The sounds of splashing from swimming pools echoed against the cadence of tennis balls and sounds of triumph. Opulent Cadillacs and Mercedes chauffeured businessmen from this cool oasis to downtown, commercial Teheran and, further up the mountains, the Palace of the Shah, Niavaran, stood in the shade of a park of old plane trees framed by the craggy peaks of the Tochal.

A month later, fleeing from the dizzy dichotomy of commuting between twentieth century Iran and sixteenth century Persia, we moved the horses from Mahmad Agha's establishment to a stable near the race track at Khargushdareh. There I ran across an old friend from Gonbad-e-Qabus. He listened sympathetically to my tale as well he should have, as I was still caring for two of his mares that he had unceremoniously dumped on our doorstep in Norouzabad one winter when he was short of feed. He reminded me of paradise on a mountain where we had once been boar hunting together. My memory dredged a vision of cool springs, endless Meadows, no fences and few inhabitants.

"Baleh Khanum, that is the place. Why don't you move all the horses there and turn them loose for the summer?" He suggested.

"But the land must belong to someone," I insisted.

"Not really," he replied, "and, anyway, arrangements can always be made." With inordinate haste and not personally checking the site again, Omid Ali and I ordered the necessary trucks and shipped all but the stallions to Pashei. This was a Turkoman village about thirty kilometres along a dirt track from Kalaleh to Maraveh Tepe near the Russian border. The horses were unloaded after the twelve hour drive and walked the remaining eleven kilometres to the top of the mountain, an area known as Ghara Balkan.

When Caren and I arrived two weeks later to spend part of the summer settling the horses, we discovered that Kiki, the mule, had 'made' our reputation with the Turkomans. Faced with roaming wild boar that he assumed were threatening his herd of mares that first evening, he charged with flailing hoofs and bared teeth. When the boar fled in terror from this child of Point Four's 'improve-the-animal-husbandry' program, the Turkomans felt that they had found the answer to the scourge of their wheat fields. Unfortunately for them, Kiki was concerned with the presence of the boar only when he felt they menaced his charges but was oblivious to the destruction of cultivation on the lower slopes of the mountain.

There was also a constant stream of Turkoman visitors who said they had come to see the "Magic Horses'.

"What Magic Horses?"

"The little ones. We used to have them long ago in the time of our ancestors but they are all gone," they said. "Legend says that with one of those you could beat any big horse, given a small head start."

So we were credited with bringing back the Magic Horses which gave us good standing with the Turkomans and ensured us a special place on the steppe.

Caren and I erected two tents, excavated the trotter-stomped spring and explored the mountains through waist high grass and scattered trees. From the top of the mountain at Ghara Balkan the view looked south over a forested range of high hills and an intensively cultivated valley. Beyond the valley there was the large wildlife park, then named after Mohamad Reza Shah, which flowed over four hundred thousand hectares of virgin oak forest, meadow and plain. There were rocky mountain ledges for goat and grassy reaches for wild sheep; deciduous paradise for deer, wild boar and bear; and everywhere leopards, cheetah, lynx and wolves.

Turning one hundred and eighty degrees to the north there was the beginning of Central Asia. Space and sky were a limitless extension of the sharp brown folds of the hills which led to the Atrek River and Soviet Turkmenistan. A region known as the 'bayer' (wasteland) was inhabited by a few small mud Turkoman villages and nomad encampments of round, black, felt 'alachekhs' (yurts). Sheep and cattle wandered seasonally over this vast area, following grass and huddling around the few sweet water springs. Large herds of Turkoman mares roamed at will. Stallions were introduced in the spring and foals were roped in the autumn. Wolves followed in their wake, cheetahs sprang out from behind tamarisk bushes, golden wild boar foraged the steep slopes of the Khalid Nabi mountains which dropped perpendicularly to the 'ghezel bayer' (red wasteland) and the mud banks of the Atrek. Partridge scuttled through Christ thorn burbling with contented chuck chuck sounds. Golden eagles surveyed the whole domain watching the two civilizations divided in a sharp line which the ancient Parthian wall (known locally as Alexander's Wall or the red snake) scored for confirmation on the boundary between the two.

We would have continued our aimless wandering submerged in the uncaptured freedom of infinity had the thought of winter not intruded. So much vegetation must surely require considerable moisture at some season of the year and the Turkomans soon confirmed the ferocity of the elements. Nouri, our host in Pashei and sometime horse trainer, observed that the snow reached "soooo high!" Sharing our concern for the horses with Hadji Avaz, he cleverly suggested that he had just the answer for us near a village he knew down on the flat steppe. Accepting his offer of help, we drove the Jeep down the mountain one day to meet with Hadji and inspect the site he proposed for winter quarters.

The first impression formed by Ghara Tepe Sheikh was one of forlorn, scorched poverty. Horses and donkeys were tied by long ropes to stakes in front of sagging huts built of broken bricks gleaned from the remains of 'Alexander's Wall'. Chickens scratched in ankle deep dust and women moved slowly about their tasks of baking bread and carrying water from the river, a steep two hundred metres below the village.

Except for a grove of closely planted trees, a legacy of the Katkhoda's father, and the broken, dusty stubble proving that there had been a harvest that year, the village was devoid of cultivation. A few bony cows were searching for bits of wheat dropped from the combine. We drove through the village of ten huts that were sufficient to give the settlement a name and stopped on a 'chaman' (natural turf steppe) to the north of the village. Alexander's Wall, which was visible a short distance further north, suggested the proximity of Ghara Tepe Sheikh to the beginning of Central Asia and a last bastion of 'settled agriculture'.

Hadji Avaz and Kari Ishan, a local mullah, dignified in his long coat and black astrakhan hat, appeared delighted with the setting. They alighted spiritedly from the Jeep to extol the virtues of the barren bit of stubble in front of us as winter quarters for the horses. Speechless with the bleak aura of poverty and hopelessness that seemed to hang like a worn blanket over this part of the steppe, I missed the arrival of the Katkhoda (headman). When I lifted my eyes from the dusty soil I, at first, thought they had met with a mirage, or a figment from the past giving mute testimony to the fertility of the land, the sleekness of the cattle and the promise of rich seasons.

All six feet of Avaz Katkhoda radiated strength, warmth and humour. His bronzed face with its twinkling, slanted Turkoman eyes, was creased with the lines of a young man who has worked in the open and his handshake was strong, self confident and painful. If such an outpost could beget the grace, power and kindness inherent in this specimen of nomad living, then there must be more to Ghara Tepe Sheikh than the choking heat, dust and poverty that were immediately obvious. Although I was somewhat sceptical about what we could accomplish with nine hectares of baked steppe, kilometres away from any all-weather roads and near a river whose high banks suggested that it spewed forth more of the muddy ooze than this season indicated. There was no bridge. Hadji Avaz's insistence and Avaz Katkhoda's enthusiasm carried their own authority. I later discovered that this was all a plot of Hadji's and Kari Ishan. They thought the Norouzabad energy and enthusiasm could transform this tired village into a model of activity. I guess that, briefly, it did but twenty plus years later two or maybe three new houses had been added and all except the revolution had passed it by. The villagers point to the stables and horses and proudly rest on their father's laurels. "WE did that!"

Caren and I returned to Teheran to put a proposition to Narcy. Would he like to own nine hectares of steppe set far from the bustle of civilization, with an unequalled view of the beginning of Central Asia? Narcy had had his hands full with Construction Company problems and had not been showing much enthusiasm or interest in equine pursuits for the past year, apart from insisting that the horses should not be sold. As important an event as investing money in a new piece of land, however, required a determined act of will and not another deceptive slide away from reality so I insisted on his collaboration in the decision.

Narcy was amenable to making the trip north to investigate. When neither Caren nor I could remember which of the many tracks leading aimlessly across the expanse of steppe was the lifeline to Ghara Tepe Sheikh and when he was finally faced with the bloated, tortuous ribbon of deep brown water that was the river, we could see his determination to enjoy the trip begin to waver. By the time we found Ghara Tepe Sheikh he was openly dubious. 'Our' nine hectares was impossible to differentiate from everybody else's as there were no lines to demarcate ownership and, of course, nowhere was a fence to be seen. Surprisingly enough, Narcy agreed to the project without hesitation (probably could not wait to get out), leaving Caren and me in the care of the Katkhoda. He shooed the mice out of the store room opposite his small brick hut and promised us the use of his bamboo 'talar' (raised platform) situated between the two. We negotiated an arrangement whereby we would provide the staples for the whole family in return for the Katkhoda's wife, Douag, preparing the meals.

Caren, Ahmand, the driver of a long-suffering Chevrolet pickup truck borrowed from the Firouz Construction Company, and I immediately began preparations for building the barn that Narcy and I had hastily designed and laid out on the bare ground in one corner of our 'farm'. To keep costs down we decided we would use nothing but local materials which meant the ground on which we stood and the chocolate water from the nearby river. Those two ingredients, mixed with straw from the previous harvest, lying matted on all the fields, and we were well into the construction business. To support the roof and keep this structure from collapsing, we dug holes and planted poles one metre into the ground. We watched them soar in graduated heights to resemble a mini Persepolis, visible for miles on the unrelieved flat of the steppe. The poles were poplars imported from Kalaleh, twenty kilometres distant, and the lime came from a kiln slightly to the west. Otherwise Ghara Tepe Sheikh provided all that was necessary in the way of raw construction material. An expatriate Russian Turkoman was brought from Gonbad-e-Qabus by Hadji Avaz to be our memar (builder). Differences of opinion were marked from the beginning but enough of a grudging relationship developed to allow work to proceed at a pace nudged by the proximity of autumn.

Aman Geldi, the memar, was initially and thereafter, appalled at the idea of working for a woman. The situation would probably have resolved itself had I promised a lump sum of money for so many square metres of mud building and taken myself back to the flesh pots of Teheran until he could hand over the completed building. That, however, was not the intention and there were matters requiring attention apart from the urgent nature of a completed barn. With a singular lack of grace, Aman Geldi eventually acceded to the inevitable, and the three meals we shared a day (and when the snow came, the same room at night) took on the atmosphere of a Salem witch hunt.

"Read books, do you?" he muttered through a fistful of rice.

"Yes, don't you?" knowing perfectly well that Aman Geldi was illiterate, but capable of fixing the intricate wires of a transistor radio with those huge, ham-like hands.

"Don't see the need for it. Waste of time," he continued, fixing me with a teasing taunt to his slant Turkoman eyes and pushing his fur hat back on his shaven skull.

"Anyway, if you did any work during the day you'd be too tired to waste YOUR time. And you're hogging all the light from the lamp," he continued.

The last was true and I pushed the kerosene lamp closer to where he was sitting cross legged on the felt covered floor.

"Quite right. You obviously need it more than I do."

The Katkhoda, Avaz, seemed happy with the state of affairs. His ego had already been shattered by an unfortunate investment in tractor and combine in partnership with a 'friend'. When the friend absconded with the money from the first harvest leaving Ahvaz holding the bag with the partly paid for machinery, Avaz was completely 'bankrupt'. The agricultural company reclaimed the machinery but the land he had sold to invest in the project was also irretrievably gone. His last nine hectares he sold to us and sex, nationality, colour of eyes to the contrary, we were his lifeline to a new existence. His determination to have this project succeed did not prevent his enjoying the evening slander sessions best camouflaged in the knuckles game of Shah, Prime Minister, Everyman and Thief which followed the chakdameh dinner (rice and mutton).

A sheep knuckle is passed around a group, in this case, of six men and me. With the luck of the roll, Elias is Shah; Avaz is Prime Minister and Aman Geldi the Thief. Araz Mahmad, Elias' brother is Everyman.

"Ah, the thief, the thief!" cries the Shah as Aman Geldi is brought before him.

"What has this despicable man done?" asks Elias of his Prime Minister, Avaz.

"It pains the soul to tell," says Avaz looking shocked and murderous at the same time.

"But you must tell!!" roars Elias, "We must fix a suitable, horrible punishment for such scum of the earth."

"Oh, Your Majesty, you should not have to hear what this insignificant issue of a burnt father has had the temerity to do in your sacred Kingdom."

"Tell all!!" says Elias, looking lascivious."He stole a sheep, Your Majesty."
"A sheep?" says Elias, "a sheep - only one sheep?"
"Well, actually, it was really more than one sheep. You see, the ewe was pregnant."

"Aha, that's better - two sheep! And what else?' says His Majesty, coaxing his Prime Minister.

"He also ran off with the shepherd's wife!"

"That's MUCH better!! What else?"

"On his way out of the encampment he slit the shepherd's throat with a knife!"

"Oh, very good, very good. Two stolen sheep, one abducted wife and one slaughtered shepherd. Yes, YES."

"What punishment do you decree, oh sacred one, for I am nothing but your slave," says Avaz grinning hugely at Aman Geldi who is trying to hunch his large frame into an attitude of servile humility.

"For these heinous crimes I find it difficult to think of a suitably horrible punishment. Stealing a man's sheep; cowardly, cowardly ... And killing the shepherd whose only crime was having a faithless wife ... no humanity! Let me see, I must have time to think."

The Shah rolls his eyes towards the murky bamboo and pole ceiling dimly lit by the flickering kerosene lamp. He pushes back his hat and scratches, tugs at an ear and finally shakes his head.

"YOU," he roars at this brother, Everyman, "what do you think?"

"THINK, Sire?'" says Araz Mahmad, shifting uncomfortably on his bottom at the unexpected attention."Me, Sire, I don't THINK. Spare me, I am your slave. I am dirt at your feet. I exist only in your shade!"

Satisfied and preening, the Shah directs his gaze at the Prime Minister and points a long finger at the Thief.

"I direct you, Prime Minister, to cut off his ears, to give him twenty sound lashes on the soles of his bare feet and then off with his head. Then get rid of that offal somewhere so I won't trip over it in the morning!"

The sentence is carried out with much merriment, the knuckle rolls again but the Shah and Prime Minister keep their positions until someone else comes up with the magic sides of the polished bone.

Elias had been hired to help Omid Ali and Mahmad Ali with the stallions in Teheran. He was also supposed to 'learn the ropes' of stable management under the capable guidance of those two competent Kurdish grooms. Elias' gap-toothed, wizened face resembled a frost-bitten golden Lebanese apple. The colour of his parchment skin, I later understood, came from years of extracting more nourishment from the fruit of the poppy than the stone-milled brown bread which others considered a staple diet. Although it was impossible not to like Elias, Omid Ali soon sent him back to Ghara Tepe Sheikh saying he thought we needed him more than he did. For a Turkoman he was a well-travelled man and a mine of information about local customs and recent history. He explained about the Russian occupation during World War 11, the ploughing up of the common grazing lands and subsequent sale to the Turkomans of small plots of their own land at vastly inflated prices. The title deeds they were given read that they were sold this land by the Shah. He also warned us about the care one should take so as not to annoy the 'djinns", those little demon creatures as ubiquitous as molecules and atoms. Even more important, Elias could speak Farsi and was reasonably literate. The ability to communicate with me was crucial as none of the other Turkomans had more than a rudimentary grasp of Farsi and misunderstandings erupted over minor issues which would have gone unnoticed had we all been speaking the same language.

Fortunately most of the people working for us picked up Farsi faster than I learned Turkoman, but the Farsi they learned was from me so if it had a shade of an American accent they were certainly to be forgiven. Ui showed up on the scene slightly later than Elias. First his oldest brother, Dungatar, worked with the horses but was considered unsuitable by everyone, including Avaz who was his brother-in-law, the stunning looking Fatemeh being Avaz' only sister and Dungatar's wife. The second brother was Golatar and he was less suitable. We hit bottom and hired the third and last brother, Uatar, who, like some Grimm fairy tale character was just fine. Ui could not have been more than twelve years old but he did the work of grown men and, too young to have the opium habit, was generally more awake.

Although Avaz assured me that this was one of the hottest, driest summers that they had ever experienced, they seemed to weather the elements far better than Caren and I. We felt withered after the first few days of dealing with the dust, which found its way into the seams of clothing, the pores of our skin and formed a uniform layer around each strand of hair. The temperature hovered around 105 degrees Fahrenheit during the day but there was no shade to escape from the scorching rays of the sun, magnified by dust particles suspended in the still air. Sweat ran in rivers through the dust, cutting little erosion channels down the back of the neck and between the shoulder blades. As there were no facilities for washing properly I became enveloped in a cocoon of sweat-soaked dust. I was excluded from the refreshing soaks that Caren and Ahmad were able to take in the river on their regular trips for water hauled back in barrels in the pickup truck. The unremitting heat raised a thirst which no amount of iced, brown river water could quell .The only advantage of these combined elements was the rapid drying of the 'kahgel' (mud, straw and water) allowing us to add layers of the material with great speed.

August proceeded with a monotony of mud dumped upon mud, broken by trips to the nearby forest for huge oak logs which we hauled to the saw mill in Gonbad-e-Qabus to be cut into posts and planks for the fence. The temporary cool relief of the dense virgin forest in Loveh was shattered on arrival in Gonbad. The damp heat created by the encircling rivers was sweltering. By the time a crane was found to unload the massive logs and the sawmill attendant had understood that we were building a fence and that we did mean posts two metres long and planks two and a half metres long and not to confuse the two, it was usually too late to try to reach Ghara Tepe Sheikh that night. We would pull wearily into Hadji Avaz' village for an evening's rest amongst his hordes of children and ever-hospitable wives. With what seemed infinite slow motion, the walls of the barn crept up towards the sky and the fence posts punctuated the level plain of the steppe. August drew to a close and September heralded the beginning of Ramadan. Haste was abandoned for survival in the scorching atmosphere as none of the Turkomans could pass drink, food or smoke between their lips from sun-up to sun-down during the holy month. It soon became apparent that the near death routine during work hours was caused more by all-night revelry and stuffing of bellies than by any abstinence during daylight hours. But custom was custom and nothing would interfere with the cycles of the moon and a decree issued with finality in the seventh century.

From my position on the talar I could hear the sounds of the midnight feasting which ceased only shortly before the first morning prayer, which more or less coincides with the second cock crow or four a.m, if you own a watch. The men would rollick over to the Masjid (mosque) across the way, chant prayers and then stagger back to bed rolling themselves in their 'lahofs' (cotton stuffed quilts) on the felt covered, hard mud floor of the room. The women had been up most of the night preparing a large meal for the men and could now snatch an hour's sleep before it was time to milk the cows, feed the children and gradually get on with the other chores. The most arduous of these chores was undoubtedly fetching water from the river. This was a monotonous task repeated every day and sometimes several times a day. Each donkey was fitted with his pack saddle and two goat skins were slung, one on either side. The women plodded through ankle-deep dust down the steep path to the river, prodding the donkeys. Trying to avoid assorted specimens of excrement floating on the surface of the gelatinous, brown ooze that barely flowed towards the latter part of the summer, they would fling their orange and black silk shawls back over their shoulders and scoop the contents in old tin cans into the neck of the goat skin. When full, the neck opening was plugged with green grass growing on the banks of the river between tiers of turtles sunning themselves on the mud. When I commented on the consistency of the 'water' the women laughed.

"You should see it when they take water upstream for cotton!" they chortled.

"Then it sits in stagnant pools and stinks. This is good water"
Something I did not yet know was that the life cycle of some parasite that lived in that river included wandering through the veins of equids. At some stage it exited through the skin of the animal leaving bloody trails. I discovered that this condition was peculiar only to the Gorgan River in the Turkoman Steppe and the Ferghana River in Soviet Central Asia (the blood-sweating horses of Ferghana), a useful rule of thumb for determining the geographical origin of a horse, but disfiguring. Some years later, Farshad Maloufi, a young veterinarian who was working with us, discovered the condition was caused by a fly, parafillarios, and his place in history became secure.

To compensate for the blistering, dry summer, winter fell out of the sky with little warning from autumn. One morning I awoke from my position on the talar thinking that the chickens had lost all their feathers, only to discover that the substance was snow. It was cold. Some cows were huddled miserably around the scant shelter afforded by the roof of the talar. The Katkhoda's mother, Ana Sultan, scurried by in the grey dawn clutching a milk bucket and slipping precariously on the mixture of snow and mud churned to a lumpy consistency by the cows' hoofs. The tough, white guard dogs were curled into tight balls and the chickens had fluffed up their feathers against a steppe wind that left no doubt as to its northern Soviet origin. The barn was still lacking a roof, although the poplar rafters and bamboo were piled nearby, ready to be installed. Over hot morning tea the Katkhoda was told that we had an emergency on our hands. He immediately mobilized the entire village. In two days the rafters were in place, the bamboo laid and tied over them and the kahgel roof hastily smoothed over.

Wasting no more time, we sprinted to the top of the mountain at Ghara Balkan and retrieved a herd of thoroughly miserable mares and foals. Their coats were thick and woolly in anticipation of winter. A five hour ride down the mountain and over the steppe to Ghara Tepe Sheikh saw them home, a haven which they gracefully accepted as their due.

With the mares snug under a roof, it was time to transfer the stallions from Teheran to the steppes. This task was performed admirably by Omid Ali. He appeared late one cold afternoon riding a large, grey Kurdish stallion affectionately known as 'Killer' and leading a skittish herd of ten other stallions haphazardly directed by a motley crew of Turkomans. As they reached the 'chaman', spurred on by all the village curs, some atavistic response triggered a concerted whinny from the group. This was immediately answered by the mares with predictable results. We rounded up the strays and the shaken Turkomans who had met the truck five kilometres to the south of the river at the last reasonably passable track. Then we closed the doors of the box stalls on the excited stallions and settled ourselves for a congratulatory tea in the living room at the end of the barn.

Left: Inside a Yurt at Ghara Balkan   Right: A Talar at Ghara Balkan

Rug weaving at Ghara Balkan

Buying stallions on the Turkoman Steppes

Roshan trying a riding horse at Gonbad-e-Qabus

Chapter 16

A Nomadic Existence and Attack by Wolves

Omid Ali and I were particularly pleased as we had now spent close to a year switching horses from one barn, sheep shed and stable to another, wondering with each day how long the reprieve would last. The satisfied munching of horses in a stable we had built, on land that we owned, was a relief. We thought we would now have time to realise why we were saving them and to what useful purpose we could put them. Elizabeth Haden answered a letter I had written to her indicating that the Caspian business was still a possibility even if we had lost the advantage of second and third generation foals. In fact, they welcomed the fresh blood of new foundation stock.

We had two Caspian stallions; Aseman and Prince Caspian. The foundation mares numbered four: Tehou and her colt foal, Simone, Zogcheh and Shirine. Since this was hardly an auspicious start for a stud which could now count on a market, I contacted the horse dealer in Babol who had inherited the Caspian post from Mahmad Ali. Gedda Ali was less flamboyant than Mamad Ali but just as willing to spend time in rice paddies if the end result guaranteed him a nest egg to start a business with more future than the horse trade.

From the spring of 1976 to the autumn of 1977, Gedda Ali regularly appeared with loads of mares and stallions. Although at least half of his animals were unsuitable, they were kept, fattened and traded in for animals from the next lot. This practice left the accounts in shambles and Gedda Ali owing me several horses by the time the Royal Horse Society once more intervened. The system was wasteful but, running the farm and making occasional appearances in Teheran left no time for searching the Caspian coast myself. By the spring of 1977, we were running a herd of twenty three Caspian mares and five Caspian stallions.

Growing up in Virginia farmland had been inadequate preparation for coping with the demands of a large herd of horses in country that resembled the wild west of the United States. I watched the Turkomans in their seasonal searches for grass to feed their cattle and sheep and blatantly copied their patterns. We spent the winters at Ghara Tepe Sheikh, where we planted barley for the horses to graze. By Norouz (March 21st) we began to move the mares north towards the Atrek river where the winter was milder and the grass grew luxuriantly green in the Khalid Nabi mountains long before the same phenomenon occurred at Ghara Tepe Sheikh. The Khalid Nabi and the steppe bordering the Atrek were designated as common grazing lands, available to anyone with a claim to property on the steppe. We joined herders from as far away as Gonbad in search of a valley where we could stake a claim. Unaware of the advantages, and disadvantages, of various locations, our search involved several complicated switches of camp before we were settled in a narrow valley which opened up at the top to broad pastures of tall grass. One of the main advantages of this spot was the proximity to Hadji's camp, an advantage which he lost no time capitalizing to his own benefit. From there on he grazed his mares with ours and was saved the expense of a chapadar (herder). I was to discover that we were popular primarily by virtue of our water tanker as sweet water springs and rivers did not exist. By early June the grass in these mountains was turning brown and the flies descended in swarming, stinging hordes. We joined the mass exodus but, instead of remaining on the steppe where the herds of sheep and cattle were left to graze the newly harvested wheat and barley, we moved the mares and stallions to Ghara Balkan Pashei.

Since our first summer in this paradise we had been encouraged to buy the mountain valley at a price that was compatible with our slender means. Title deeds did not accompany the purchase. We had scraps of paper with thumb prints which were locally considered sufficient evidence of ownership. I was not too concerned as I had been witness to the takeover of properties whose proof of possession was neatly wrapped in stamped government certificates. I was under no illusion about the tenuousness of any form of land ownership. If we could harvest the hay for two years and graze the mares for the same amount of time I felt that the investment would have paid off handsomely.

The social whirl of Teheran was far from my mind as I let the seasons sweep me from one grazing ground to another. The creak of a saddle and the soft plodding of horses' hoofs mingled with the chatter of happy Turkomans. Life was controlled by the elements and political exigencies were part of someone else's life.

Sometime in late February, 1976, the peace was shattered by the news that Omid Ali had been jailed in Teheran for something that sounded vaguely connected with me. Dropping everything, I left immediately. I discovered on arrival in Teheran that the situation looked gloomy indeed. I had allowed myself to forget that the Royal Horse Society existed somewhere back in the metropolis of Teheran and I had forgotten that politics often substituted for callouses. I was unprepared for the charade which gradually unfolded.

Late one night five yearling Caspians were found to be missing from their stable at Norouzabad. The count was actually four, one having broken both front legs when it was chased by local stray dogs and mercifully shot by the manager of Norouzabad. The Royal Horse Society decided that Omid Ali, Mahmad Agha and I had arranged to steal the yearlings to sell to Elizabeth Haden in England. With a promptness that belied the usual lethargic pace of the Royal Horse Society, they arrested Omid Ali, Mahmad Agha and one of the grooms from Norouzabad. They were locked up in the maximum security of Agahi prison for political prisoners.

This had happened on a Sunday, so that by the time I slipped into Teheran late Wednesday night, Narcy already had the dossier number for Omid Ali. I telephoned Mr. Atabai at his home in the Royal Stables compound to ask that he arrange the release of the people who had been imprisoned. He denied all knowledge of the arrest, although not of the missing ponies, and I realised that we would have to pursue the matter without the co-operation of the Royal Horse Society. A further call the following morning confirmed that, even if they were not convinced that we were responsible for the theft, we would do as the victims.

Narcy then discovered that Omid Ali had been remanded from Agahi prison to the Nematabad garrison, a short distance south of Norouzabad on the Saveh road. I drove down to see what I could do to arrange his release. On arrival I found that the sergeant in charge was an old acquaintance from happier days at Norouzabad.

He was as puzzled as I about the matter. Two hours of talk produced no concrete results and his calls to the Royal Horse Society appeared to be as frustrating as mine had been. It was not until an accountant from the Royal Horse Society materialized that we began to make progress.

The sweet urbanity hardly matched the circumstances. There were sharp cries from bludgeoned prisoners clearly audible over the sipping of tea. Soon there was a promise of Omid Ali's immediate release. The accountant, who later spent a year in jail as a scapegoat for whoever was actually responsible for this charade, pledged to deliver Omid Ali to his home as soon as certain formalities had been completed. With this assurance, I asked permission to see Omid Ali and explain the circumstances of his release.

A sigh of relief escaped his lips as I approached him in the prisoners' yard, but he was less optimistic about the outcome.

"It's not really me they want, ' he said. "They have spent three days interrogating us to force us to admit that you arranged the theft of the ponies."

Continuing swiftly but with agitation; "They are convinced, or at least they would like us to confirm, that you arranged the theft and that Mahmad Agha and I were carrying out your orders. Apparently they don't really know what happened and if you leave us here they will apply more pressure until we confess."

"As it is," he said, trembling, "we've been through a terrible time and they have forced us to give all the names of the Turkomans who work for you in the north. If you don't clear this matter up now they will be in trouble too."

"Anyway," he continued, "I've told them that the Khanum (lady) may be crazy but she's not stupid. How could she possibly steal five well-known yearlings and expect to get export certificates from the Royal Horse Society? If nothing else, she would have to give a proper pedigree, and how could she if they were yours?" Armed with this information, I returned to the main interrogation room and offered myself for arrest. There was considerable embarrassment upon receipt of this sacrificial offer and, within the hour, Omid Ali, Mahmad Agha and the Norouzabad groom were in my car and headed with speed for home. Over tea in Omid Ali's house he told me what he knew had happened.

Apparently two grooms at Norouzabad were feuding and, unable to settle their differences, one of them released five yearling Caspians one night in order to be able to blame the other. Fierce barking of some local stray dogs frightened the groom and he woke the night watchman who was snoring in his sleep. Together they went to find the ponies. They found one, lying in an irrigation ditch with both front legs broken. They carried the yearling back to the stable and woke the manager who shot the unfortunate pony.

In the meantime, the remaining four ponies fled in terror and took refuge in the garden of a large vegetable oil refinery to the near north. These ponies would have been returned but for the helicopters, police cars and two-way radios that appeared on the scene early the following morning along with the cry that "someone has stolen the Shah's horses!" The grooms were too terrified to admit their part and the workers in the factory were frightened lest they be blamed for harbouring the Shah's horses and thus become guilty by association. Eventually, they chose a dark night, persuaded the ponies to leave and, locking the gate firmly, hoped they would return home, which they did.

I called the manager of Norouzabad to tell him what appeared to be the truth behind the episode and left as soon as possible for the relative sanity of the steppes.

In spite of this ominous setback, the Caspians seemed to have started once more in a direction that might promise success, and we turned our attention to the other horses. Two of the children's show jumpers were Turkomans of a superior cast and one of Narcy's Fars colts showed promise of speed when it came time to train him. Elias and I decided we should condition them for racing which might, at least, mollify our neighbours about the number of horses we were feeding without visible results.

We harrowed a short oval track in one of the barley fields and embarked on a program of fitness for our three 'race horses'. Day by day the muscles became more pronounced, the bellies tighter and the horses almost impossible to hold. We persevered, the bright lights of Gonbad an alluring incentive.

The problem of registering as a trainer in that all-male preserve was neatly solved by the Teheran Racing Company's Alex Bergl, the racing manager in Gonbad. He did not seem particularly interested in the sex of the trainer or, if he did, it certainly had nothing to do with horses. The local trainers were not quite so sanguine about my gender.

They had closed ranks to wage a war of attrition on the Teheran Racing Company (an Australian-Hong Kong based venture in partnership with the Royal Horse Society). This feud was encouraged by the Royal Horse Society which had hired the foreigners to run the track after they found they were unable to do so themselves. It was a typically Persian example of cutting off your nose to spite your face.

A poignant example of the bickering was revealed one Saturday morning when I went to register our horses for the following Friday's races. As I stepped up to the registration window under the grandstand, I was waylaid by one of the trainers from Hadji Avaz's village. He quietly indicated that I should not sign up our horses. I asked him "why not?" He seized my arm and led me out of earshot of the other trainers gathered around incurious groups.

"It's a little bit difficult to explain," he said.

"Why don't you try?" I answered.

"We're on strike against the Sherikat (TRC) and we want to impress on every trainer that it is very important that we show solidarity by all joining."

"You could have simply told me," I said, still puzzled.

"That's difficult" he said, looking embarrassed.

"Look, if you're going to keep me out here standing in the sun you might as well tell me why I can't sign up my horses for the races Friday." I was becoming increasingly annoyed at the shuffling feet and the Turkoman's inability to look me in the eye.

"Well, it's this way. In order to impress on everyone the seriousness of the occasion we swore a 'Ghassam' (holy oath on the Koran). Anyone who breaks the oath and signs up his horses will be too unclean to approach his wife."

"Why didn't you tell me?" I asked.

"You don't have a wife!" he answered.

He had a point, but I was intrigued by the solemnity of the occasion.

"Tell me," I said, "why are you striking this time?"

"We want more two-year-old races," he said.

"Then why don't you tell Mr. Bergl you want more two-year-old races?"

"Because he might give them to us."

By now I was a bit confused but also fascinated. It seemed there was more to this than met the eye - my usual naive reaction to situations involving anything to do with the Royal Horse Society. Obviously the Teheran Racing Company and the Royal Horse Society were reaching an impasse in the ongoing feud, but involving the trainers in a 'ghassan' was a serious matter.

Testing my theory that the Royal Horse Society was behind the trouble, I asked the trainer "who told you to swear a Ghassan?"

"The Major (Manager for the Royal Horse Society in Gonbad)," he answered.

That established, I suggested that a representative group of trainers accompany me to see Alex Bergl. When they told him they were on strike (a fact of which he was unaware) because they wanted more two-year-old races, he readily agreed. The Turkomans had been right!

Alex Bergl's Irish tact mollified the trainers and we all trooped out of his office to sign up our horses for the races.

Elias was particularly proud of Gholli Dagh. He was a large, grey Turkoman gelding that belonged to Roshan. He was in superb shape, and looked it; the tiny, new racing saddle looked dwarfed on his back. No-one was surprised when the gamblers unanimously made him the favourite. Gholli Dagh's subsequent performance, however, convinced us that we should stick to breeding horses, not racing them. Gholli Dagh leapt from the starting gate with enthusiasm, faltered, seemed to get his stride, and then ran disappointingly in the middle of the pack.

When the jockey brought him back he explained that a stirrup strap had broken as they left the gate. It was all he could do to stay on, much less win, he said. When I inspected the saddle I saw that I had attached the stirrups the wrong way. Out-of-pocket gamblers did not believe this story and were convinced that we had 'thrown' the race. Elias and I retreated rapidly with irate gamblers at our heels. This was not quite the end of my career as a racing trainer but the indication was clear that we should take racing seriously or leave it alone.

We now had our hands really full. We were maintaining a herd of over sixty mares, foals and stallions. The Caspians and the Turkoman horses, along with normal farming duties, left us little leisure time for attending race meetings and conditioning horses. The migrations to seasonal pastures were a nightmare of organisation; striking camp, trucking, cooking equipment, bedding, tents and 'alachekhs' to the new location and setting up once more. Herding the horses from one location to the other was a pleasant, if tiring, occupation. The Turkomans laughed and chattered and loved nothing better than to gallop through someone else's watermelon patch or waist-high wheat to round up the strays. Invariably the strays were the Caspian mares that preferred the dust-free front of the herd. They set a spine-shattering, dog-trot pace and were always the first to spot water or something particularly edible, preferably cultivated. As barbed wire fencing was fortunately very rare we could resemble a herd of locusts unless we kept tight control on the Caspians.

From our valley near the Atrek, Yangi, to Ghara Tepe Sheikh, the ride was three hours and cultivation relatively sparse. From Ghara Tepe Sheikh to the Pashei, along Alexander's Wall, and over the rich steppe, the situation was fraught with potential disaster to the farmers during the spring trek. By the time we reached Pashei and were ready to start climbing the eleven kilometres to the mountain pastures, the horses were tired and behaving although, by that time, the effect on crops was negligible, as cultivation dwindled with altitude.

Completing the migration from spring to summer quarters in one day was a deadly, exhausting eight-hour ride which would have been a strain on the young foals. We usually broke the trip for a night at Ghara Tepe Sheikh, continuing early the next morning in order to avoid the worst of the heat. Although we tried enticing friends from Teheran into joining us, we managed only once to persuade someone to do the ride twice. Jane Wynn was the staunch survivor of two migrations. She later admitted that the second time was only because Narcy and I had brought her nail clippers for her Salukis from London. She thought it would be churlish to refuse.

As the seasons moved we settled into a routine of grazing and survival. The adobe living room at the west end of the barn in Ghara Tepe Sheikh was refuge from the fierce storms of winter. Snow lashed across the steppe, driven by winds whose origins were lodged somewhere in the vastness of Russia. Spring announced itself in February as the first crocuses were followed by iris, narcissus, red tulips and black lilies. Then came the red poppies which, viewed from the back of a horse, had a hypnotic effect, red, brilliant and shimmering. When the wild gladioli turned the wheat fields to mauve it was time to move from the Khalid Nabi to Ghara Balkan where summer switched in dappled shades from the yellow and white daisies to pink blackberry blossoms. There were yellow hollyhocks and bright orange wild pomegranate flowers.

The birds followed the seasons and flowers. Giant Dorna (Great Blue Crane) with their high-pitched honking, shattered the high sky. Flocks of geese, ducks and grouse wintered along the Gorgan River and seasonal ponds on the steppe. In summer, crested meadow larks sang in the wheat. There were swallows, hoopos and magpies and the rainbow hues of bee eaters and rollers. Over the mountain pastures two golden eagles kept sentinel all summer, oblivious to the hovering kestrels intent on scurrying mice. Pheasant and chukker abounded in mouth-watering abundance in the mountains while doves and pigeons were ubiquitous in all settings. Equally at home from the banks of the Atrek to the Alborz Mountains, wild boar rooted for sustenance and ravaged the wheat fields. Wolves roamed at will, stalking herds of sheep and horses. The mournful howl of the jackal was peculiar to Ghara Balkan and Ghara Tepe Sheikh. At night headlights would pick out the scavenging, long-quilled porcupine, his short-quilled cousin, the hedgehog, and the sly steppe cat on his way to raid a chicken roost.

Sitting around a communal dish of rice and lamb (chakdameh) we would discuss who was riding which horse and leading which yearling the next day. We would estimate how many sheep the village had lost to the wolves the previous night, the village curs' unrestrained cacophony having heralded the nightly raid. What sort of barley harvest could we expect? Who was the latest victim of the government's crack-down on opium smugglers?

We had built an eight-stall stable at Ghara Balkan. One of the stalls acted as my room and the kitchen. There was an adobe fireplace which dispelled the damp that accompanied the rain whenever we were haying. The fireplace smoked so consistently that it was a choice between being comfortably warm or breathing.

We also built a cantilevered 'talar' (bamboo platform) which boasted an unequalled view of the Khalid Nabi and the beginning of Central Asia. At night we could occasionally see a large, expanding ball of light which, I was told, was Russians testing new devices across the border. There were 'alachekhs' and tents for the grooms. There was also an elegant bamboo outdoor toilet with a splendid view of Central Asia. We called it the easement,

The past was a constant intrusion on the present: ancient burial mounds and tepes lining the ageless tracks, beaten by hooves from the time man first domesticated animals. Terraced mountains attested to the energy of the Parthians two thousand years ago.

Bowls and pitchers from excavated mounds were put to immediate use in alachekhs. Everywhere one went shards of dull, red pottery poked invitingly from the ground. The more recent mounds speckled with the iridescent blue and green of Islamic age pottery. Old bronze pestles, small statuettes and treasures of gold were not unusual finds and everyone knew how to glue an old pot together. The remains of Alexander's Wall, built by the Parthians, was both a source of construction material and a reminder of even recent times when the Turkomans, successors of Genghis Khan, were a scourge to settled agriculture.

As late as 1977, few gendarmes dared intrude north of the Gorgan River. Even if their Jeeps were subsequently found, their mortal remains seldom appeared. There were too many deep holes in the steep canyons of the steppe to warrant a search. Opium smuggling was rife as was its ingestion and smoking. The proximity of Afghanistan made transport of the contraband by horseback a simple matter over country that was roadless and without communication. Against this background of pastoral activity we continued to work with our herd of horses. We paid particular attention to the seven Caspians which Elizabeth Haden and her partners in the Caspian Stud (UK) had indicated would be suitable for import. Farah, Simone, Shirine, Doueez, Fatemeh, Pari and Anamarat had been chosen for their distinctive Caspian characteristics: fineness, gazelle-like features and intelligence. As they were all Foundation Stock and, with the exception of Simone and Shirine, had not foaled with us, we knew we were taking a chance. In spite of certain inner concern, we felt reasonably sure that they would do well in England. Fatemeh we never doubted would be as full of opinionated self-confidence as she was a leader of every seasonal trek. Doueez was sweet and beautiful and Farah looked as if she had stepped out of a

Persian miniature. Simone was a proven brood mare with a handsome, kind tempered colt foal.

By late August of 1977, the water in the springs at Ghara Balkan had dried up. The horses were struggling to maintain condition, trekking each day eleven kilometres down the mountain to a spring at Pashei and grazing their way back. We decided it was a losing battle. We moved the herd to Ghara Tepe Sheikh in early September to take advantage of the muddy brown of the Gorgan River which was water even in that form. There were also rotting watermelon rinds which were a tasty adjunct to the dry straw.

Our arrival at Ghara Tepe Sheikh coincided with a heat wave that seemed determined to suck the last bit of moisture and sustenance from man and beast alike. Gasping for air on the steppe, I did not see how we could subject the mares to the confines of the stable at night; much better to leave them loose to graze on the harvested barley, I thought. The Turkomans warned me that I was exposing the mares and foals to the insatiable appetites of the wolves. I laughed,

"There can't possibly be wolves now," I said, "it's much too warm."

"Nothing to do with the weather," growled Elias", if you leave those mares loose out there tonight you'll find one is missing in the morning."

I followed my own instincts and, by noon the next day, as I was watching the mares returning from drinking at the river, I noticed that Farah was missing. She was one of the best of the new foundation mares and had been especially well fed and prepared for her trip to England. She was of an exquisitely fine form and the closest we had found to the ancient graphic picture of a Caspian. I asked Ui, the youngest of the grooms, to see if he could find where she had gone. I was preparing lunch when he returned to say that she was in a valley at the end of the barley field. She had been partly eaten by wolves.

I rushed out of the stable and followed the direction Ui had indicated. Over the rise and into the valley I saw what remained of Farah - from the rib cage up. After lunch, Mahmad Ali, a Kurdish groom who had remained after Norouzabad, and I returned to study the scene of the killing and try to understand a bit more of what had happened. This time Kiki, the mule, saw us coming and trotted over. His long brown ears were waggling with concern. Making sure that we were following him he led the way to Farah. He stood two metres away from her body and gazed with agitation at all that was left of one of his charges. Even after Mahmad Ali and I had left he stayed by the pitiful bit that remained.

After this lesson the mares were firmly locked into the stables at night.

But Simone and her five-month old foal, Anamarat, managed to escape a few nights later. Once more their absence went unnoticed until noon when Ui set off to search for them. He returned with Anamarat's halter, the blood stained brown against dusty white nylon. I had no need to ask him what had happened. With Mahmad Ali, I returned to the same spot to discover Simone eaten from the rib cage down and her foal fifty metres away. He was facing towards the stables which he must have been trying to reach in a last panic-stricken dash. All three of the Caspians had been killed in the same fashion. They had been herded to the same spot by nips on their necks and legs. Then they had been choked to death.

In the space of one month, three donkeys, three Caspians and a stray mare that had joined our herd were killed by wolves, all within three hundred metres of the stable. I was approaching a state of total exhaustion, sitting up at night with a shotgun over the corpses and working during the day to make the barns more secure. Narcy arrived to help hunt the wolves. We searched the crevices of the canyons in the Khalid Nabi Mountains by day and hid around the vicinity of the kills at night but never saw a single wolf.

The only wolf that was killed was by accident. A group of revelling Turkomans were returning from a wedding late at night when they spotted a pack of fourteen wolves near Alexander's Wall. They chased them and ran over one in a watermelon patch near our farm. They seemed to know about our problems and drove to the barn to wake me up. They suggested we take guns and hunt for the rest of the pack.

An uncle of Narcy's, Ghaffar Farmanfarmaian woke at the sounds and happily leapt for his gun and his Jeep. Half the wedding party left with him and I joined the rest in their Jeep. We tore out of the yard and into the black maw of the steppe. The headlights were not much protection against hurtling into the precipitous ravines which bisect the otherwise flat steppe with unpredictable and treacherous suddenness.

First we picked up the dead wolf in the watermelon patch. Then we coursed back and forth over ploughed fields, watermelons, sunflowers and steppe grass trying to find the rest of the pack. Ghaffar later said he had seen them and given chase along Alexander's Wall for a kilometre but they had disappeared over the wall and he couldn't follow. We never did see them. We did shut off the engine at some point and sat listening for sounds. From somewhere nearby came the long, drawn-out wail of wolves. Presumably they were mourning the victim of the Jeep. The sound sent shivers down everyone's backs and snuffed out much of the enthusiasm for continuing the chase.

We decided to check with Narcy who was waiting for the wolves at the horse corpses. He was sound asleep, his arm curled around the rifle.

A section of a stone rubbing taken by Louise at Persepolis

Above: Fatemeh Below: Doueez –
Mares exported to the U. K. with the 'wolf shipment'

Farah – killed by wolves. She was intended for the UK

Making bread in Ghara Tepe Sheikh – photo: Brenda Dalton

Ghezeli with Louise' granddaughter at Alexander's wall - Ghara Tepe
Sheikh is in the background, framed by the incredible light of Iran
Photo: Ruth Staines

Deep chasms and flat barley fields - Riding out from Ghara Tepe Sheikh
(Louise Firouz, Brenda Dalton and grooms)
Photo: Maziar Jamshydkhani

Chapter 17

<u>The 'Wolf Shipment' Leads to Confiscation of the Herd</u>

Winter appeared in the abrupt fashion of the steppe and, although the wolves soon ignored us, as if tired of horse-meat, I despaired of ever delivering any Caspians to the British in one piece. I decided that some prodding was in order and drove to Teheran through nine hours of rain, mud and snow to place an urgent phone call to Elizabeth Haden. I was still covered with the grime of travel when I stood by the telephone to be told that Liz, 'Jaffa', 'Griff' and 'Twink' were being received at Buckingham Palace, They were presenting Roy Reynolds' painting of Prince Philip's Caspians, Rostam and Khorshid Kola. I suppressed a passing moment of envy at their rather more enjoyable surroundings, left an urgent message that they contact me as soon as possible and took a long bath.

With typical efficiency they were back on the line to Teheran within the hour. We made plans for the speedy transfer of seven Caspians to England. The story of the wolves and the rare Caspians would later hit the press in England, introducing an element of publicity in Iran that would have been better left-buried.

Once more we became immersed in the complexities of arranging quarantine certificates, blood samples and Customs releases. I was unaware of the growing consternation of the Royal Horse Society viz-a-viz our herd of Caspians.

We were finally able to load the Caspians on a Caledonia Airlines flight arranged by Liz and the British Bloodstock Agency. There were sufficient troubles at Mehrabad Airport to convince the Captain of the flight that this was his first and last experiment with Persian procedure. In addition to the Captain's own problems, IranAir, handler for all cargo at Mehrabad Airport, at the last minute required an additional five thousand dollars handling charge. Liz, through the British Board of Agriculture, had already paid exorbitant fees for the privilege of shipping horses out by air from Iran and this unexpected, final 'sweetener' came as a blow. Not in the habit of carrying large amounts of cash around in my pockets, I appealed to Fritzi Riahi, who had come to the airport to say goodbye, to rush into Teheran and borrow the money from her husband, Manucher. She returned with a cheque which proved unacceptable and had to dash back to exchange the incriminating piece of paper for cash.

We landed in Gatwick to the accompaniment of full press coverage and a typical British downpour. Fortunately for me, I was under doctor's orders to proceed with all speed to the London Clinic for the removal of a potentially serious source of trouble. I was able to slip away from a net of newsmen and television cameras, all reflecting the sympathy of the British for depleted wildlife and valuable forms of early domestic animals. Unfortunately the Royal Horse Society viewed the picture from a different angle and took the press coverage as a deliberate insult to their own talents for saving rare horses. The result was an immediate ban on exports of Caspians 'in order to preserve this rare national heritage (Caspian) from extinction.' Survival obviously meant different things to different people.

I had left Teheran in November, 1976, and did not return to Iran until late January, 1977. When I arrived I found that a World Caspian Association had been founded by the Royal Horse Society and that all the Caspians extant in Iran were to become the property of the Royal Horse Society. Although there were probably more Caspians in the forests of Mazanderan, mine were the only ones they bothered to nationalise. Committee meetings and legal procedures ate through most of February and March with no visible evidence of any concrete Association actually emerging.

In the meantime, there were some valuable Caspians in Ghara Tepe Sheikh eating their way through quantities of our hay. By June we were facing bankruptcy. The Royal Horse Society was still talking and we were still feeding. I wrote them a letter suggesting that the nationalisation of the herd should include the facilities at Ghara Tepe Sheikh as I was simply not able to finance the maintenance of what was claimed a national heritage.

By July, the Royal Horse Society agreed to a certain monetary compensation for our animals that covered the feed they had eaten since they had been nationalised. The Royal Horse Society was not interested in our farm at Ghara Tepe Sheikh, claiming it was too primitive a place in which to keep horses. There was still no water, electricity or all-weather road. And we were still living in the one room in the barn.

The Royal Horse Society wanted the horses to go to their facilities in Gonbad. In return for having paid for the feed, the Ghara Tepe Sheikh staff and I were to accompany the animals and work for a period of four months establishing the stud and training their staff.

This move had none of the frenetic quality of our departure from Norouzabad but we were a bit pressed for time. The mares had returned from the Khalid Nabi in early June and were due to make the migration to Ghara Balkan. As the discussion culminating in the July 5th takeover were in process, it seemed a needless waste to subject all of us to the gruelling trek if we were but to turn around and double the distance to Gonbad. In the end, we rushed through the barley harvest and kept the mares down on the steppe grazing the stubble until the decision of our destination was clear. We were also still numbed by the tragic death of Avaz Katkhoda in April. He had neglected to put our tractor into first gear descending the steep track to the river, had lost control, and was crushed by the overturning tractor. Ghara Tepe Sheikh was still in mourning and we moved through the preparations for departure in a dazed state.

Elias, Ui, Walli, Caren and I cleaned out the barns and offered for sale everything that was not bolted to solid construction on the grounds that it would probably disappear anyway during our four months absence. We considered driving the herd of thirty Caspians and twenty odd Turkoman mares to the Royal Horse Society facilities in Gonbad. The thought of disrupting traffic in Gonbad with our unruly herd was tempting but was over-ridden by an unusual attack of common sense combined with mental exhaustion. The Turkoman stock was included in the equine package as the Royal Horse Society had neglected to clar-ify my horse-owning status. I had been told that I was prohibited from owning any more Caspians. It was not clear whether the interdiction included all members of the horse family.

We loaded our riding horses onto a truck and shipped them to Tehe-ran. They were tied to trees lining the outer walls of my brother David's garden in Punack. They were offered for sale. Ateshe was in charge of this project. She rose each morning at four o'clock to exercise the eight horses before Teheran's summer heat made the task unbearable.

We found a truck in Kalaleh that could transport the Caspians in two loads. I left Elias in charge of loading the animals in Ghara Tepe Sheikh. I drove to Gonbad to await their arrival and oversee the un-loading and stabling. In the meantime the Royal Horse Society had shipped the Norouzabad Caspian stallions to Gonbad where we were to practice our managerial talents in the elegant facilities of the Royal Horse Society Stud.

Renewing my acquaintance with old friends amongst the stallions, I was dismayed to find that the kind nicker I had been accustomed to expect had been replaced by a tendency to attack with vicious swipes of the forefeet and bared teeth. I decided to cope with this problem later and left the caged animals to contemplate their new surroundings.

The Caspians from Ghara Tepe Sheikh arrived in various stages of disarray. Elias had evidently thought that separating the stallions and mares was unnecessary but that separating mares and foals would cause no problem. The truck contained milling, screaming horses. We cleaned the cuts and abrasions as best we could. The stallions were stabled two by two in stalls to lessen the shock of being parted from the herd. The mares we turned loose in one of the adjacent paddocks. Ui and I stayed with the Caspians while Elias, Caren, Gelich and Walli returned to Ghara Tepe Sheikh to ride the Turkoman mares and Khorshid, our Akhal Teke stallion, to Gonbad the next day .Ui and I strolled around the Royal Horse Society Stud to see what was available in the way of pastures, training areas and stabling. The evening was warm and the air scented with the blooms of hundreds of rose bushes. They were both scattered about and planted in neat rows as if the blooms were to be sent to Teheran's flower shops. Plane trees and acacias, planted by the Royal Horse Society after they had acquired the property from the gendarmerie and Air Taxi, lined the roads and hugged the buildings; a shock after the unblemished turf of the open steppe. I felt as if I had accidentally blundered into a budding Kew garden. I had no idea how Ui felt. He declined to comment. We were agreed, however, that we would be hard put to find a place to work the stallions. We could also see no possibility of stabling the mares when the winter rains turned the cultivated fields into an ocean of mud.

The following morning we moved the mares to the harvested wheat fields belonging to the Royal Horse Society. These backed upon a four-hectare area of 'unimproved' steppe adjacent to the grandstand and race- track. These mares were soon joined by the remaining Caspians from Norouzabad. We erected our own tent that we used for spring and summer migrations and installed Walli in his traditional post as herder. Then we started to try to find some way of taming the little horrors from Norouzabad in the confines of narrow paths and rose bushes, while dodging the Royal Horse Society' Akhal Teke stallions and mares. The project was definitely a losing battle. There was no clear indication whether the rose bushes or the stallions would emerge victorious. What was certain was that we, the grooms, had no chance of achieving our aim and remain unscathed in those surroundings.

The only clear working space was transformed overnight into another flower bed, and two grooms were treated at the Red Lion and Sun hospital in Gonbad for severe injuries to their faces from the remarkably accurate front feet of the Caspian stallions. Then I decided we should employ a drastic but more humane solution to our problem.

We moved all the stallions to the four-hectare remnant of steppe and staked them out on long ropes. We set up a tent for ourselves and slept under the clear stars of Central Asia with a breeze that had been unable to penetrate the barrier of roses.

Two days of struggling with the unaccustomed ropes, alternately tangling their legs in an effective self-hobble or charging to the end of the tether with intent to murder either one of their own species or one of ours, and the stallions gave in with good grace. They received their water buckets with nickers of pleasure and their feed bags with equal enthusiasm. Not a single groom was bitten, kicked or treated with anything but polite respect. In two days we had transformed fifteen man-eaters into a semblance of the kind of children's ponies we had left at Norouzabad.

We sent to Ghara Tepe Sheikh for three small boys to ride the ponies for the summer. When they arrived we spent a week re-arranging their riding style from donkey to horse. Then we turned them loose to join the early morning work-outs of equal sized jockeys on the large, felt-draped race horses. They were a fine, proud sight; the small boys with their black, astrakhan hats and the dancing stallions, miniatures in the steppe landscape.

Meanwhile, Ui had been busy repairing the small dog cart which had originally been assembled from spare doroshkeh parts at Norouzabad. We discovered that we could take an unbroken three-year-old stallion from Norouzabad and have him trotting the dog-cart up and down the macadam road to the race- track in the space of one week. So eager were the stallions to learn that we restrained ourselves with difficulty from breaking our own training schedule for fear the word might leak out to more conservative circles. When one of our graduates later that summer danced with the Sadler's Wells Ballet in Rudaki Hall in Teheran, however, we displayed no false modesty about the achievement.

Ateshe had arrived from Teheran with some friends to join Caren for a week in Gonbad. They helped with the stallion project: their undivided attention to the ponies' training and welfare made the difference between success and failure. Ateshe had been the mainstay of the Caspian project at Norouzabad and it was evident that dealing with Irish show jumpers had blunted none of her enthusiasm or talent for working with Caspians. She organized Caren and Ui, parcelling out duties and instructing Ui in the use of long lines and the elements of driving.

The Royal Horse Society had donated one of their trainees to the Caspian project. Taghi Damadji was an engaging young man who quickly pointed out that he was not a groom and knew nothing about it. He also said he knew nothing about training or riding. He said his instructions were to give instructions. We were somewhat awed by this announcement. I tried to interest him in bringing the Caspian records up to date and setting up a system that would simplify the necessary future information. Taghi watched while activity hummed happily around our patch of green. The horses were being trained and exercised and I, bent over the books, was trying to imagine what had happened during our three years absence from Norouzabad. I transferred the solid bits of information to a Master Stud Book that would also include the herd from Ghara Tepe Sheikh but there were large holes in the information from the original herd. Obviously the Royal Horse Society had not been keeping records.

After we left, Taghi worked hard to preserve the Caspians. He had grown fond of them and the indifference of the Royal Horse Society management to their steadily worsening plight disturbed him. They were not interested in augmenting the herd, nor exporting, nor feeding what they had. Taghi fought to save them and it was not his fault that they eventually perished.

I made repeated trips to Teheran in attempts to persuade the Royal Horse Society to provide a barn for the mares during the winter months. A token attempt at appeasing my crusading zeal was made in the form of approaching a firm of architect-engineers to design a stable appropriate for brood mares. Master plans for the entire stud were drawn up and abandoned. Stables were designed and discarded by committee decision. The whole project eventually fell victim to the grand scheme of a forty-hectare golf course. This coincided with the discovery that the firm contracted for the Caspian project was not the firm that was actually doing the work.

Before it was clear that the Royal Horse Society was, in fact, reluctant to do anything constructive with the Caspians, I had suggested that Sherri Platt be employed for the autumn to help train the stallions to pull a variety of carts and carriages in different combinations. Sherri had had some experience in this field and was familiar with Caspians so she seemed a logical choice. In order to be ready for Sherri's arrival from Washington, D.C. where her husband was currently stationed and for the speedy implementation of the driving program, carts and harness were ordered through the Royal Horse Society for immediate delivery.

When Sherri did arrive, however, we discovered that the Royal Horse Society had neglected to put the order through although, for some reason, they had not cancelled her contract to put the order to practical use. She occupied the first week of her employment standing in the wings of Rudaki Hall with Ui catching Prince Caspian as he emerged from the arms of adoring ballerinas of the Sadler's Wells. Following this experience, Prince Caspian was transferred from our tiny town garden near Rudaki to Norouzabad to await the annual 'Arya Mehr' show.

The Arya Mehr show jumping competition was an annual event started by Kambiz Atabai in 1970. In the beginning it was a friendly affair dominated by local teams of riders competing on the indigenous breeds of horses. As the Royal Stables and wealthy devotees of the sport began combing Europe and Ireland for experienced horses, the tone of the 'show-jumping set' gradually changed to what appeared more a race for prestige than a competition of skill. By 1977, foreign riders of Olympic stature (the D'Inzeo' brothers, David Broom and Kathy Kusner to name but a few) along with their world class show jumping horses, were flown to Teheran at government expense to 'compete' with local riders. Iran's breeds of horses became nothing more than an exhibition in between the rounds of jumping.

Much the same happened to racing. What had once been the province of the Turkoman and Plateau Persian horses was replaced by Thoroughbreds, imported from England and Australia. Although Turkoman races still occupied part of the racing card, the distances were calculated for the benefit of the Totaliser and pure Turkomans found themselves at a disadvantage as crossbred began mixing in as 'purebred' Turkomans. Bred to cover long distances, the short sprints of the modern track at Farahabad were not designed for their long, slim bodies. The focus of Iran's riding world had inadvertently switched from its own breeds to those produced by the west. Tribal and village breeders found themselves with a surplus of unsaleable animals while Turkoman breeders were forced to use the Thoroughbred stallions scattered around the steppe. The long term effect of this program was the almost total disappearance of local breeds in Teheran's sporting scene. Even polo ponies succumbed to the glitter of the 'western' horse, Argentinian polo ponies gradually appearing to replace the sturdy Kurdish horse. For a country that had been providing the world with the best horses for over three thousand years this was a tragedy of major proportions. Sherri and I drove to Gonbad to see what we could accomplish with bits of rope - that being the advice of the Royal Horse Society on training for four-in-hands. For all practical purposes, the remainder of our tenure with the Royal Horse Society consisted of waiting for the Arya Mehr show and the conclusion of the four month contract. No progress had been made on winter stabling for the mares. No progress could be made in driving beyond what could be accomplished with our dog cart, our ancient harness and by long reining the ponies.

Autumn had arrived, although the muggy heat of Gonbad did little to dispel the notion that summer would never end. The haunting mating call of the maral (red deer) in the nearby forest and the vivid red of the changing dogwood leaves suggested that the weather was crisp in the higher elevations. Four months of paved roads, meticulous rose beds, washing stable windows and lack of freedom of initiative, was sufficient for all of us to yearn for open spaces.

We returned to Ghara Balkan to bring the Turkoman mares, which the Royal Horse Society had dismissed, down from the mountains to Ghara Tepe Sheikh. The first evening, brewing tea high up near the top, we watched the shadows fade on the Khalid Nabi. The first wild boar ventured out and the pheasant cocks gave a last challenge to the day. The next day, wending our way down the steep, grassy slopes with the foals chasing each other around bushes and the choughs crying in large black flocks high overhead, we all settled deeply into our saddles and let our eyes stray complacently to nothing more important than the odd ripe wild pomegranate or flicker hungrily over a far, scurrying partridge.

Preparations for the Arya Mehr show were underway. I had driven to Teheran earlier, leaving Sherri in Gonbad to cope with transporting the three Caspian stallions which were to be part of a breed show. The Royal Horse Society still had not given us any tack with which to work. I tried to persuade them to loan some equipment from their tack shop for the prestigious display of native breeds they planned before an international audience and the Shah. After much wrangling, equipment was provided although I had to pay for the alterations myself.

Sherri telephoned frantically from Gonbad that the truck found by the Royal Horse Society for transporting the Caspians and one Akhal Teke stallion had a defective floor. No amount of argument could persuade the Royal Horse Society to switch trucks. It was one hour before the telephone rang once more from Gonbad. One of the Caspians had slipped partly through the floor of the truck which, fortunately, had turned back to the stud. Instead of ordering a new truck, a piece of metal sheeting was laid over the hole. By this time, the Akhal Teke stallion was nervous so, as the story has it, his front legs were hobbled to restrain his movements and he was somehow led onto the truck. As his feet touched the unfamiliar metal sheeting he reared and threw himself over the side of the truck. Unable to brace himself with his closely tied front legs, he broke the fall with his neck. Nothing daunted, the three Caspians were loaded and sent to Teheran. Sherri was left to find her own transportation and that of the three young riders.

When they arrived in Teheran we discovered that no arrangements had been made for their lodging. We hastily bundled together some bedding, fed them supper and put the boys to sleep in our house. The following day we found the stables where the ponies were being housed at Kuhak. We set up a training schedule to keep all occupied until the show some two weeks hence. As the boys and the ponies were already on a form of schedule, only a small adaptation to the physical surroundings and their role in the show was required. For the first week nobody noticed our presence. Both the boys and the ponies improved noticeably with the uninterrupted attention.

By the end of the week various people 'in charge' appeared. Soon the Caspians hooves were pared down to a point where they could not cope with the stony ground. Early one morning we found a new group of 'helpers' chasing them around on a lunge. The Turkomans were standing to one side looking on with helpless wonder. Soon, our quiet ponies had reverted to their early Gonbad days and it was no longer safe to mount the boys on them. No amount of pleading or threats seemed to dent the impassive armour of this strange group of people. It was as if the Royal Horse Society was bent on purposefully destroying what they had nationalised to preserve.

I was uneasy that the Turkoman boys would be hurt by the increasingly ill-mannered behaviour of the Caspians and resigned from Royal Horse Society employ. Our four- month bond was over anyway. I did not attend the gala performance of the Arya Mehr show where the Caspians were to put on a dazzling display between rounds of the D'Inzeo brothers, Harvey Smith and other riders jumping in the competitions. I was told later that anyone who bought a Caspian after that effort would have had a mini rodeo in mind.

Sherri sighed with relief and returned to Washington. I arranged what was left at Ghara Tepe Sheikh and left for England en route to spend Christmas with the children who were in University in the U.S. I took with me the results of the summer's hard research on the Caspian records so that Liz and I could compile the Second International Stud Book while there was still some solid information from the Persian contingent.

When I returned to Iran in late January 1977, I was told that the Caspian mares were not faring well in Gonbad. Their winter quarters were a dripping mud hut that had once been used to house sheep and a muddy open courtyard surrounded by barbed wire. The confined space and constant standing in mud up to their hocks, plus a diet limited to straw, eventually led to some form of epidemic which wiped out an unconfirmed number of these rare mares.

The Turkomans, who had become quite fond of the Caspians, were full of disturbing rumours concerning the welfare of the Caspians at the Royal Horse Society stud. Evidently, according to the Turkomans, a large number of the stallions were gelded as they were considered unmanageable and no effort was being made to train the young stock.

When I next visited the stud in late June with Helen Rattray, who was visiting from New Zealand, I noticed that the remaining stallions were all securely tied in their box stalls and that the mares ran in an un-groomed, motley herd on the race- track. No one appeared to know their names. Although Mrs. Rattray was anxious to purchase a number for a Caspian Stud in New Zealand, there was no one who would agree to the sale. This was in spite of the cancellation of the ban on exports shortly after the Caspian takeover in July of the previous year. Helen and I jointly invested in a lovely, small grey Caspian that we had found in Amol on our way from Teheran to the steppes. We had him trucked to Pashei. The following morning we rode down from the mountain pastures of Ghara Balkan to lead him up to his new home. Ui was waiting for us by the stable when we rounded the last bend in the track. There was a broad, happy smile on his face as he caught sight of the Caspian.

Helen Rattray at Ghara Balkan where she bought the aptly named Zeeland (right) Ironically, she was never able to take him to New Zealand

Zeeland, the only Caspian remaining after the revolution –Louise loaned him to a farmer who hastily returned him due to his inexhaustible energy

The villagers who built the barn at Ghara Tepe Sheikh (GTS)
"WE did that"

Narcy at Ghara Tepe Sheik with a phallic symbol from the Khalid Nabi
(right)

Chapter 18

<u>Revolution, Arrest and Hunger Strike</u>

One dismal, snowy day in early January, 1985, I took my typewriter to a shop on Villa Avenue to be serviced. The usual groups of shabby redundant men were sitting on rickety chairs drinking glasses of tea, puffing acrid smelling cigarettes and entertaining each other with desultory conversation. They looked up as I entered and seemed cheered by the sight of a foreigner, scenting a new topic. Each ragged overcoat said "salaam" and one said he was in charge of the shop. Having established that the typewriter could not be serviced owing to the technician's probably permanent trip to Turkey, I turned to go. The overcoats seemed loath to let me escape. They probed with questions; "where do you live, where do you work, where are you from, why do you stay in Iran?" When they heard that I was attempting to write a book about horses in Iran, one of them asked if I had ever heard of a small horse from Mazanderan called the Caspian pony.

Interested, I said, "yes, I have heard of it, but how do you know about this breed?

"Oh," he said, "a long time ago there was someone by the name of Mrs. Firouz who used to work with them. I like horses and I read about it." He paused and seemed to be looking at long memories. "By the way, you wouldn't know what happened to her?"

Taken aback, it was my turn to pause. Finally I admitted that I was, in fact, the Mrs. Firouz in question.

The Islamic uniform must have confused him. "My God," he said, "I don't believe it!" Peering up under my scarf he asked "Is everybody hiding behind these things?"

Everybody on that dreary day certainly was not. Most were a long way away from Villa Avenue in Teheran. They were in the U.S., Britain or France. Or they had been executed, or they were in prison. I felt an island unto myself trudging the pot-holed pavements in my decorous black scarf and long, muddy raincoat, dodging women blinded by their cocoon-like, funereal chadors. There were Afghan refugees in tattered shreds and Kurds swaggering in their balloon-like pants. What crazy compulsions had driven everybody in the giddy, lopsided, monomaniacal days of the seventies when the suddenly escalated oil revenues made everything seem possible? Overnight, where did they disappear in the Islamic explosion of 1979? A good question. Where was everybody?

There were those of us who thought we could see the storm clouds of revolution looming on some distant horizon back in 1978 but, for the most part, the revolution seemed to come as a surprise even though all of the ingredients were visibly there. Workers who had struggled out of the dismal poverty of small, rural agricultural plots, only to see their opportunities and futures whisked from them in front of their eyes by the whim of power hungry court favourites, were fertile soil for any sort of revolution. There were the students, their numbers swelled by the Shah's literacy campaign, pouring into the streets from newly created Universities in Teheran, Mashad, Tabriz and Shiraz. They were ripe in age and education for rebellion.

Industrial workers were concentrated in large numbers in factories and oil refineries; they were a force that could be manipulated in a way that scattered peasants never could. A growing middle class had the money and education to shrug feudal ties with the monarchy. The bazaar, with its age-old tentacles still gripping the commercial reins, was backing the clergy, morally and financially.

Military conscription was liberating young men from the parochial social structures of their remote villages, familiarising them with diverse ethnic groups and stimulating a desire for more freedom and the benefits of a material society that had been denied their fathers. All these elements were simmering with dissatisfaction. They were urged on by the clergy, by the National Front Party, by the Mujahedeen and the Fedayeen. As the pressure built, high government officials, members of the Royal family, Savak and the armed forces seemed curiously indifferent, detached and, eventually, impotent. The real surprise was that the revolution was such a rout. Like Topsy, it grew and grew and no one seemed to know what to do about it. We were all caught up in the whirlwind of dissension. We were more fascinated than appalled because everything in the decade of the seventies had been larger than life. There was the gigantic celebration of two thousand five hundred years of Monarchy. There were showcase dams, the Khuzestan industrial-agricultural development, the largest air force in the Middle East, Bell helicopter factories and U.S. army personnel swarming the streets, protected by the unpopular 'Status of Forces Agreement'.

We had become distracted from the realities of Iran. We had listened to the Shah's rhetoric and absorbed it, ignoring the voices from the clergy, the bazaar and the tribes which cautioned less profligacy. Not a western oriented, Middle Eastern super power - Persia, not Iran.

But there was a revolution burgeoning and the Shah, helpless to control the strikes, the marches and the civil disobedience, eventually left in early January, 1979. He had departed in this manner once before, when Mossadegh forced the issue in August, 1953. That time he returned a little over a week later. This time there was no return. He died in Cairo on July 27th, 1980, and was buried beside his father, Reza Shah, in the El Rifei Mosque.

Before that happened, however, his presence in a New York city hospital was to trigger one of the more debasing diplomatic episodes of recent history: the taking of sixty U.S. hostages, all but two employed at the Embassy and Consulate in Teheran. Fifty of these were held for four hundred and forty four days and the world realised that it was possible to pluck a feather from the Eagle's tail with impunity. Slogans sprouted on walls in Teheran taunting "THE U.S. CAN'T DO A DAMN THING"

I was farming on the Turkoman Steppes when all this started in January, 1978. There was a demonstration in Tabriz in Azerbaijan ending with deaths amongst students of the University. On the fortieth day of mourning there were more demonstrations and they spread amongst students all over the country. It seemed that each fire ignited a new one and they were erupting spontaneously.

I stayed on the steppes, paying little attention to the growing dissent, concentrating more on the harvest and a break in the weather to start haying. By July, 1978, I took the advice of some local Turkomans and self-exiled Iraqi Kurds employed by the Game Department. They said the situation was very serious and that I should consider leaving. They mentioned the throats of several school children had been slit in Kalaleh and this was being blamed on the Bahai's, a splinter religious sect that was especially singled out for persecution. No one believed the Bahai's had done it but provocation often precedes a diametrically opposite action. A number of books and all the research on the Caspians were shipped out to England. Apart from some dogs and horses, they were my only important possessions. I also left and spent until early October, taking Caren from his school in Scotland to one in the U.S. There were some rare weeks together with the children in Berkeley, California.

When I returned to Iran in October, I found the country in a state of euphoria. It was as if the occupants of a giant kindergarten had seized the reins, the teachers powerless to stop their charges from overturning and incinerating cars and buses, defacing walls, chopping down trees to block roads and, everywhere, dashing vigilantes speeding on motor bikes Paul Revere-like announcing the approach of authority. To the cry of "Azadi" (freedom), the emancipated crowds cheered each other on. Although there was anger evident, the prevalent mood was buoyant and it was impossible to escape the sense of convivial joy exhibited by everyone but the authorities.

There was fascination in what was happening. I abandoned my earlier intention of returning to the U.S. and joined with others in watching the cataclysmic explosion. Except for five weeks in December and January when I joined the children for Christmas in California, I remained possessed by the spectacle of anarchy.

Khomeini returned to Iran from fifteen years of exile on February the first, 1979. The short battle between the Shah's Prime Minister, Shapour Bakhtiar (himself a member-in-not-good-standing of the National Front as a result of accepting the job) and Khomeini was waged more as a personal slanging match than a fight. Bakhtiar lost and left for France whence Khomeini had just come.

There followed a brief period of freedom of the press and a longer period of executions, death photos of the victims prominently displayed in the daily newspapers. Why so many government officials and senior members of the armed forces remained in Iran after the Shah fled was a puzzle. The reasons behind this slaughter may always remain an enigma, but it was an appalling host of executions.

Narcy and I had been planting potatoes at Ghara Tepe Sheikh in mid-February, 1979, and were returning to Teheran when the fragile dam burst on the night of February 22nd. Homafars (technical airmen) of the Doshan Tepe air base in east Teheran, near the Royal Stables at Farahabad, revolted. This was the signal for the end of the uneasy truce of two governments running the country; Bakhtiar's Shah–and–armed forces backed faction and Khomeini's clergy-and-popular faction.

By the time we reached Teheran from the Khorrasan road at 11 o'clock in the morning, having spent the previous night with Azizeh Azodi in Shahrud, a column of dark smoke was rising over the barracks of Eshratabad in the middle of the city. Buses and cars formed flaming slalom posts down the main streets. Chieftain tanks, immobilized by Molotov cocktails, slewed drunkenly over sidewalks. Small children squatted on their front door steps authoritatively manufacturing fresh gas bombs. The usual lethargic Teheran crowds were milling purposefully in opposite directions. Posters had sprouted overnight instructing the uninitiated in minute detail how to assemble G3's, Kalashnikovs and Uzi's. Small groups were crowded around AWOL soldiers holding street seminars on how to fire a rifle. So altered was the face of Teheran that Narcy and I perforce gave a lift to two hitch hiking revolutionaries as guides in the general direction of our house on Avenue Damghan. They were solicitous and warned of roads we should avoid when they got out of the car near the flaming ruins of Eshratabad.

We reached home with relief but, propelled by curiosity, we ventured out and joined the crowds lining Teheran's main east-west avenue, Shah Reza. They were watching the victory parade of the vanquishers of Eshratabad. Men and boys were dressed in a motley assortment of uniforms. There were conscript caps, battle boots, ceremonial swords and band- leaders' jackets. Hawkers along the sidewalks were already offering individual tracer bullets, bandoleers of machine gun bullets, canteens and army blankets. An armoured personnel carrier appeared weaving tentatively down the avenue, pedestrians scurrying for safety as pinched but happy faces roared from their precarious perches that the driver's nearest relative, the donkey, was more competent. An army truck, loaded with a mass of gesticulating humanity hurtled past; a ragged man perched on the bonnet waving a sword urged all to follow them to Bagh-e-Shah (another garrison near the palaces) where the next battle was even now waging. The crowds surged west in the wake, carrying us along.

The next day we heard that Evin, the largest of Teheran's prisons, set up against the mountains west of Shemran, was being stormed. We decided to include this on our revolutionary itinerary. We joined a stream of traffic carrying enthusiastic sightseers. We were borne along the newly completed Shah-an-Shahi boulevard to the north. Cars bristling with guns honked their horns to pass the tourists, brusquely instructing non-fighters to stay in the right lane. Eventually spectators and revolutionaries all became embroiled in a tight-knit snarl of boiling radiators. We were carried away from Evin by the tide and deposited at Qasr prison in time for the break-in and freeing of prisoners. Later, reading Ken Follet's book, 'On Wings of Eagles', I was appalled to find myself anonymously described as one of the faceless angry mob rather than victims of the same traffic jam. Eventually we tired of the jostling and eased the car through winding back streets, halting occasionally to allow the shooting to abate before crossing an intersection. We went home for lunch.

That evening Mahmad Agha telephoned to say that he and his fellow horse dealers were concerned about the safety of Norouzabad.

"They are stealing the horses," he said.

"It's none of my business," I replied.

"It's everyone's business! Where have you been the last few days?' he roared, his voice screaming down the line.

I called Colonel Shaki whose stables were adjacent to Evin Prison. Although I was unaware of it at the time, he was in the midst of the battle for Evin Prison and did not sound in the mood for a chat. He suggested that anything we wanted to do we 'get on with it'.

"All right Mahmad Agha," I said when I called back, "do what you think is best."

By ten p.m. he was telephoning from Norouzabad to say he and fifteen other horse dealers had 'secured' the property.

Our gardener, Sayed, and I drove out the next morning to be met by sixteen horse dealers, bristling with arms, patrolling the stables and looking very proud of themselves. A jubilant cry of "here comes Mrs. Firouz" alerted the Royal Horse Society officials who appeared less than impressed by our invasion. The occupation lasted forty eight hours, by which time discretion dictated a tactful retreat.

Neither Sayed nor I were anxious to remain the centre of attention at this siege. We left shortly for Teheran where we were caught in a traffic jam at the cross-roads of Takht-e-Jamshid and Fisherabad avenues. Sayed was pointing to cloth-wrapped heads darting on roof-tops when a barrage of bullets whipped over the tops of the cars. Stray bullets were smacking into windscreens. Two blocks to the east we could see the U.S. Embassy under attack. From the jubes to the west of us rifles were aimed at the attackers on the roof-tops. Caught in the cross-fire of angry ammunition we could only lower our heads and hope the Volvo lived up to its solid specifications, although I did not recall that 'bullet proof' was one of them. Eventually the traffic moved and we pulled into the garden of our house with relief.

My brother David's departure for the U.S. to attend our father's funeral coincided with the first evacuation of Americans from the Embassy. Although David had intended to return, his papers were confiscated at the airport, abruptly terminating the Iran phase of his life. Adding to the confusion, I smashed my ankle tripping in the living room. I had been trying to talk to Roshan in San Francisco on the telephone and answer a frantic summons at the door from a British friend who was fleeing stray bullets ricocheting in the street outside our door.

Taken to a hospital by way of numerous road blocks, I was put in a room overlooking a five story building across the street. During the evening a nurse came to lower the blinds. She explained that the rest of the patients had been evacuated to the other side as a battle over the opposite building was expected.

"What about me?" I asked.

"You'll be all right," she said, "the blinds will keep out the bullets."

Later, much groaning heralded the arrival of a woman in the throes of childbirth. She was placed in a room adjacent to mine. She delivered at six a.m. and was in my room at eight a.m. telling me about her journey to the hospital through the road- blocks.

"The easiest part of the night was having the baby," she sighed.

After several days I was back home with a pin in my ankle and a cast firmly holding it all together. Two weeks later Narcy and I left Teheran to spend Norouz at Ghara Tepe Sheikh. We were concentrating on the traffic negotiating through Maidan Ferdowsi when we were stopped by armed Revolutionary Guards. (Pasdaran). They jumped into the Volvo and announced that we were under arrest.

"Turn right, turn left, stop here."

We were outside a mosque. They ordered us to disembark and march in. That smooth retreat was denied me as I had not yet mastered the art of crutches and lurched precariously over jubes and against gun-toting guards. Inside the mosque, long queues of people stood arguing with mullahs and guards. A small group of guards was playing soccer in the court-yard using old kerosene cans for goal posts. I sagged against a wall awaiting the outcome of the detention, my leg throbbing painfully from the unaccustomed downhill position. After half an hour I slipped to the floor elevating the cast and trying to look miserable, which was not hard. Much talk and much "let's send them to the Central Committee" ended with releasing us. The Volvo was the culprit. Apparently Savak, the Shah's Secret Police, had ordered large quantities for their own use before the revolution and it was assumed we had been too stupid to turn in our official car for something less conspicuous.

Night and we reached Ghara Tepe Sheikh with grateful thanks for no more diversions. Spring had arrived bringing daffodils, iris and tulips. They waved gently amongst the green shoots of grass. Migrating birds were appearing. The sounds of lambs from our neighbours' flocks throbbed over the warm earth.

In five days ominous news passed along the steppe.

"Did you know there are counter-revolutionaries in Gonbad," said Elias.

"I never knew there were any revolutionaries," I said, still amazed that the Turkomans, whose land had all been confiscated by the Pahlavis, had stayed faithful to the Monarchy until the end.

"There weren't any revolutionaries. That's why there are now counter-revolutionaries," he said with cool logic.

I asked him what they were doing.

"I'm not sure. They weren't revolutionaries, but they weren't for the Shah and now they seem to be an opposition force to the revolution. But, whoever they are, there seems to be trouble." He had a twinkle in his eye that must have lit many a Mongol face before a major battle.

An announcement on the radio informed the people of Gonbad to surrender or they would be obliterated with artillery from the ground and bombs from the air. Shortly after the sound of heavy guns could be heard, followed by refugees from the town using any form of transportation at hand from Peykan cars to horse and oxen drawn carts. They streamed out over the steppe pushing cars and carts through deep muddy ruts. They camped in the occasional mud and brick villages along Alexander's Wall or in nomad encampments along the Atrek River.

The guns continued to boom forty kilometres away in Gonbad and the radio warned that the deadline for surrender was two p.m. We were watching the skies over Gonbad as two planes circled lazily, like vultures watching the death throes of a bloated, defenceless cow. The radio, tuned to the local Gorgan station, announced that the deadline had been extended until five p.m. Still the planes circled. Shortly after they were replaced by two other planes, as the first flew back for fuel. When five o'clock came and no bombs had been dropped, we heard over the radio that Gonbad had capitulated. We also heard that Kalaleh, our nearest town ten kilometres away, had been captured by the air force. The entire region was isolated. No one could enter and no one could leave. We were quarantined.

This was no punishment. The weather had turned warm and sunny again after a brief period of rain and there was plenty to do. Narcy entertained himself with vegetables and I devised a way to ride for half an hour at a time using a rope sling instead of a stirrup for the casted leg.

Within a week the 'quarantine' was lifted and we loaded the car to return to Teheran. At the outskirts of Kalaleh, a group of smartly clad, blue uniformed air force officers were halting traffic from the restricted area. One of the officers came up to our car, peered in, stared briefly, and called to a companion in a perfect Texan drawl: "look what we've caught!" They were graduates of Lubbock air force base in Texas and could not have been more delighted to have captured an American. Laughing, they let us go.

In Shahrud, where we stopped to see Azizeh, the atmosphere was less congenial.

"You could have called," she said, "we were worried stiff."

"We don't have a telephone," we reminded her and the subject was dropped.

When we returned to Teheran we found that Narcy's brother had been arrested, the start of a six-year sojourn as a guest of the government. Although people tended to disappear with no warning, on the surface, life in Teheran continued unchanged for the majority. Work limped on, parties were regular affairs and play reading, initiated by the staff of the British Embassy, provided weekly entertainment.

But many people we knew had either been executed or were languishing in jails. Mary Gharagozlou had been arrested in Khuzestan in February and was said to be in Qasr prison in Teheran. No communication was possible. All information was relayed by rumour or from those who had recently been discharged.

Upon Mary's release, after four months of detention, she took up residence in the ex-Royal Stables at Farahabad where she and the grooms struggled to save the Royal Horse Society Arabs and the horses which had belonged to the Shah. During the chaos of the revolution some fanatics had attempted to execute the Shah's horses on the grounds that they were 'Monarchist'. Fortunately the grooms in the Royal Stables were able to prevent this massacre.

The Caspians, in the meantime, were not doing well in Gonbad. Initially neglected, they were now relegated to a barbed wire enclosure at the back of the stud where they stood hock deep in mud. They were gradually dying from lack of even straw and water. Roshan and I made repeated trips to the stud to plead for the Caspians. We argued that if they were not going to feed them they should at least let them go to fend for themselves on the steppe. Or they could shoot them. But the Revolutionary guards in charge had no orders and were powerless to do anything. They were not allowed to feed them and they were not allowed to shoot them. There was no malicious plan behind this decimation.

Once the Caspians had been segregated to their squalid ghetto there was no one to rescind the order. Bar another revolution they were doomed to extinction. The Revolutionary guards were finally benumbed by this pathetic sight and an auction was organized to sell the survivors. Unfortunately the Horse Society did not inform me of the auction and I was not there to bid on any of the Caspians. I was later told by someone who worked at the stud in Gonbad that they were sold for between fifty and one hundred toumans each (three to six pounds sterling). They were bought mainly by Kazakhs, a horse eating tribe from Central Asia. Because they were so cheap they took them home, slit their throats, and ate them.

At that time my position in Turkoman country was precarious. All the 'foreigners' (Fars) had fled, leaving their land and possessions behind. Large numbers of 'Feodals', or prosperous farmers, a name also applied to the Russian 'Kulaks' (twenty million of whom had been killed in the Russian revolution) had been dispossessed and many of them executed. Certainly, anyone who owned Amlak land (grazing land confiscated from the Turkomans by the Pahlavis) was nowhere to be seen. Fortunately the land I owned had been bought from the Turkomans themselves, but the diverse revolutionary groups in charge were sceptical about my continued presence. I was an American - why had I not left - I was not allowed to keep more than one horse - dogs were luxuries. The Turkomans of Ghara Tepe Sheikh defended me. They said I was a part of them and not 'Feodal'. So I kept my Kurdish horse, Almeh, and the Caspian stallion, Zeeland. We reluctantly dismissed any notion of maintaining an orphanage for Caspians and the large herd of Turkoman mares we had collected was turned loose.

The scene on the steppe simulated the Russian communisation of agriculture in the Don sixty years previously. We had village Soviets (Shora) which farmed the confiscated land, dividing some of the profits amongst the villagers. Permission to purchase seed grain, fertilizer or tractors had to be obtained from the District Soviet (Heyat-e-Haft-Nafari - Committee of seven), based on a letter from the village Soviet. The system did not crystallize in the way it did to the north as parliament (the Majless) was unable to reach an agreement on legislation for land ownership. Gradually the more energetic farmers began to lease land, building up their acreage and assuming the trappings of capital enterprise.

Abruptly in November, 1979, Teheran's uneasy peace was shattered by the taking of hostages in the U.S. Embassy. Overnight, TV crews arrived from the U.S., Britain, France, Germany, Japan and even Mexico. The Intercontinental Hotel was crowded with TV cables, handsome anchormen and black market dealers. The avenue in front of the U.S. Embassy (renamed the 'Den of Spies') was blocked off and soon sprouted fast food stands to satisfy the appetites of thousands of fascinated onlookers enjoying the spectacle of militant bands of fist wavers being recorded for history by competing TV crews. Effigies of Uncle Sam, President Carter and the Shah, dangled by their necks from lamp posts. Only missing from this forum were the lions - the Christians were out of sight in the red brick chancellery building.

This sad affair continued for four hundred and forty four days, punctuated by the grisly aftermath of the attempted rescue by U.S. special troops. This ended in dusty and flaming disaster in the desert outside Tabas in east Iran.

In September, 1980, I had planned to go briefly to London and the U.S. with Roshan. She had returned in 1979 and had been working with various news agencies. I wanted to see the other children and there was a rumour in the air that Roshan and a young British diplomat with the Embassy in Teheran, were thinking of getting engaged.

My travel documents were ready, including the airline ticket. I was only waiting for Narcy to return from Ahwaz in Khuzestan where he was still struggling with the installation of a sewage system. Roshan left for London a few days early to visit friends so I was alone on that Saturday in late September when at eight in the morning, the door-bell rang and the door was given several hearty blows.

I opened the door to a group of uniformed revolutionary guards. One of them waved a tattered, hand-written search warrant in my face.

"Police," he said in English.

"Not dressed yet," I replied in Persian and closed the door.

They gave me five minutes and then resumed running up the electricity bill: several, more athletic, members climbed over the garden wall. By this time I had a cup of coffee and some proper clothes plus the morning English language Kayhan newspaper which one of the pasdars (Revolutionary Guard) had brought from the doorstep.

By one o'clock they had Narcy's considerable collection of hunting rifles, ammunition and knives artfully arranged on the bed. It was reminiscent of photographs of guerrilla's lairs, 'captured after a fierce battle'. There were light-hearted games involving hunting knives which drew blood and the bathroom had been ransacked for band-aids. I had been through an initial interrogation based, it seemed, on eliciting the names of all the people I knew. I was soon disabused of levity when I answered that "most of the people I know have left, been shot or are in jail". I could not think of anyone. Temporarily stuck, my interrogator suggested a few names that led me to conclude that they had not come unprepared.

Narcy opened the front door at this point and stared in disbelief at the receiving committee of eighteen or twenty pasdars. He was immediately ushered into another room for a separate interrogation while I was allowed to scramble some eggs for lunch. The pasdars were served separately by a van delivering mobile lunches to their far-flung crews. At four o'clock we were instructed to pack an extra set of underwear and toilet articles for an indeterminate stay with them. I found a package of cornflakes that I opened for our four dogs, which were locked into a room, and filled a bowl with water.

We were blindfolded as soon as we were seated in the back of a car. We were instructed to keep our heads out of sight and not to talk. Half an hour later, the car stopped and I was led stumbling along a path, up some steps, along a tiled floor and down more steps through several doors which clanged ominously on opening and closing.

My blindfold was removed inside a grey-walled cell. There were two cots bolted to the floor and a small, narrow window high up near the ceiling. I rubbed some feeling back into my eyes and they gradually swam into focus. In front of me was a headless body, a Palestinian scarf hiding the stump. I assumed the intent was to terrify me and it did. The blindly swerving ride up the hill, unable to see, and this apparition removed all sense of reality.

I had no idea where we were. There had been a constant changing of gears on the ride and my ears had popped several times. That, I assumed, meant we were going up into the mountains. But where? Or did it really matter? That 'we' were in the same place was only an assumption. I did not know whether Narcy had been taken out of the car at the same place or not. Apart from the guard locking the door to my cell and then unlocking and locking what sounded like three barred gates, there were no sounds of life.

I sat down on one of the cots and tried not to feel claustrophobic in the solitary confinement.

Dinner was brought two hours later but I did not feel hungry and declined to eat.

"That's all right," said the guard, "most prisoners feel this way their first night. You'll soon get over it."

I was not sure I wanted the time to get over 'it'. The dogs were alone in the house with no one to feed them. Roshan was expecting me in England on Monday. No one knew where we were and this was one experience I felt I could definitely do without.

A friend who represented the London Times in Teheran had only the day before been released from ten days in prison. His advice to those caught in like circumstances was to abstain from eating while avoiding the confrontation of a hunger strike. He had done this for the last five days of his detention and was not only free to tell the tale but he had a considerably improved figure. I took heart from his example and decided not to eat. There was a legitimate excuse. Ui had served mounds of fresh green grapes at his wedding the week before and I had found them delicious, but the effects were only too apparent.

That first night I was led blindfolded to the bathroom that was through one locked gate adjacent to my cell. In the dim light it seemed respectable enough. The next morning I was first in, of what turned out to be a line of six cells. By early light, hundreds of baby cockroaches were visible swarming over three wash basins and a heap of garbage from the prisoners' meal trays thrown in the corner. I scraped a place in one basin and brushed my teeth and washed my face. Then I banged on the door to have the guard lead me back to my cell. Other prisoners, all male, were led past my cell one by one in varying stages of complaint, coughs and anger. One of them, by the sounds of the cough, was Narcy, but no one ever admitted whether this was so or not.

Breakfast was tea, bread and butter. I drank the tea but remained faithful to the fast. Lunch looked delicious. It was a khoresht of meat and vegetables on rice. I was sorely tempted but honour demanded that I equal the London Times, at least on a hunger strike. After five days of this I had outlasted the Times but was no longer tempted by food.

To the guards' credit, they were worried by my lack of appetite. They offered pills and homemade remedies to cure the results of what they considered had been my intemperate appetite at the wedding. I agreed with the Times that claiming a hunger strike would not advance the cause of freedom, but was grateful to the guards for their solicitude. They were, in fact, polite and courteous throughout my stay.

The interrogations started on Sunday, the day after my arrival. A young man with his head swathed entered the cell and sat down on the opposite cot. His manner was civil, reserved and precise. He explained that as soon as a number of matters were clarified, I should be free to leave. That looked encouraging and I quickly mentioned that I had a reservation on the following day's flight to London. "Don't worry about that," he said, "you won't be able to go."

"Why not?" I asked, "I'm booked on that flight."

"The airport is closed," the smile fairly oozing from behind the mask, "because we've just gone to war with Iraq."

I had thought I had heard much excitement that day over my head. There had been stomping of feet and the clatter of guns being loaded but I had mistaken this for normal prison procedure.

"Now that you know there is no hurry, we can relax and get this over with."

I wondered how long 'this' would take. I was convinced by now that the dogs would be trying to chew their way through the door of the room and causing a howling racket in No. 10 Damghan. My faceless interrogator was not worried.

"For as long as it takes."

I cannot compare these interrogations with any other than entering U.S. immigration at Dulles airport, Washington D.C. in 1981, after not leaving Iran when President Carter had apparently ordered all U.S. citizens capable of leaving to depart Iran in 1980. The Dulles interrogation took about two hours and was not pleasant. This one took two weeks and was not pleasant either, but I had not expected it to be,

The almost daily sessions with my faceless questioner were relieved by daily air raids. They usually started between seven and eight at night. My view was limited to the narrow strip of window near the ceiling. The orchestral display of 'son et lumiere' relieved the tedium of the evenings. There was the anti-aircraft fire that sounded with uneven booms. The machine guns would come in swells like violins and the deep percussion was provided from the occasional bombs. It was impressive but a thunderstorm one night shook me out of my lethargy. Until I heard the rain I entertained the numbing thought that we might have switched to nuclear warfare.

During the day distraction was provided by the cats and kittens in the air conditioning system. The cats screamed at each other and the kittens howled. They scratched their claws in the metal ducts. The noise grated, amplified by the length of the system. I begged the guards to do something about either saving the kittens or me. They laughed, and claimed each had equal rights to a share of the prison.

The only other distraction was the interrogator. He eventually shed his scarf when he lost face, by being unable to sit cross-legged as long as I could. It was unfair - I had been seven years in Turkoman country sitting on the floor and he had been seven years sitting behind a desk at Texas A. and M. University.

After two weeks, an allowance of two showers, and smelling abominably in my one shirt and blue jeans, I was told I had two hours to collect my things and I would be released. My things consisted of an extra pair of underpants, Barbara Tuchman's 'A Distant Mirror' and a tooth brush.

I collected them; made sure the blanket was neatly folded on the cot and sat dizzily waiting for the moment. By this time I had lost so much weight that my clothes were hanging in loose folds and I could only keep the jeans up by clutching them around the waist. I was blindfolded and led upstairs. I was dumped into the back seat of a car where once more I was ordered to keep my head down.

Just before reaching Damghan Avenue the blindfold was removed. I was taken to the door of our house by two guards who were unsuccessfully averting their unshielded faces. This attempted anonymity was short-lived as the two house servants, Hormoz and Ismail, were sitting on the door-step in front of a sealed door. They were complaining that they had no way in. The guards with me did not have permission to break the seal either. Someone went to telephone the Central Committee for permission to break the seal and the two guards played soccer with local boys in the street.

Somebody finally came with permission to open the door. It was a mistake. The inside of the house was piled knee high in debris. There were books, slides, papers, melon rinds and clothes all mixed together as if by a giant churn. Cockroaches were feasting happily on all the edible bits. The kitchen was heaped with dirty dishes and uneaten, rotting food. The bedrooms had 'DEATH TO AMERICA' and 'ALLAH AKBAR' written in flowing script over the closets with lipstick and blue eye shadow. The bathroom had similar sentiments on the tile walls written in excrement. The guards apologized briefly, disclaimed responsibility and asked for a list of missing items to be prepared by the next morning. Missing indeed! Without even looking I knew there was one husband, the Toyota Jeep they took with the guns and, in that mess, who would ever know.

Hormoz and I cleared narrow paths through the debris in a 'fox and goose' fashion just to be able to move from the telephone to the kitchen and to bed and bath.

We had just finished when the air raid siren sounded and shouts of "khamoush kon" (lights off) sounded in the street. I was too tired to break the two week fast but I did telephone some friends to ask them to contact Roshan and explain what had happened.

Narcy lasted a further six weeks in detention mainly, I suspect, because he ate all they gave him. The dogs survived the experience and had even grown fat, fed by the pasdars and the neighbours who had felt sorry for them.

When the Turkomans discovered that I was in jail, Ghara Balkan fell to the beaver-like axes of Nouri and his brother Avaz. They so devastated that mountain top that it would serve as an illustration for Malraux's 'The Walnut Trees of Altenburg'. Ghara Tepe Sheikh survived with Elias helpfully removing all felt carpets and household goods to his place in case we should not return.

Chapter 19

War with Iraq and an Argument with a Scud

Whilst life on the whole in Teheran returned to the normal frenetic bustle of an Oriental city shortly after the Revolution, there were some inevitable changes.

The avenue in front of the American Embassy became the 'Den of Spies' and was closed to vehicular traffic. Renamed from Takht-e Jamshid to Taleghani (Throne of Jamshid to Ayatollah Taleghani), the space in front of the red-brick Chancery was permanently occupied by demonstrators waving clenched fists and chanting "Death to America", "Death to Carter", "Death to Hypocrites" and whatever else appealed. The hypnotic chant must have been unnerving for the American Diplomats caged within, as even the most illiterate of them must have understood this much Persian. They had no way of knowing whether this was a personal threat or morale building for the slightly uneasy Revolutionary Government of the Islamic Republic of Iran, themselves at a loss to know America's intentions.

The pace and temper of activity in front of the Embassy seemed to depend on how negotiations between Iran and the U.S. were faring. The abortive raid to free the hostages that came to grief near the desert town of Tabas rated huge demonstrations. These included the sacrifice of a large camel by the front gate. The carcass was then dragged with a tractor to the west- side road of the Embassy compound leaving a wide, bloody trail. Just inside a small gate leading off this road into the compound was a Mullah, poking through the body bags of U.S. servicemen brought back from the Tabas crash scene.

Roshan, who was at that time working for The BBC, and I, just happened to be walking past. On the same day we also just happened to be walking past the Amjadiyeh Stadium on the east -side of the U.S. Embassy compound and noticed that it was festooned with yellow ribbons. Who had hung these premature standards of relief and joy?

At any rate, none of this made any apparent difference to the time of detention. After four hundred and forty days in captivity, I do not suppose the hostages cared if Oliver North had baked the Iranian authorities a chocolate cake or arms had been clandestinely shifted to Iran through Israel for their struggle against Iraq in an attempt to bribe their freedom.

Of overwhelming importance to Iran was not some hostage crisis. The procrastination at the beginning of that episode ensured they would be left to languish in a jail of their own construction. Iran was in a life and death struggle for its own survival. Already faced with shortages of food and fuel, the war put a cruel strain on the populace and the infrastructure.

The government was composed of differing factions, none with any experience in governing. The army had dissolved itself, the Generals had either fled or been executed. The only item of food still readily available was bread but, at that, there were long bread lines every morning and evening. There was no meat, butter, milk, eggs. There were no vegetables and no fruit. The only edible item left seemed to be golden caviar – the Royal Court no longer having a monopoly, it flooded the market but only a few were left who had developed a taste for this delicacy and it went unsold. Narcy and I and a few friends ate this for breakfast, lunch and dinner washed down with the remaining bottles of Chivas Regal until the sight of both made us nauseous.

Amazingly, Iran rallied to the threat posed by Iraq. Soldiers who had thrown down their rifles in disgust during the Revolution picked them up and marched enthusiastically to the front. Urban citizens complaining about the deprivations caused by the Revolution, tightened their belts, contributed the gold of their wedding rings to the cause and joined the Baseej (local Militia) to protect the cities, while their sons marched to confront the Iraqis on the battlefield. Differences were forgotten while everyone rallied to protect Iran.

If there was ever any question about the longevity of the Revolution the Iraqis provided the solution. No one was going to let the Arabs into Persian land again. Martial law, of course, is also a major deterrent to opposition. A counter-revolutionary can be summarily dealt with under times of crisis; and that this undoubtedly was. All of a sudden there seemed to be a lot of counter-revolutionaries.

The war came home to the inhabitants of Teheran with the Iraqi bombing of the city from aeroplanes. Every night at about seven o'clock the air raid sirens would fill our ears. Shortly after, the sound of bombs exploding further shattered our ear-drums. Our fox terriers became shivering wrecks as they dived under the furniture. We listened as the bombs walked their way towards us wondering if, this time, we were the ones to be unlucky. Tinky, one of the most vociferous of the fox terriers was fingered as an enemy spy.

"He tells the Iraqis where we are," complained one Revolutionary Guard to our servant, Ibrahim.

"We will have to shoot him," they added, trying to squeeze past Ibrahim into the house.

"No, please, I will tell Khanum and I am sure she will make him stop," he cried, terrified lest something happen to the dog while we were away.

At that time we were on the Turkoman Steppes trying to sort out some chaos and had trouble returning because of the mass exodus of citizens turning the road to the north one way, their way.

"That's all right, Ibrahim," I told him. "You tell the Pasdars that Tinky is a watch-dog and he is warning them of the Iraqis arrival and then barking to chase them off."

That mollified the Pasdars and we heard no more about canine counter-revolutionary activities.

While the bombs caused widespread damage to the cities it was the Scud missiles which struck terror into everyone's hearts. They came without warning at any time of the day or night. There was no pattern to the devastation, as if the Scuds had been sent off to find targets at will. Gradually, large vacuums appeared between the buildings. Where yesterday there had been a department store today there was a crater. Where the day before there had been an apartment building today the bulldozers had created an instant parking lot. Bulldozers raced ambulances to the scenes of devastation. Ambulatory victims of the bombing scrambled over debris to reach the outside before the bulldozers flattened the damage. No one could understand why the hurry to create more parking lots in a city where most of the denizens had fled. Teheran, which has always had a traffic problem, suddenly became a paradise of open boulevards and unfettered roads. Whereas it usually took up to two hours to cross Teheran, the same journey was now accomplished in half an hour of relaxed driving. Everyone who could escape fled to the Caspian or to outlying towns. Some were simply pitched up in the hills, sleeping at night curled up in blankets on the hard ground. Instant millionaires were made from selling water, kerosene and bread. A tent rented for ten thousand toumans a night (one hundred U.S. dollars) and an articulated van for thirty thousand. Some speculated that more people had died from snake bites than from Scuds.

Coupons were issued, gas rationing was instituted and kerosene became non-existent. Even fabric became scarce as more and more was needed for shrouds as the bodies began coming back. Mourning a victim was not allowed. The telephone call that announced the death of a soldier congratulated the family on achieving a martyr and rewarded the families with chickens and eggs and permission to shop in special stores. Later, the families of martyrs were given more special privileges, places in University, opportunities to buy cars, start businesses, export permits and other inducements to smother any anger at the waste of human life.

Although the war finally stopped in 1988, the bodies were still coming back in the year 2000 and prisoners of war were still being exchanged. Within two years of Iran declaring a truce, they started to exchange friendly visits. This was probably due to Desert Storm where the Iraqis faced their previous allies and lost so badly. That time it was the Kuwaitis with their latest model up-grade cars that were making one-way traffic east and battling with the snakes at night. Proof that 'my enemy's enemy' can become my friend and, indeed, in rapid turn-around order.

It was the arrival of the motor of a Scud missile through the roof of our house in Avenue Damghan that persuaded me that I would rather not end my life in Teheran. The smoking metal remains landed by the dining room table shortly after we had left it. Narcy was out in the street enjoying the commotion attendant to a Scud strike and I was probably cowering in the basement with the dogs.

Pasdars rushed into the house with a blanket to claim the treasure. Narcy was stoutly defending what was his by right of domain. He lost, and the Pasdars bore their booty off in triumph.

The Iraqis seemed to be finally getting their range, somewhere around the immediate vicinity of our house that was conveniently situated in the middle of downtown Teheran. We were one short block from Ferdowsi Square that was one long block from the British Embassy in one direction and three blocks from the American Embassy in the other. I thought it was high time we joined the general exodus.

Narcy was enjoying the anarchy and chaos too much to contemplate removing himself from the fray. His Construction Company had been confiscated, much to his relief, and much to the chagrin of his confiscators when they discovered all his assets were attached by a catholic assortment of banks. For the first time in years he was free of worry and he intended to savour life to the full.

I liked savouring life too but did not feel that what we were doing was contributing in any large measure to the furthering of it.

Providence in the form of a bright new Islamic Republic of Iran passport allowed Narcy to finally leave the country after eight years. He had not seen his parents since they left for Paris in 1978; his father having died in the meantime. He had also not seen Ateshe and Caren for several years.

Roshan had married David Reddaway, Third Secretary of the British Embassy in Teheran, and Narcy had missed the London wedding which was known as the 'other wedding' coming shortly after that of Prince Charles and Lady Diana.

After he left for a five-month tour of family and friends I began looking for land a safe commuting distance from Teheran. My father had died in 1979, leaving me a small legacy. I thought he would be pleased to know I was using it to save my life – if not my wits.

Farhad Seif, a friend with whom I had left some horses in Teheran, and I together bought a small fruit garden in Kurdan. This was a village on the slopes of the Alborz, mountains fifty-five kilometres west of Teheran. We built a stable and started on the foundations of a house, helped by Roger Cooper who was waiting for an exit permit to return to Dubai.

Narcy eventually returned and was appalled at what I had done; Roger was taken to jail for six years – nothing to do with helping in the nefarious garden project – and Farhad decided to take his stake and move up-river. Although after some months the situation calmed down, Narcy never moved his clothes from No.10 Damghan although he took over the running of what he called "this waste of time." As it turned out, it was Narcy who initiated the final big plunge into Caspians.

Kurdan in the foothills of the Alborz mountains
Photo: Brenda Dalton

Louise in her living room at Kurdan and (right) in the stallion yard –
photo: Brenda Dalton

Buying Caspians from the Revolutionary Guard at Jallilabad
A final foray into Caspians following the war with Iraq

 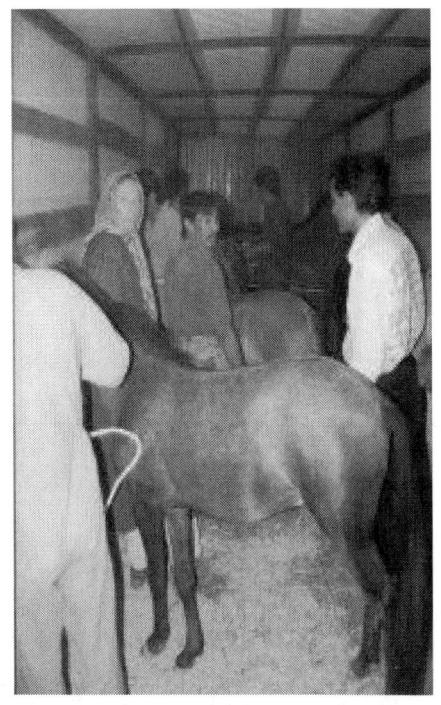

Left: Secandar Gol – a stallion purchased from the Revolutionary Guard
Right: The 1994 shipment leaving for the U.K. (They arrived in 1995)

Chapter 20

Kurdan, War horses and Great Personal Loss

The revolution had a rejuvenating effect on Narcy. Perhaps we had become complacent with the comforts, luxury and abundance of material goods under the Shah's regime. Under the new administration we were forced to forego such frivolous niceties as food, soap powder and gasoline. Ration coupons were issued and long lines formed outside shops. A Zoroastrian friend of ours used to join any queue he found, on the grounds that he did not want to miss anything. This same Zoroastrian lived in an ancient house near the British Embassy compound where he would invite us for dinner, give us a shovel and tell us to dig up our own cocktails. Buried in the long-disused flower- beds was a cornucopia of Johnny Walker Black Label and Remy Martin.

Narcy cheerfully admitted that he had not felt so young since College. "I think it was taking my clothes to the dry cleaners," he said. "It reminds me of my University days."

There had always been servants to do the laundry, cook, clean the house and deal with red tape. Now there was only us; the servants having all departed for the front with the exception of one. He stayed by the front door and eventually made a lot of money selling vodka to the Pasdars. The Teheran Tower Hotel across the street from us was taken over by the Revolutionary Guards, as was the French Club, one garden to the east of our house. Chains were stretched over the road on both sides of our block to prevent access to any traffic but official Revolutionary cars. Fortunately our garden had a back gate that led to a narrow alley and what used to be called Shah Reza became either Freedom or Revolution Avenue. I had trouble remembering all the new names of the streets, especially as they tended to change every few months from Ayatollah to Martyr so I stuck to the original names adding 'sabegh' or 'formerly known as'.

There was a Persian version of a Polish joke making the rounds; "A Rashti (person from Rasht in northern Iran) was in Teheran for the first time since the Revolution, carefully watching how people were taking taxis. He saw them hail the orange cabs and yell "such and such a street, sabegh". Wanting to travel several kilometres along the same street he yelled "straight ahead, sabegh.""

In addition to our enforced regime or diet we were discouraged from acting as if we were having a good time. Music and singing were outlawed.

So was laughing publicly. I once saw several boys hauled off for having a snowball fight in the street. Video films were prohibited (which meant the black market was thriving), cinemas were closed, satellite TV had yet to arrive but when it did and we had all become addicted to the 'Soaps', it too was prohibited. Alcohol was prohibited which meant we all learned how to make it and there was a run on pressure cookers and a shortage of raisins. Narcy made delicious 'mead' out of honey but his beer bottles had a tendency to explode, sounding suspiciously like the start of another revolution. Women were required to wear scarves and a long coat, like a house –coat, or a chador which is like a scarf that runs from the top of your head to the tips of your toes. It is about as impractical a garment as was ever devised although it does make shoplifting easier. Socks or stockings must be worn, but not flesh toned. Make-up was not allowed although by 2001 this restriction appeared to have been lifted and spectacular 'designer' models of chadors had appeared, only to disappear again very soon after.

After our ancient Toyota Jeep had been returned by the Pasdars we parked it in the garden and used buses. The thirty litres of gasoline a month we were allowed was just enough to keep the battery turning over. Eventually we joined the black market game and travelled with a sixty-litre barrel of gasoline in the back from which we syphoned off gas as needed. I once pumped more than thirty litres into the tank at a gas station, my attention having wandered. My driving licence was confiscated until I could come up with the necessary extra coupons and exchange them for my papers. Feeling guilty became a way of life.

With the purchase of the land in Kurdan, I cheerfully abandoned the house at no. 10 Damghan Avenue. The house was rented from a Zoroastrian lady who had fled to Florida with the first whiff of tear gas. Various groups of Pasdars visited the house and considered its confiscation but fortunately for Narcy the premises were considered too shabby: far more palatial residences that could now be occupied were abundant. Kurdan was an undiscovered paradise. It was an old village nestled in amongst groves of ancient mulberry trees at the base of the mountains. The worn mud walls of the gardens hid apple trees, pear and cherry. Huge wooden gates ensured absolute privacy. The narrow, dirt alleys were just wide enough for two donkeys to pass. Every family had at least one cow, some chickens and a vegetable garden. All of a sudden we re-discovered butter and cheese. After I had devoured a whole day's supply of cheese in a neighbour's house, it was suggested that we buy our own cow.

She was a lovely little black cow and came along with her heifer calf. Accustomed to making butter back in my youth in Virginia I happily separated cream and churned butter. Roshan sent me some cheese starter from London and we were once more eating. We bought two young steers, fattened them and added them to the freezer. We bought some chickens and ducks and planted a vegetable garden. We planted cherry, apple, pear and apricot trees. We had never eaten so well in our lives nor enjoyed the process of growing, harvesting and preparing food as much. We suddenly discovered friends we never knew we had.

Our dogs took a new lease on life. They discovered mice and rats, hares, foxes and jackals. They shuddered at the distant sound of Scud strikes and bombs but no longer dived under beds. The Scuds did not look so menacing as they flew over the valley heading for Teheran, resembling a lit cigarette travelling backwards.

We kept a few of our own horses in the stables but sent the bulk back to Ghara Tepe Sheikh. As there were extra stalls we rented them out to friends which, by now, were mainly diplomats – Persians having departed for kinder shores. The Kurdan River flowed near the farm and on the other side there were the foothills of the Alborz. The valley of the Assassins was over the mountains, where the remains of Noah's Ark were believed to nestle undiscovered.

Having diplomats for friends was nice because they were allowed to import all sorts of luxuries that they called necessities and they were kind enough to share with us. They always looked so neat with their beautifully laundered, new clothes (their washing powder was better than ours) driving their latest model, air-conditioned cars. The only draw-back to these friends was their propensity to feel that because they boarded a horse they could stay the night too, cultivating this habit with regularity every time there was a Scud strike, their servants fled and their dogs couldn't take it any longer. As late as midnight there would be a crash by the front door, a furious dogfight and an apologetic hail.

"So sorry!" We didn't wake you, did we?"

"Of course not! How nice to see you", pulling apart three fox terriers and a visiting behemoth of a Great Dane.

"We just didn't know what to do. Our servants fled, there is nothing to eat and all of a sudden three Scuds hit right near the Embassy Residence."

There is really nothing more distraught than an upset Diplomat. For some reason they think diplomatic immunity should apply to bombs which, as far as the German Embassy Residence was concerned, was correct: their scud didn't explode. The British did not fare so well as they lost one bungalow completely and suffered a fairly shattered Residence. This explosion also took out the shard room of the British Institute for Persian Studies.

The Norwegian First Secretary, Oystein Steiro and his statuesque wife Berit became very good friends throughout what must have been, for them, a trying time. Eventually a distraught Berit was obliged to escort the evacuating Norwegian Ambassador's wife over the border to Turkey in the middle of a harsh winter storm but until then the Steiros, their two horses and their pet wolf were regular inhabitants of our house. Oystein was two metres tall, owned a 16 hand, chestnut Turkoman stallion and took his wolf riding with him in the hills. People used to park by our gate to wait for Oystein to return from his rides just to watch this unusual Viking. He was stopped once by some Pasdars who tried to prevent him from getting out of his car in Kurdan. The wolf herded them back to their car and the Pasdars never returned.

One evening, after the war with Iraq had ended, a friend we had not seen for many years came in through the door. Bahman Aliari had stayed in touch with the Horse Society people and still stabled his horse at the ex-Royal Stables in Farahabad. He was, he said, in contact with the Revolutionary Guards who had taken over the old Army Remount Station in Jallilabad near Varamin fifty kilometres south of Teheran.

"They want to meet you," he said, indicating me.

"Why?"

"They think you may be able to help them with a problem they are having with all those horses they have collected," he said.

Somewhat churlishly I hoped they were having a lot of problems. The Revolutionary Guards had attempted a clean sweep of all the horses in the province of Mazanderan at some point during the war. Having denied them our horses I had gone after the rest, complaining to the Horse Society and anyone else who would listen. The horses were destined for the front where, it was hoped, they, instead of the soldiers, would detonate the land mines. The reluctance of the horses to walk on the land mines had more to do with halting this practice than my complaints but, at any rate, large numbers of horses ended up in the corrals of Jallilabad. The Revolutionary Guards thought I might be able to help them dispose of these horses in a profitable way. They had heard about Caspian horses and their popularity in England.

A time was arranged and Bahman, Ateshe, who was visiting from the U.S, Narcy and I drove to Jallilabad. The road wound south of Teheran through some mud slums, past crumbling factories and into the open countryside. There were neat plots of ground where fresh herbs were grown, rows of tomatoes and cucumbers. There were mud-walled villages, an occasional horse-drawn cart full of produce and donkeys staggering under heavy loads. There was a string of camels carrying manure towards the city and a few flocks of sheep.

During the time of various Shahs, Jallilabad had been a thriving Remount Centre for the cavalry. American Military advisors had counseled against keeping the horses on the grounds that this was the twentieth century, but the anachronism had persisted and horses were still being produced at the time of the Revolution. Shortly thereafter economy dictated that they no longer be fed and they were released into the Great Salt Desert (Dasht-e-Kavir). Shortly after that the war with Iraq started and the Generals hit upon the idea of sending animals over the mine-fields. They tried donkeys with no success; they rounded up private horses (the released Remount horses having mainly succumbed to wolves and leopards) and sent them to the front with similar negative results. Somebody suggested that since there were so many wild boar, they could be rounded up and sent to detonate the mines. That last idea never germinated as no one could figure out how to capture that many wild boar, much less transport and persuade them to join the Iraqis.

Now that the war was over something had to be done with all of these horses, by this time totally wild. We looked over the mud walls of the large corrals at hundreds of milling horses. There were six of these enclosures, each about a hectare in size and each holding around three hundred horses standing knee-deep in a mixture of fine dust and dried manure. There were mangers along all four sides and the horses had obviously been well fed. Tractors pulling trailers of fresh alfalfa and straw were driving into the corrals and depositing the contents for the eager horses.

It was explained to me by the Captain in charge that I was to go into the corrals one by one and pick out likely looking Caspians. When I had selected one he would send his 'soldiers' to catch it. As I tried to move quietly towards the horses they threw up their heads, snorted and stampeded for the far side of their lot. This raised a cloud of dust that completely obscured them. I waited for the dust to settle and tried once more to get close. The rush to distance themselves was repeated and I was left sneezing and rubbing water from my eyes. Eventually I spotted a small creature hiding amongst the legs of its larger cousins and cried "Talley Ho". Five soldiers were sent in with ropes to catch the unfortunate animal. If I had thought my lone presence was terrifying for the horses, the attack formation of the soldiers petrified them. They went round and round and I was sure they would melt into ghee. Suddenly, out of the cloud of impenetrable dust emerged one small kicking horse dragging five bruised and battered soldiers. And it was a Caspian.

This process was repeated for four more hours during which time we managed to isolate eight horses of Caspian appearance. The heat was scorching, the dust was choking and no one thought to bring any water. It was not until I was soaking my head in a horse trough that one of the soldiers was dispatched to bring some ice-cold lemonade. I have never been so grateful for something to drink.

At this point we were invited into an air-conditioned trailer which served as an office, offered tea and began the serious business of deciding how we were going to set this venture up. Gradually I began to understand that the Pasdars had a partnership in mind. We would go half-and-half, they finding the horses and we paying a nominal sum for them as well as stabling, feeding, breaking and finding markets for them. I thought I made it clear to the Pasdars that these horses could not be shipped to the British just like this. First they had to prove themselves as good breeding stock and then we would sell and send the foals. Either they did not wish to believe this or they deliberately misunderstood.

The terror at being manhandled did not abate with removal from the herd and long upturned hooves had to be treated by drastic action with a saw before any semblance of a hoof shape returned.

After some months of working with these horses, during which time we kept the emergency ward of the local hospital fully occupied with broken bones, the Pasdars decided we were ready to begin bringing in the large profits they envisioned. When I told them this was not possible, that first we had to establish the breeding herd, they lost interest. Narcy bought out their fifty percent share and we now owned quite a large herd of Caspians as more forays into the Jallilabad herds had been made since that first trip.

Narcy had inherited a small amount of money when his father died. He used this to add several hectares of land in Kurdan and to build a barn for the new Caspians. The Pony Company, as it was called, expanded to supposedly include imports and exports of goods other than horses. In the end further business did not materialise and it remained simply a holding company for these horses. As was envisioned, the horses multiplied and thrived and pretty soon we did have some horses to export. Rather grudgingly the Horse Society gave us seven export permits and we prepared to send them to England where we were assured buyers were eagerly awaiting this new Foundation Stock blood.

How to get them to England was the big question. Since the Revolution our quarantine status had lapsed into a state of decay. Apparently the veterinarians who were supposed to send six-monthly reports to the World Organisation for Animal Health (O.I.E) had neglected to do this. We were crossed off the list of 'clean' countries that could export their animals to EC countries. Christina Dodwell who had been our guest in Iran when she was researching for her book, 'A Traveller on Horseback', wrote that she had found an answer to our problem. She said there was a man called Ron Meddes who regularly brought horses in from Russia and he was willing to quarantine the seven Caspians in Belarus for a long enough period for them to become, in effect, Russian horses. He said that six weeks was sufficient. Somehow naively I believed this and little did I think we would 'lose' them for eight months.

We found a transport company that was willing to take the horses in one of its large articulated Scania tractor-trailers. We loaded enough feed and water for ten days and then squeezed in the seven Caspians: four stallions and three mares. I accompanied the truck as far as Astara on the Persian-Russian Azerbaijan border. A bit of palm greasing got them through Customs and they disappeared down a dusty road on their way through Daghestan, Chechnia and up to Belarus. The drivers refused to take me any further lest my presence should attract the attentions of the warring factors en route. The Turkoman groom we had sent with the horses returned six weeks later. His visa had run out and he had gotten himself lost in the wilds of Russia trying to get back to Iran. There was one telephone call from Moscow with a plaintive cry for help but there was not much I could do from that distance. When he finally limped back into Ghara Tepe Sheikh he swore he would never work with horses again; and he has not.

Six months later the horses finally reached England. They had been driven in an open truck to Moscow to have their papers stamped and then retraced their steps in the middle of winter across Russia and northern Europe. They left Iran in September and arrived in England in February, luckily not much the worse for wear.

Unfortunately I had not made my position clear to the owners and breeders of Caspians in England. I was under the impression that they were desperately anxious for fresh breeding stock; that without it their stud programmes could not proceed without too much inbreeding. The cost to us was three thousand pounds sterling per Caspian and this was the price I was charging. Only two buyers paid this price for the four hors-es they took. The other three were 'auctioned' at five hundred pounds each. Narcy and I were faced with a large deficit that we could ill afford. In an attempt to cut our costs with the Caspians, we trucked them to Ghara Tepe Sheikh where they could graze outside for most of the year and thus cost us less.

In the spring of 1994, disaster struck. First our dog, Capie, was bitten by a rabid dog and died; but not before I had become contaminated and had to be given the rabies vaccination. The shots were of ten days duration. During this time, the helicopter in which my sister-in-law, Barbara Schell, a Diplomat with the U.S. mission for the Kurds sta-tioned in Incirlik, Turkey, was travelling was shot down by mistake over northern Iraq. Narcy was distraught when I phoned him, having heard the news on the television. He insisted I return to Teheran but I was still getting rabies shots and did not think the competent author-ities would continue them there. On the last day of the shots, as I was driving to the hospital, I was stopped by a friend who had received a telephone call from my son, Caren, saying Narcy was desperately ill and in the hospital. I asked him to tell the Turkomans at the farm that I would continue to Teheran without coming back.

I arrived in Kurdan to find the house empty and still. Narcy was in a hospital in Teheran. The next morning I drove to the hospital and finally found Narcy lying comatose and the doctors saying he had gone into kidney failure. The doctors told me that there was no hope. Narcy rallied for ten days and then his heart stopped. During this period he was barely able to speak and the only words he uttered were; "I want to go home."

I wish I had taken him home. Intensive care is not a good place to die. We buried Narcy in the little village grave yard in Kurdan. The Tur-komans held a ceremony on the steppes to honour him. Kambiz Atabai overcame his reluctance to communicate with anyone in Iran and sent a long fax via the British Embassy remembering all of the things Narcy had done to help the children of Iran to learn to love horses. The British Caspian Society sent a large floral wreath.

Unbeknownst to me Narcy's accountant suddenly claimed that Nar-cy had borrowed a large sum of money and this should be paid back immediately. I was convinced that Narcy would have told me if this was true but there was no longer any way to check this. There were no cheques and no IOU's but the family decided that honour demanded that this sum be paid. I sold some land and sold the Caspians to the

Ministry of Jehad Sassandeghi (Ministry of Reconstruction) and paid the money.

Narcy was one of a kind; irresistible, charming and highly respected by everyone. His inherent kindness and generosity, and that of his family, was all-enduring.

Chapter 21

A Failed Export Attempt and Trekking on the Turkoman Steppes

The property at Kurdan was divided up between the children. Roshan and her husband, David, built a lovely Persian style house on their 'quarter' and Ateshe sold her land, on which stood one of the large stable blocks, complete with flat. I continued to run the house, which was to become Caren's, and the property at Ghara Tepe Sheikh, some ten hours distant, and commuted between the two.

John Schneider-Merke, a friend of Narcy's, bought Ateshe's part of the inheritance and asked if I would find, and manage, a herd of Caspians there on his behalf. John's father had been a veterinary surgeon and assisted in saving the Austrian Lipizzaner horses during World War ll. I think he felt obliged to keep up the family tradition. I pointed out to John that starting a Caspian herd from scratch was a tricky proposition. Of the original horses purchased for breeding over fifty percent are generally culled within the first four months; of those kept for breeding a further fifty percent are culled after their foals prove unacceptable. Horse dealers from all over northern Iran soon heard that we were looking for horses and would arrive with half starved specimens of all shapes and sizes, at any time of the day or night. After we had sent a few of them away with a flea in their ear, they became more discerning and started to bring suitable horses, a few of which were extremely good. Whilst most of them recovered, with lots of loving care and ill-afforded barley, some had little or no chance of survival. The horses that bred true to type were kept in the herd and the ones of suspect origin that failed to produce Caspian type stock were sold or given to local children to ride.

Life continued to be interspersed with the effects of the revolution. The authorities were still confiscating properties and it was hardly a surprise when one of Narcy's cousins arrived on my doorstep one morning, distraught because his house had just been confiscated.

John Simpson, the BBC's foreign correspondent, who had dedicated one of his books to Narcy, came for lunch at Kurdan the day after the elections, early in 2001, and did a twenty four minute interview on Turkoman and Caspian horses. His camera crew had been beaten and taken to jail the night before while they were filming the victory celebrations in Park Mellat in Teheran.

Whilst the Ministry of Jehad continued to breed the Persicus herd that they bought following Narcy's death and included Zeeland,, John's herd eventually reached almost sixty in strength. He ran into problems when he removed his horses from my control and they were sold by my successor, without his permission. It was a problem that took almost four years and several court cases to resolve in his favour but John never did get his horses back.

In the meantime, the USA had started to purchase horses from the UK and Australia and it was obvious that, if faults were not to appear through inbreeding, further bloodlines needed to be exported from Iran.

The authorities toyed with the idea of granting further export licences but, despite a visit from the International Registrar, Brenda Dalton, from the UK, to explain that a lack of new bloodlines in the west would eventually lead to inbreeding, they never finally agreed.

Although I decided not to raise Caspians any more, one day a young Canadian, whose main equestrian interest was long distance riding, came to visit and bought some of the Jehad Caspians. Brent Seufert and I trawled the areas where Caspian ponies might still be found and Brent made several visits to Iran finding and purchasing Turkoman stock. Only by filling a chartered plane could the transport costs be justified.

Three times, preliminary permission was granted, only to be rescinded at the next level. On one occasion the shipment was approved at the second stage and the horses were moved to Kurdan for quarantine purposes.

For three weeks, forty horses were quarantined in my yard at Kurdan waiting for export permission. Brent was unable to order the aeroplane to take them to Canada until the final export papers were signed. At my request, Brenda Dalton wrote to the Minister reiterating the point that without new bloodlines in the west there would eventually be problems with inbreeding. I started to wake up at hourly intervals during the night agonising over the forty horses in quarantine standing in snow, ice and mud outside my bedroom window. The adviser to the Ministry of Jehad denied permission for Brent's Caspians to go to Canada on the grounds that they were foundation stock. He asked for an additional registration system to include foundation animals and their offspring. Only when this stock had a specified number of offspring could the foals be considered for export.

The proceeds of sales from breeding the Turkoman horses and the funds raised from keeping horses for friends were barely sufficient to keep me afloat, let alone buy the fodder to maintain the mares and stallions during the winter months. I had to find a new way to keep myself and my horses.

It was suggested to me that the amazing rides through the forests of Golestan enjoyed by myself, friends and family could be extended to include paying visitors and, to that end, I established a relationship with a company called 'Magic Carpet Travel' and later another named 'In the Saddle', who found riders from far flung places to come and enjoy the glorious terrain of the national park and to experience the occasional sightings of wild boar, bear and leopard along the way.

One of the early ventures attracted only one visitor, Ruth Staines from England. "You can still come" I told her "as long as you don't mind exploring". We were accompanied by Roshan and her family. It was the second of five visits that Ruth eventually made.

A visit from an Australian group was accompanied by a film crew for a series called 'The Grey Voyagers'. The screening gave us valuable publicity and encouraged several more guests from Australia to visit us.

My grandson, Alex, and various friends, including Maziar Jamshydkhani, a young Iranian rider who had learned to ride on Caspians, often accompanied us on horseback. Shortly before Brenda's visit he had won the National Jumping Championships before promptly breaking his leg in a non-horse related incident which relegated him to practising his photography skills from the back-up truck.

We were usually accompanied by two Turkoman grooms, whilst another drove the truck carrying tents, food and the occasional non-riding guest. Young horses were led or ran loose, alongside ridden horses, to give them experience as future mounts. We would often ride for eight to ten hours at a time. At night we tethered the horses and shared the companionship of local villagers, who were always surprised and delighted to have us visit. It was safer to stay close to a village at night to avoid unwelcome visits from bear, wolf, boar or snakes. Each ride turned into a new adventure and we often took directions and advice from the villagers where we spent the night, although I had usually ridden the trails with the grooms in advance.

The terrain was varied and unfolded continually from narrow tracks within side-stepping distance of deep ravines, and possible disaster, to vast open spaces, green with the young shoots of barley. High up on vast rock faces were the entrances to caves where, centuries before, those incapable of completing nomadic drives were hidden, out of reach of predators, with sufficient food to live out their few remaining days.

I had long planned to ride to Jargalan, where Dr. Ghiadi, a breeder and supporter of the Caspian and Turkoman, kept his horses, two hundred miles away across the mountains and close to the border with Turkmenistan. Ruth came once more with a party of riders from England. Amongst the party was Bridget Tempest, an artist, who sketched and painted her way to Jargalan, returning at the end of the treck to paint the horses at Ghara Tepe Sheikh.

We left Ghara Tepe Sheikh with two of the grooms leading spare horses at the rear. Turning our backs to the ancient ramparts of Alexander's Wall, we followed the vast dry river valley, the dust rolling up like November fog from the feet of the horses in front, forming a thick crust on the sweaty flanks of those behind.

A long, hard climb for the horses brought us on to high downland of wheat fields speckled with poppies and edged with hawthorn, split by an arrow-straight track of beaten earth. Rollers, gaudy birds that look like jays in kingfishers' clothing, flitted ahead of us among the bushes, and invisible quails chuckled in the corn.

Blind valleys and Parthian terraces bore two thousand year old crops of pomegranates and vines. We escaped the burning sun by riding through cool forests of beech, oak and sycamore and camped close to a waterfall, where two streams merged to form a rocky pool in which to cool off and remove the dust from the day's ride. One of the grooms, on back-up duty in the truck, waited with a crate of alcohol-free beer and slices of watermelon. We rugged the horses and tethered them with a nosebag of rolled barley.

Next morning we began a two thousand foot climb out of the forest. At intervals we met donkeys, almost invisible under loads of fresh grass, or men and women struggling out of the thickets with armfuls to lay beside the road, ready for collection, as hay, by nightfall.

The little mare Ghezeli became a victim of the parasite parafilaira multipapillosa from the Gorgan River and began to bleed heavily from the neck. The rapidly-maturing effect of hot muscle caused the grub to emerge with the oozing sweat. By evening the blood-sweating was complete and the wound had closed without trace.

Bridget, who was an accomplished rider, discarded her mount when it struggled to keep up and opted for one of the pack horses; Ghyzyl Khan, a Yabou, a Central Asian type not as elegant as the Turkoman, with a straight neck and an upright shoulder. His legs were 'feathered' (hairy) but the breed is tough, feisty and able to go all day.

That night, we camped in a water meadow below the village of Jambulak. By damming the trickle through the meadow we created pools for washing, watering the horses, and filling the tea pots that simmered constantly in the fire to combat the dust from the trail.

That evening, hordes of villagers came strolling down the road to inspect the foreigners. After supper, we had a more sinister visitation. "Head scarves!" I called urgently, as a green and white truck drew up by the camp, out of which stepped two menacing looking policemen. Despite my careful preparations they had not been told that we would be passing through. They obviously considered that ladies riding horses were not very important in the great scheme of things and quickly dismissed us for better crimes.

The damp shady woods of ancient, gnarled hawthorn trees wore long beards of lichen that provided shelter the following morning. Two radar scanners loomed high on top of the highest mountain in the district and served as a guide. We dropped down into a deep valley where a tiny stream split a hillside rough with granite. Its clean, hard rock was refreshing after days of crumbling mud hillsides. We watered the horses at the ford in the village, where children clammered to gape at us open-mouthed and women with babies on their hips came from mud-brick houses to watch us pass. Finally, we reached the summit and looked down on to the vastness of an arid valley some four thousand feet below and more miles across than we could guess. A few hundred feet below us, a vulture circled.

If Iran had advanced sufficiently to impose Health and Safety laws, the path down from the summit would most certainly not have passed. The recent heavy rains had cracked the mud, splitting it into flaking chunks that might at any moment break off and sledge down the mountainside, taking the horses, and us, with them. We looked down on to new country: barren desert of low brown hills dotted with scrub, broken here and there by dull grey crags and scree. In the small village at the bottom, the tinkling of goat bells vied with the rant of a mullah, hammering through an open window from someone's radio. The watercourse was dry. The horses remained thirsty.

Crossing one dry stream bed after another, we began to climb again, slowly, towards the head of the valley, where tiny settlements clustered at the feet of small sharp-pointed hills, and wheat grew doggedly wherever the land levelled out for a few yards. Still there was no water. At last we turned off into a side valley and found a tiny spring feeding a series of stone troughs. The horses sank their noses and drank. We banged their tether pegs into hard shale, while the grooms went to work erecting our tents under pomegranate trees at the foot of sandstone cliffs.

Overnight rain had damped down the dust. In this hostile region every available inch had been heavily fertilised and sown, with cornfield abruptly meeting desert in a series of intricate sweeping curves, like the interlocking of a jigsaw puzzle. There was no in-between, no fringe territory for the goatherd. Golden Orioles almost lost themselves among the brilliant yellow blossom of the Christ thorn bushes, and skylarks bubbled overhead.

We dropped abruptly and unexpectedly into a hidden canyon, a narrow crack in the rocks where the horses had to pass in single file, picking their way carefully over paths of slate and shale. Completely disorientated by a corkscrew series of paths, we took the wrong exit, and the unfortunate horses had to retrace their steps and climb out again by a different route. At last from the advantage of high ground we had a majestic view down to the Atrek River, which for much of its length marks the boundary between Turkmenistan and Iran.

Even the mighty Atrek, when we reached it, was no more than a shallow stream. The horses drank deeply then easily forded it, scorning the new metal bridge downstream. We crossed only the second tarmac road in a week. Scarves on and sleeves rolled down, we hustled quickly through the first sizeable village of our trek and climbed over a hump to find the mess tent already pitched for us in a natural amphitheatre of barren hills. The village headman followed us.

"This is no accommodation for ladies," he said, generously offering us hospitality in his own house. I declined his generous offer.

"The rougher it is, the better they like it."

Departure the next morning was slightly delayed whilst the grooms carried out a small farriery job on Ruth's mare, after which we left the Atrek valley to return to the highlands, where there were no villages, just scattered farmers' huts. Whole families had turned out to harvest the cumin crop, scything, stacking, threshing and carrying away.

The huts were small and spartan, puddled with mud to keep out the worst of the rain and with a thin triangular slit for entry. Inside was an oil stove, on a beaten earth floor.

An old lady, a Turkoman of the Göklan tribe, came to visit from a neighbouring hut. We sat drinking tea and looking out over the stunning view: to our right, the magnificent ridge of the Bozdag range, while to the left only the Razyndag now separated us from Jargalan. While we chatted to the old lady, Bridget was sketching her, giving her the finished painting. Part of the fascination of the steppe is its ever-changing landscape. We veered north along the ridge, east into the valley by the village of Kallata Mohammedberdi, and up again into the Razyndag. The scene changed: sharp, jagged rock colonised by sa'ul trees, the remains of a great forest, standing out cleanly against a washed blue sky, draped with shreds of cloud. Up through a narrow gorge and downward, teetering on the sheer edges of another great riverbed and we rode on into Jargalan.

Tidy settlements of mud-brick, their yards guarded by bleached wooden doors, warped and buckled with antiquity. Poplars hid them from the sun, walnuts and pomegranates grew in their well-stocked gardens, surrounded by mud-brick walls strong enough to retain the water, when it flowed.

We found a sizeable village and a shop; a shop stocked with fruit juice, which we drank greedily while the whole population, it seemed, gathered to look at us. The ladies found it impossible to turn their backs on this western style luxury. We camped just outside, in a meadow where the output of a spring had been skilfully guided through channels to the nearby gardens. For our last campfire the grooms piled the wood high, throwing on monstrous tree trunks that they had somehow managed to find.

Next morning we passed a natural bowl in the hills, where a dusty track formed an almost flat circle, the grandstand of Jargalan Racecourse. Another two hours riding found us at the home of Dr. Abdul Zalil Ghiadi, who had managed to find room to preserve some of the horses from Brent Seufert's failed shipment, along with his own Caspian and Turkoman horses.

The proceeds of the ride kept the horses for the rest of the year. Brent had been trying for two years to get permission to export his horses. During this time he had been paying fees to various farms for their keep and board. Finally, with several offers of export licences behind him but no guarantee in the offing, it proved too expensive and the venture had to be abandoned. When the money for keep dried up, so did the feed. Brent, working from Canada, with as much help as I could give him, tried desperately to find homes for the horses. Some of the 'lucky' ones did find homes, whilst the least malnourished ones that survived the funeral pyres were offered shelter by Dr. Ghiadi. This venture again proved the dangers of amassing a significant number of rare animals in one place and left Brent very disillusioned and seriously out of pocket.

Meanwhile, the market for Caspians in the UK was struggling to expand and it was only the interest in the US that stimulated breeding in Europe at that time. When they held an International Conference in Texas in 1999, I was honoured to be invited to speak there and it was there that Brenda's first book on the Caspian horse was launched.

At the end of 2003, my friend, Sina, was on his way from Bam to Kurdan, to deliver ten tons of dates to supplement the horse feed over winter, when he received a call to return home. Several of his family and eight of his ten horses had died in a dreadful earthquake which had all but annihilated the ancient city of Bam and its infamous Citadel. All had died in the suffocating dust of the buildings that crumbled as they slept. I was without words and, unable to think of anything better, found myself offering to take the two remaining horses but he said he had found a place to keep them. What made everything much worse was that I couldn't afford to pay him for the dates, which he sent a few days later.

I was now living very much 'hand to mouth' and it didn't help when, at the beginning of 2004, I cracked a pelvic bone in an avalanche of yearlings which had already rounded a block of stables at the gallop by the time I heard them coming.

The financial position that I found myself in forced me to take a partner, in order to try to safeguard the future of the stud and the horses that I had spent most of my life trying to save. It was a mistaken trust that would eventually lead to several court cases, my bank account being blocked and my car being impounded.

The second International Caspian Conference took place in Rutland, England in August 2004, where new Caspian owners from the U.S.A, Scandinavia and Europe were also present, along with Gus Cothran from Kentucky University. His research work had now proved that the Caspian and the Turkoman breeds held the most ancestral position in the history of the horse, pre-dating the Arabian and the Thoroughbred. Two vets from Iran also accepted invitations to speak there.

I was now no longer involved with Brent's export hopes and was spending all my time at Ghara Tepe Sheikh, raising horses and taking out trekking parties, when political climes allowed. The rides appealed to people from all walks of life, and authors, long distance riders, film-makers and journalists miraculously found their way to Ghara Tepe Sheikh on a fairly regular basis.

Unfortunately for me, during one of our more ambitious rides, a forest guide became lost and we found ourselves at the bottom of a deep ravine with the option to turn back or to jump our horses ledge by ledge until we reached the track on the opposite side. It was a bad decision. We had almost reached the top when my horse missed his footing, falling sideways as he landed on one of the ledges, almost sliding back down into the ravine. Fortunately a tree halted his fall sufficiently for two of the riders to take a strong hold on his tail and haul his legs back onto terra firma. As he scrambled back to his feet, releasing my leg, I realised that I had done something fairly serious. My arm was also severely scraped and was causing more pain than the leg. A doctor, who happened to be riding with the party, was sure that the leg was broken; the guide and another rider set off to find the Jeep.

The leg was set at the hospital in Gonbad but the break was more serious than first thought and I was taken to Teheran where the bone was re-broken and re-set. It was only the next day that pristine patients in nearly beds started to complain.

"Get that woman out of those clothes".

I had ridden for days and had gone through two operations, in two hospitals, and I was still dressed in the same clothes!

Alex, Maziar and some of their friends once more offered help during the time that I was incapacitated. However, I soon found it easier to ride than to walk or drive and I couldn't afford to be long out of the saddle.

A long drought that summer was followed by a huge rain storm. The river overflowed, killing large numbers of people and livestock from the villages upstream. The weight of the water washed out the bridge that was vital on the route to Teheran. It was some time before I was able to get Alex out of Ghara Tepe Sheikh for a return flight to London.

Managing both Kurdan and Ghara Tepe Sheikh was becoming financially and physically difficult and no longer seemed to make any sense. Caren took over Kurdan and I concentrated solely on managing the farm at Ghara Tepe Sheikh. The numbers of riding guests proved sporadic. When the political scene was quiet I was able to attract sufficient guests to pay for the horses and the wages of the grooms but whenever there was political sabre-rattling, the income was severely curtailed and I never quite knew where the next load of forage was coming from.

It was during one of these anti-American episodes, that came thick and fast during the western invasion of Iraq, when I had to escape a bombardment of stones via the back door of my local veterinarian's surgery in Kalaleh. Never before had I felt the wrath of the Turkomans, who had always totally embraced me and referred to me with affection as 'the American'. This experience was new.

Another fall from my horse in 2006, caused by a suspiciously loose girth, seriously damaged a shoulder. The swelling and pain from three breaks and a dislocation disguised a fourth break, and a severed tendon, for some time before they were discovered. The severity of the injury forced me into the truck during the few rides that we were still able to make, since foreign governments were periodically advising their citizens not to venture into Iran.

When I finally felt that I could get back into the saddle my doctor told me that I was extremely foolish to be riding at my age (seventy two). "No", I told him, "I was only foolish to fall off".

The shoulder continues to cause problems and, despite surgery to correct the tendon, has never fully recovered, forcing me to abandon riding and the trekking that provided the means to keep the horses. At the moment I rely on scant fees from the occasional mare being brought to stud or the sale of a yearling, which is rare since we still do not have permission to export.

Friends think that I am quite mad to remain here and beg me to move away from the steppes, but people in the West who think they are free have never experienced the true freedom of the Turkoman Steppes on horseback. They cannot imagine the exquisite beauty of the primeval forests that still exist in north eastern Iran.

Today, I still live on the Turkoman Steppes with my dogs and my horses, and with the trees that Narcy and I planted. His memory is forever green and his favourite mare stands proudly on the mound in front of my window.

Louise Firouz
2008

The splendour …

… and the rigour of the Turkoman Steppes
Photo: Maziar Jamshydkhani

The Firouz farm at Ghara Tepe Sheikh, seen from the edge of a deep gorge. The house is on the left and the mare, Roya, is standing on the mound (right)
photo: Brenda Dalton

Filming for 'Alexander the Great', one of several films and documentaries for which Louise provided horses and riders

EPILOGUE

Brenda Dalton

Over the thirty years that I knew Louise Firouz it became increasingly obvious that she had a unique magnetism.

Louise had a beguiling personality. She was charming, intelligent and adventurous. She maintained a dignified elegance and composure, yet she was sociable and fun loving, with a sharp wit and a ready sense of humour.

Louise had the ability to pass seamlessly among all walks of life. She had an all-consuming love of horses, an independent spirit and stubbornly refused to accept defeat. Louise inspired loyalty, admiration and respect. Even in her seventies she had an energy denied to most forty-year-olds. She didn't suffer fools gladly, yet she had a naive faith in human nature that was sometimes misplaced and occasionally worked to her disadvantage.

When she discovered the remnants of a lost horse breed she could easily have accepted the verdicts of sceptics but, against all odds, she succeeded in arousing the interests of geneticists and archaeologists and eventually convinced them that she had, in the Caspian, probably discovered the original Oriental horse. She became absorbed in the culture of ancient Persia and its people and, despite being American, was accepted by diverse populations, both rich and poor. Most of all Louise developed a fascination with the horse breeds of Central Asia. While Iranians were scrambling to leave Iran for the 'freedom' of the west, the magnetic pull of the little horse that she called her unicorn kept her in Iran at the time of the revolution when it was commonplace for people to be arrested simply for association with the West or aristocracy. Friends and relatives fled Iran. More were detained and some never returned or, if they did, they found that their accusers had taken over their property or confiscated their possessions.

Louise was American, female, and married to a Persian Prince, leaving her vulnerable to the opposing groups of revolutionaries from whom no-one could be considered safe.

During her lifetime, the manuscript of her memoirs was accepted for publication by two leading publishers, both of whom had asked her to "personalise" her work. She told me that, through all the pitfalls and setbacks that befell her, she had developed an aptitude for stepping back and looking at her life from a distance, a trait that never left her. She conceded that it was this detachment that kept her "sane". As a result, she understated her problems, experiences and achievements. Almost every paragraph in these memoirs is worthy of a chapter in its own right.

For the last twenty one years of her life I worked closely with Louise as Registrar for the International Caspian Stud Book. She stayed with me in England on several occasions and, through endless correspondence and telephone calls, usually beginning "Brenda, we have a problem", I got to know her extremely well.

When she telephoned me at the turn of the millennium and requested that I should visit her in Iran to meet with the officials at the Ministry of Jehad (who had purchased the Persicus herd following the death of her husband, Narcy), there seemed to be only one answer, which, when showered with the full force of her enthusuasm, was not the one I gave. Although I entered Iran with apprehension, the warmth of my reception, by the officials at the Persicus Stud, the University of Teheran, the various individuals that I met there, and Louise herself, re-assured me that my revised answer had been the right one.

During the short time that I spent riding with Louise on the Turkoman Steppes I had a brief glimpse of the intense calm and freedom that meant so much to her and I basked in her amazing knowledge of her adopted country. Perhaps, too, it was the latent memory of her childhood in Virginia, riding in the heavily forested landscape surrounding the Potomac River that helped to cultivate her love for the vastness of the Golestan Forest and her life, and eventual resting place, at Ghara Tepe Sheikh in north eastern Iran.

Louise Firouz - *'your place is empty'*

Stallion viewing at the first International Conference in Texas 2000
(Front row: Barbara Smathers, U.K, Pandora Best, U.K, Louise Firouz,
Chuck Stull, U.S.A. Back row: behind Louise, Pat Bowles UK, right:
Shauna Mills-Swart Australia – photo: Brenda Dalton

International Conference UK 2004 - Seated from left: Maureen Byrne,
Australia (then Chairman, ICS), Pat Bowles (then Chairman of the
CHS and organiser of the Conference), Louise Firouz, Brenda Dalton (then Registrar ICS, current Chairman ICS) Liz Webster, current
Chairman of the CHS and importer of the majority of the original
foundation stock from Iran to the UK. Joan Taplin (Bermuda) stands
behind Louise Firouz

Louise Firouz with Elizabeth Mansfield (Rotherwood Stud, U.K.) judging at the Caspian Horse Society Show in the UK (2004)

The legacy of Louise Firouz - A group of Caspian colts in Texas
Photo: Stine - courtesy of Anne and Les Stevens

Susiana – exported from Iran to Australia via the UK

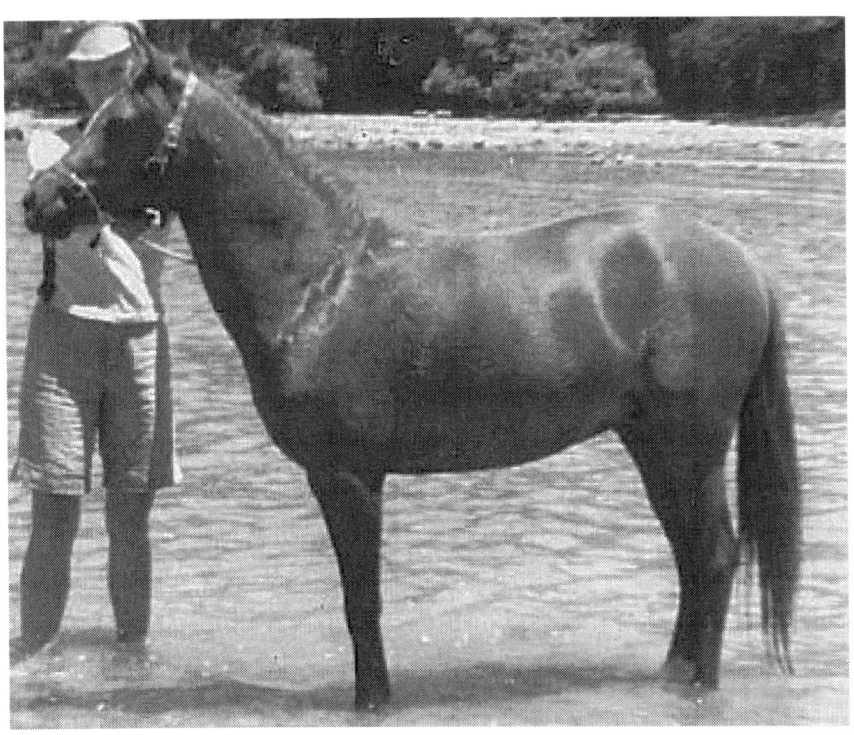

Hopstone Atesh, a son of Khorshid Kola and the stallion, Karoun
He was exported from the U.K. to New Zealand by Helen Rattray
where, bred to Thoroughbred and Arab mares, he produced many
good competition animals

Lanhill Ferrer – a stallion bred by the Scott family, whose Henden and
Lanhill Studs are influential in U.K. breeding
Photo: Brenda Dalton

Left: Chippendale Bahram - Photo: Dru Harper – courtesy of MCC Farms
Right: Marida Dadan - Photo: Stine – courtesy of Anne and Les Stevens
Both stallions were bred in Australia and exported to the U.S.A.

Translations

Agha - Mister
alachekh – Yurt, felt tent
chador – head-to-toe covering for women
Chay khaneh – tea house
chakdameh – mutton and rice dish
chaman – natural grass or pasture
chapadar – literally 'keeper of four-footed animals. Also Buzkashi rider
doroshkeh – horse drawn carriage
Ghassam – Holy oath
Hadji – one who has made the Hadj to Mecca
jube – irrigation or drainage ditch
kahgel – straw-mud mixture for construction
kaleh-pacheh – stew made from the head of an animal
Katkhoda – Head-man
kebab – barbecued meat
Kebabi – place where kebab is sold and served
khamoush kon – lights out
Khanoum – Lady
khoresht – meat or vegetable stew served with rice
lahof – quilt
Masjid – Mosque
Moharam – Holy month
Mullah – Moslem priest
Norouz – vernal equinox, Persian New Year
Pasdar – Revolutionary Guard
Peykan – Iranian made car
Sherkat – company (as in Firouz Construction Company)
talar – raised platform for sitting and sleeping outside
tapeh – ancient mound

BIBLIOGRAPHY

Bokonyi, S. 1970"Tepe Nushi-Jan", Second Interim Report in Roaf M. and Stronach D., Iran Xl, p.140.

Bokonyi, S.,1972 "Once more on the osteological differences of the horse, the half-ass and the ass, 1972, in L. Firouz, The Caspian Miniature Horse of Iran, Field Research Projects, Miami, Florida pp 12-23.

Bokonyi, S.1978, "Excavations at Tepe Nushi Jan, Part 3 The Animal Remains, A preliminary Report, 1973", Iran, vol. 16, pp.24-8

Cothran, E.Gus and Long, Y.G., 1993, "A new phenogroup in the horse D system of red cell alloantigens found in the Caspian pony," U. of Kentucky, Lexington , unpublished.

Cothran, E. Gus, 1994, "Genetic Variability of a Rare Breed of Domestic Horse, the Caspian Pony." unpublished.

Duerst, J.U., 1908, "Animal remains from the excavations at Anau and the horse of Anau in its relation to the races of domestic horses," in R. Pumpelly, Recent Explorations in Turkestan, Expedition of 1904, Vol. ll,pp.339-442, Washington.

Firouz, L.,1969, "Conservation of a Domestic Breed", Biological Conservation, Vol. 2, Oct. 1969

Firouz, L.,1972 The Caspian Miniature Horse of Iran, Field Research Projects, Miami, Florida.

Firouz, L. 1973,"Osteological and historical implications of the Caspian miniature horse to early horse domestication in Iran", in Matolcsi,J. (ed,) Domestikations Forschung und Geschichte der Haustiere, Internationales Symposium in Budapest,1971, .Budapest,pp.309-15

Firouz, L. 1995, "Origins of the Oriental Horse", Horse Keepers of the Eurasian Steppes, Institute for Ancient Equestrian Studies, Conference in Petropavlovsk, Kazakkhstan, 1995

Firouz, L. 1998, "Original Ancestors of the Turkoman, Caspian Horses,

First Int'l Conference on Turkoman Horses", Ashgabat, 1998

Firouz, L. 1999, "Foundation Stock Caspians", First Int'l Congress of Caspian Horses, Houston, Texas

Hosseinion,M. and Shahresevi,H.,1972,"A Preliminary report on the basic skeletal differences of the Caspian miniature horse as compared to other Iranian and European breeds", Appendix B in L.

Littauer,M.A., 1971,"The figured evidence for a small pony in the Ancient Near East," Iraq, Vol.XXXlll,Spring, pp. 24-30.

Littauer, M.A., Crouwel, J.H., 1979, Wheeled Vehicles and Ridden Animals in the Ancient Near East, Leidon/Koln, E.J. Brill

Maloufi, F. 1995, "Equine Parafilariosis in Iran", in Veterinary Parasitology, 56 (1995) pp. 189-197.

Moorey,P.R.S.,1970,"Pictorial evidence for the history of horse-riding in Iraq before the Kassite Period," Iraq, Vol. XXXll,Spring, pp.36-50.

Dalton, B. 1999, (reprinted 2005) The Caspian Horse" ISBN 978-0-9549362-2-8, Plausible Publishing

Dalton, B, 2000, (reprinted 2004) "Allen Guides to Horse and Pony Breeds – The Caspian Horse" ISBN O.85131.797. J A Allen an imprint of Robert Hale Ltd.

International Caspian Society and International Caspian Stud Book website: http://www.caspianhorses.org/

Printed in Great Britain
by Amazon